COMPETENCIES
FOR
GERONTOLOGICAL COUNSELING

Jane E. Myers
and
Valerie L. Schwiebert

AMERICAN COUNSELING ASSOCIATION

5999 Stevenson Avenue
Alexandria, VA 22304-3300

COMPETENCIES FOR GERONTOLOGICAL COUNSELING

10 9 8 7 6 5 4 3 2 1

American Counseling Association
5999 Stevenson Avenue
Alexandria, VA 22304

Acquisitions and Development Editor
Carolyn Baker

Managing Editor
Michael Comlish

Copyeditor
Heather Jefferson

Cover design by Brian Gallagher

Library of Congress Cataloging-in-Publication Data

Myers. Jane E.
    Competencies for gerontological counseling / by Jane E. Myers & Valerie L. Schwiebert.
      p. cm.
    Includes bibliographical references and index.
    ISBN 1-55620-149-4
    1. Aged—Counseling of.   I. Schwiebert, Valerie L.   II. Title.
HV1451.M94   1995
362.1'9897—dc20   95-41681
                                          CIP

dedicated to gerontological counselors
and
their clients

The authors wish to express appreciation to the following persons for their support and encouragement in the development of this book: Tom Sweeney, Michael Garrett, Ryan Schwiebert, and Kristie.

Contents

Preface

G erontological counseling as a counseling specialty is relatively new, spanning only 20 years. The article reprinted as chapter 1
of this book chronicles the historical development of gerontological
counseling as a counseling specialty. The development of this specialty
covers a span of time beginning in the late 1970s and continuing
through the present. In addition to the documentation of need for the
specialty, the author notes that, given the present extent of underservice
of mental health needs among older persons, the training of specialists
is only one possible avenue for helping to meet those needs, and the
training of specialists alone is insufficient to improve the mental health
of a large segment of the older population. In addition to training
specialists, it is important or essential that *all* counselors graduate from
entry-level training programs with basic knowledge of the mental
health needs of older persons and how to begin to meet those needs.
Gerontological counseling specialists require more intensive and in-depth
study of older persons to perform their work in a competent manner.

The 16 Minimum Essential Competencies for Gerontological Counselors described in chapter 1 were developed with broad-based input
from counselors, counselor educators, and personnel working directly
with older persons in community and institutional settings. The competencies have been endorsed by the Association for Adult Development
and Aging (AADA) and the National Board for Certified Counselors
(NBCC); they form the basis for the Gerontological Counseling accreditation standards of the Council for Accreditation of Counseling and
Related Educational Programs (CACREP). These specialty competencies comprise the organizing framework for this book.

In fact, the unique contribution of this book to the training of gerontological counselors lies in the competency-based format. Use of this book is intended to provide a foundation of the knowledge and skills required in an accredited training program in gerontological counseling. Further, counselors who possess knowledge and skills in these areas will find them essential in the pursuit of national credentialing as a gerontological counseling specialist. Of course, counselors who work with older persons will find a need to continue their learning beyond what can be provided in one book. Consequently, the authors have provided a variety of resources to facilitate continued learning about older persons and how best to assist them through counseling interventions.

In this book, one chapter is devoted to each of the 16 competencies. Information is provided to assist those preparing for a specialty in gerontological counseling to meet the needs of their older clients. Each chapter begins with a restatement of the specialty competency, followed by an overview of the chapter's contents. Important terms are defined, and the knowledge and skills required for a competent gerontological counselor are described. One or more case studies are provided, in which the knowledge and skills may be applied. Commentary concerning the case studies is provided. Each chapter ends with a series of questions for consideration and discussion, as well as references for additional study and information. A supplemental reading list is included at the end of the book.

Although the term *counselor* is used throughout the text, we use it interchangeably with terms such as *professional counselor, licensed professional counselor,* and *licensed professional mental health counselor.* The information in each chapter is intended to provide both counselors in training and professional counselors with the basic information required to provide effective and competent counseling services to older clients. Of course, those who seek specialty certification in gerontological counseling will want to seek both additional courses of study and supervised work experiences. This book is a beginning; it should contribute to an increase in knowledge as well as skill among professional counselors, and thus improve the quality of counseling services provided to older individuals.

—*Jane E. Myers & Valerie L. Schwiebert*

Author Biographies

Jane E. Myers is a professor of counselor education at the University of North Carolina at Greensboro. She received her bachelor's degree in psychology from the University of California at Berkeley, a master's in rehabilitation counseling, specialist in counseling and educational administration, and doctorate in counselor education with a graduate certificate in gerontology from the University of Florida.

Dr. Myers has worked as a rehabilitation counselor and administrator of aging programs in the state of Florida. She directed five national projects on aging for the American Counseling Association (ACA). These projects developed curriculum materials to train counselors to work with older persons, provided continuing education for more than 3,200 practicing professional counselors in gerontological issues, developed a model and curriculum resources for infusion of gerontological counseling into counselor education, and a statement of competencies for training of gerontological counselors. The competencies form the basis for the National Certified Gerontological Counselor credential available through the National Board for Certified Counselors, and the gerontological counseling accreditation standards of the Council for Accreditation of Counseling and Related Educational Programs. These competencies also are the basis of this book.

Dr. Myers is a National Certified Counselor, a National Certified Gerontological Counselor, a Certified Rehabilitation Counselor, and a Licensed Professional Counselor in North Carolina. She was president of the American Association for Counseling and Development, now the American Counseling Association, in 1990–1991. She has been president of two ACA divisions, the Association for Assessment in Counseling and the Association for Adult Development and Aging, for which she served as founding president. She also served as president of Chi Sigma Iota, the international honor society in counseling, and chair of the Counseling and Human Development Foundation and the Council for Accreditation of Counseling and Related Educational Programs.

Dr. Myers has written and edited numerous publications, including more than 16 books and monographs, over 60 refereed journal articles, and more than 30 additional publications. She also co-produced seven training videotapes for gerontological counseling. Among her numerous honors are the ACA Research Award, the ACA Arthur A. Hitchcock Distinguished Professional Service Award, the ACA Gilbert and Kathleen Wrenn Humanitarian and Caring Person Award, and the Distinguished Service Awards of both the National Rehabilitation Counseling Association and the American Rehabilitation Counseling Association. She is a Fellow of the Gerontological Society of America and the National Rehabilitation Counseling Association.

Valerie L. Schwiebert is an assistant professor of counseling in the Department of Human Services at Western Carolina University. Dr. Schwiebert received her master's degree in rehabilitation counseling, specialist in counselor education, and doctorate in counselor education with a graduate certificate in gerontology from the University of Florida in Gainesville. Her areas of doctoral specialization include adult development and aging, and death and dying. Dr. Schwiebert is a National Certified Counselor, a National Certified Gerontological Counselor, and a Certified Rehabilitation Counselor.

She is a recipient of the AADA and Chi Sigma Iota Research Awards for her research in the area of adult children providing caregiving for aging parents. Dr. Schwiebert has written several articles and two books on aging and aging parents.

1

From "Forgotten and Ignored" to Standards and Certification:

Gerontological Counseling Comes of Age

T he specialty of gerontological counseling has a 20-year history that began with a dearth of information and has progressed to the development of preparation standards and a national certification, both based on a nationally endorsed statement of competencies for gerontological counselors. The question of whether generalization or a specialization will best serve the needs of older persons continues to be central to the development of this specialization.

Blake and Kaplan (1975, p. 156) issued a challenge to the counseling profession that began with the statement that "Older people are the forgotten and ignored of APGA" (the American Personnel Guidance Association; now the American Counseling Association, ACA). This article describes two decades of response to that challenge, including five national projects on aging, interest groups in each ACA division, a new division with the adult years as a focus, new graduate courses, a statement of competencies, professional preparation standards, specialty accreditation, and a national certification in gerontological counseling. These developments have led to the emergence of gerontological counseling as a recognized specialty within the counseling profession. This article provides an overview of the historical development of gerontological counseling and the current status of this specialty.

This chapter was published in the *Journal of Counseling and Development*, November/December, 1995. It is reprinted here in its entirety, and includes the minimum essential gerontological competencies for all counselors, as well as for gerontological counseling specialists. The content describes the historical development and current status of gerontological counseling as a specialty within professional counseling.

The Need for a Specialty

The aging of the U.S. population is a frequent topic of conversation in both formal and informal gatherings. Whereas only 4% of the population in the United States were over age 65 in 1900, almost 13% are over 65 today (American Association of Retired Persons, 1995). It is estimated that 20% of the population will be in this age group by the year 2050, and an estimated 50% of persons will be over the age of 50 by the year 2000 (Special Committee on Aging, 1983). There are few aspects of society untouched by these demographic shifts. As a result, most academic disciplines and professions have begun to study the older population and the aging process.

As the life span has increased, counselors have moved from a primary focus on school populations to an equally strong emphasis on community-based programs addressing the mental health concerns of persons across the life span (Palmo, Weikel, & Brooks, 1995). Counselors have begun to work with older persons, and the question has emerged of whether and how such work is different from counseling with any other population. Burns and Taube (1990) noted that the extent of mental health needs does not seem to change with age, and Knight (1989) determined that psychotherapy is as effective with older persons as with people of any age group. If age is not a factor in therapy outcome, as Thompson (1987) suggested, then it could be argued that special training to work with older people may not be necessary.

On the other hand, Waters (1984) identified both similarities and differences in counseling with older and younger persons. Numerous authors have written concerning specialized techniques for use with older people (e.g., Brammer, 1985; Burnside, 1984; Herr & Weakland, 1979), presumably based on different needs of this population. A major difference is the reluctance of older persons to seek counseling (Cohen, 1977). In addition, the reluctance of therapists to treat older people has been documented (Poggi & Berland, 1985). As a group, older people are substantially underserved by mental health practitioners (Flemming, Rickards, Santos, & West, 1986), in part because of negative attitudes (Piggrem & Schmidt, 1982) and in part because of lack of specialized training (Myers & Blake, 1986). Kunkel and Williams (1991) identified an additional barrier to services as the lack of research-informed theoretical perspectives on how to provide mental health services most effectively to older people and how to encourage older people to use such services. In short, the numbers of older persons have continued to increase, whereas mental health services for this population have remained uniformly inadequate.

Historical Development of Gerontological Counseling

In 1972, the ACA (then APGA) Senate passed a resolution mandating the association to develop guidelines for curriculum planning to train counselors to work with older people (Howard-Jasper, 1981). The following year, ACA established a special committee to serve for 1 year to develop a strategy for implementing this resolution. The Commission on Middle-Aged and Older Persons survived in some form as a special committee for the next 16 consecutive years, finally being called the "Committee on Adult Development and Aging."

In 1975, only 18, or 6%, of all counselor preparation programs reported offering even an elective course in gerontological counseling (Salisbury, 1975). Prior to that time, there were few articles in the professional counseling literature addressing the counseling needs of older clients. Most of these articles dealt with "older workers," the group the federal government defines as persons aged 40 years and above. The lack of training programs, the growth of the older population, and the challenge issued by Blake and Kaplan (1975) merged to create a climate within which specialized counseling for older persons began to be explored.

ACA responded to the dearth of information related to counseling with older persons by seeking funding from the U.S. Administration on Aging (AoA) to develop curricula for training counselors to work with older persons. Between 1978 and 1990, the AoA funded five national projects on aging to ACA, for a total of more than $1 million. Each of these projects addressed a different but related area, used the knowledge base developed in the preceding projects to educate project participants, and helped to raise the consciousness of counseling professionals of the need for services to the expanding older population. In addition, the cumulative effect of these national projects and the involvement of counselors and counselor educators nationwide led to a significant change in the organizational structure of ACA as reflected in a new division focused on adult development and aging.

Aging Project 1 (1978–1979)

ACA's first national project on aging was written in response to the 1972 ACA Senate resolution, as well as Salisbury's (1975) research and the identified lack of professional preparation opportunities in gerontological counseling. The basic argument presented to the AoA was that counselors were not being trained in this area because of lack of curricular resources to do so. Curriculum materials for preservice preparation of counselors were needed.

Counselors and counselor educators were identified and were brought together in four national workshops to review and evaluate a series of modules written by experts in aging and counseling, which were combined to form *Counseling Older Persons: A Training Syllabus for Educators* (Ganikos, 1979). Also produced was *A Handbook for Conducting Workshops on the Counseling Needs of Older Persons* (Ganikos et al., 1979) and a slide tape presentation titled *Hey, Don't Pass Me By!* The syllabus and handbook were disseminated to all counselor education programs (N = approximately 475) with a request that counselor educators develop coursework and use the syllabus as a textbook for gerontological counseling training.

Aging Project 2 (1979–1981)

It would be unrealistic to expect all counselor preparation programs to add new courses in gerontological issues. Even if all of them did so, the numbers of trained counselors could not be expected to be large enough to meet the mental health needs of the older population. ACA's second national project on aging approached these needs from the perspective of training paraprofessional and peer counselors to work with older persons. Such trained individuals could provide a minimal level of helping interventions, as well as referral for needed therapy before problems became severe (Waters, Reiter, White, & Dates, 1979).

Three training manuals were produced in the second aging project, authored by both practitioners and researchers. The manuals were field tested in a series of five national workshops attended by counselors, counselor educators, and aging network personnel selected on the basis of identified expertise and interest in aging. When completed, the project materials were disseminated free of charge to all counselor preparation programs. The three *Counseling Older Persons* manuals were the following: *Volume I: Guidelines for a Team Approach to Training* (Myers,

Finnerty-Fried, & Graves, 1981), *Volume II: Basic Helping Skills for Service Providers* (Myers & Ganikos, 1981), and *Volume III: A Trainer's Manual for Basic Helping Skills* (Myers, 1981). In addition, this project developed a national network of training programs using counselor educators, continuing education offices, and aging network staff to jointly plan and implement training programs for service providers to older persons.

Aging Project 3 (1983–1984)

In 1983, most counseling professionals working in the field had no specific training in gerontological counseling, because few counselor training programs provided courses in this area. This project attempted to increase the level of training and competence in gerontological issues among practitioners. Sixty counselors were selected from over 600 applicants (Phase I) to become gerontological counseling trainers (GCTs). The 60 GCTs were divided into four groups of 15 each and were provided with 2 days of intensive training in gerontological issues (Phase II). Each GCT then conducted at least two 1-day workshops in their local area for counseling practitioners (Phase III). By the time the project was completed, the GCTs had trained over 3,200 practicing professional counselors in basic aspects of aging and gerontological counseling, using curriculum materials developed in the first two national projects.

Aging Project 4 (1988–1989)

The fourth national project was based on the fact that persons live three fourths of their lives as adults and one third or more as older persons (over age 60). Thus, it is increasingly likely that all counselors, regardless of work setting, will encounter older persons and their families as clients. All counselors, therefore, should graduate and enter the profession with some basic knowledge of the needs of older persons and how to address those needs. By 1988, a fairly large volume of research was available concerning older persons. The challenge was to determine what information would be most relevant for all counselors, as opposed to those specializing in work with older people, and how best to integrate this information into existing counselor preparation curricula.

This project used the preparation standards of the Council for Accreditation of Counseling and Related Educational Programs (CACREP) as a basis for development of curricular units for training in gerontological issues. One unit on relevant gerontological issues was developed for infusion into each of the eight core curricular areas specified in the CACREP standards, including goals corresponding to the standards, a brief and extensive literature review and references, suggestions for audiovisual materials, classroom activities, and evaluation criteria. Guidelines for practica and internships as well as specialty training in gerontological counseling were included.

As part of this project, an extensive review of gerontological literature was conducted over a 1-year period. This literature is summarized in *Infusing Gerontological Counseling Into Counselor Preparation: Curriculum Guide* (Myers, 1989). A set of videotapes was developed to accompany the written *Guide* (Sweeney & Myers, 1989, 1990). All of these materials were field tested in five regional workshops attended by a select group of practicing counselors, counselor educators, and aging network administrators and staff. At the conclusion of the project, the *Guide* was sent free of charge to all counselor preparation programs.

Aging Project 5 (1989–1990)

The fifth and last aging project focused on training outcomes as well as curricula. Using the materials developed in preceding projects, the project staff attempted to define competence in gerontological counseling. Two perspectives were addressed. First, what competencies relative to older persons could be expected of a counselor who graduated from any preparation program, assuming that gerontological issues had indeed been infused into the core curricula as defined by CACREP using the *Guide* developed in the fourth national aging project? Second, what competencies could be expected of a counselor who graduated with an intent to specialize in work with older people?

In developing a statement of gerontological competencies for counselors, a major challenge was to define what a counselor would be expected to know at the time they graduated with an entry-level degree, as opposed to what would be expected of an experienced practitioner. The competencies were developed through a series of five think-tank meetings attended by invited gerontological counselors, counselor educators, gerontologists, aging network personnel, and older persons.

To further disseminate the gerontological infusion model, a part of the fifth national project was the development of multiple-choice items, based on the generic competencies, which were submitted to the National Board for Certified Counselors (NBCC) for inclusion in the item pool for the National Counselor Examination. Items were also submitted for inclusion in the item pool for the National Certified Career Counselor examination. All of the items were field tested before submission to NBCC.

Other Developments in ACA

The five national projects described here were highly successful in stimulating interest in the counseling needs and concerns of older persons. ACA itself had supported a special committee on aging since the early 1970s. Over the years, the special committee identified as a major goal the development of interest groups on aging within each ACA division. Lack of support for standing committee status led to an alternative route to achieve association-wide support: the development of an organizational affiliate on adult development and aging. The ACA requirements for affiliates were that a minimum of 400 members be identified (and submit dues), 200 of which were new members to ACA. Within a year of its inception, the Association for Adult Development and Aging (AADA) gained more than 1,000 members, meeting the requirements for division status in 1986. The AADA now has more than 2,000 members and continues to grow.

Although many ACA divisions have maintained their interest groups on adult development and aging stimulated by the former national ACA committee, the AADA is the focal point within ACA for adult development and aging concerns. AADA formally endorsed the gerontological competencies, which have since served as the foundation for specialty preparation standards as well as specialty certification.

Specialty Standards for Gerontological Counseling

The AADA Committee on Standards used the competency statements, the *Curriculum Guide,* and available literature in gerontological counseling as the basis for developing a statement of professional preparation standards. This statement was submitted to the CACREP Board in 1990 and was revised for resubmission in 1991. After a review of the standards proposal by accredited training programs, CACREP voted in March of 1992 to approve the standards as a specialty emphasis within the existing community counseling standards. Counselor education training programs that are accredited in community counseling may elect to apply for the gerontological counseling specialty, if they meet the accreditation standards. At the time of this writing, several counselor education programs are known to be in the process of self-study to obtain recognition in this specialty, and one program has received recognition by CACREP in April 1995. The standards closely parallel the competency statements developed through the fifth ACA aging project. (A copy of the new standards is available from CACREP as part of the 1994 standards [Council for Accreditation of Counseling and Related Educational Programs, 1994].)

National Certified Gerontological Counselor Credential

A final and significant part of ACA's fifth national aging project was the submission and presentation by project staff of a proposal to the NBCC to develop a specialty certification in gerontological counseling. Before voting in favor of the National Certified Gerontological Counselor (NCGC) proposal, the NBCC and the project staff conducted a survey of the (then) 1,700 members of AADA to determine need for and interest in a national specialty in gerontological counseling. The survey included five parts: (a) questions concerning intent to seek certification if available, (b) criteria the respondent thought should be required for individual certification (e.g., standards), (c) the respondent's training and experience in gerontological counseling, (d) demographic data, and (e) a self-assessment of competence for each of the minimum essential gerontological competencies.

Survey respondents ($N = 346$) expressed sufficient interest in a specialty certification to warrant the NBCC endorsing the proposal. Slightly over half of the 346 respondents ($n = 177$, 51%) considered themselves to be qualified gerontological counseling practitioners, and more than half ($n = 180$, 52%) indicated that they would seek a specialty certification in gerontological counseling if it were available. Only 10% ($n = 35$) said they would not, whereas 38% ($n = 132$) were undecided.

Over half of the respondents ($n = 201$, 58%) did not think a nationally certified counselor should be a requirement for the specialty certification, although this certainly is a requirement of the NBCC. Slightly fewer than half of the respondents ($n = 166$, 48%) thought there should be an examination. Most of the respondents thought that appropriate training ($n = 301$, 87%) and experience ($n = 242$, 70%) should be required. Only 53% ($n = 183$) thought that appropriate supervision should be necessary. Letters of endorsement were considered most needed from supervisors ($n = 156$, 45%) and least needed from employers ($n = 59$, 17%). Audiotapes and videotapes were unpopular requirements, as evidenced by the fact that only 7% and 5% of respondents ($n = 24$ and $n = 17$, respectively) chose these two items.

The NBCC voted to approve a national certification in gerontological counseling in January 1990. The NCGC credential is now awarded on the basis of a rigorous review of credentials and without a specialty examination. A major part of the application process is an assessment of competence by the applicant and his or her references based on the gerontological competency statements described in the next section. At the time of this writing, approximately 200 nationally certified counselors have received the NCGC credential, and NBCC is considering ways to recruit more persons to this specialty, or to alter the nature of the specialty to include mid-life as well as later life development (Elinor Waters, personal communication, July 11, 1994).

Gerontological Competencies for Counselors

Gerontological Competencies for Counselors and Human Development Professionals (Myers & Sweeney, 1990), the product of the fifth national ACA aging project, is a 38-page document that includes gerontological competencies in two areas: those for all counselors (generic), and those for counselors specializing (specialty) in work with older persons. The competencies, which were developed with broad input from counselors, gerontologists, practitioners, administrators, and researchers, are arranged according to each of the core curricular areas as well as identified areas of specialty preparation. They can be used by counselor educators in developing curricula and by practitioners to determine areas of competence for counseling with older persons.

To encourage dissemination and use of the competency statements by counselor educators (38 pages of competency statements is somewhat formidable), the project staff and participants developed a set of minimum essential gerontological competencies. Counselor educators developing gerontological curricula can use the full set of competencies or specific subsets as guidelines; however, it was anticipated that most educators would respond more favorably to a shorter and more easily assimilated document. Shown in Table 1, the minimum essential statements constitute a "short form" of the gerontological counseling competency statements. Gerontological counselor specialists are expected to demonstrate both generic and specialty competencies, whereas counselors not electing to specialize in gerontological counseling would, ideally, demonstrate the minimum essential competencies for all counselors (generic). In reviewing these competencies, the reader should note that they are based on a model for infusion of concepts on aging into existing counselor preparation curricula as defined by CACREP.

Respondents to the NBCC survey mentioned earlier were asked to complete a self-assessment of their competence for each of the minimum essential gerontological competencies, using a 5-point Likert scale as follows: 1 = *very competent, able to perform at a high level;* 2 = *competent, able to perform adequately;* 3 = *somewhat competent, more training required;* 4 = *not competent, not able to perform at this time;* and 5 = *not able to judge competence.* The results of their self-assessments are shown in Table 2. In terms of generic competencies, the greatest level of competence was expressed for having positive, wellness-enhancing attitudes toward older persons (*M* = 1.2). This area also had the least variability of any of the competencies (*SD* = 0.56). The areas in which least competence was expressed were appraisal (*M* = 2.3), research (*M* = 2.3), and group procedures (*M* = 2.2). These also were the areas with the greatest amount of variability in responses (*SDs* = 0.96, 0.94, and 0.94, respectively).

The greatest amount of competence in the specialty area was expressed for having positive, wellness-enhancing attitudes and a concern for empowerment over the life span (*M* = 1.4). Again, there was little variability in the response to this item (*SD* = 0.72). The next highest ratings were given for competencies in the areas of human growth and development and the ability to function in multiple roles in working with older persons (*M* = 1.9). Variability in these two areas tended to be lower than in others (*SD* = 0.90 and 0.91, respectively). Areas in which the least amount of competence was expressed, and also which had the greatest variability in responses, were appraisal (*M* = 2.5, *SD* = 1.00), research (*M* = 2.4, *SD* = 1.01), and group procedures (*M* = 2.4, *SD* = 1.03).

The average amount of competence expressed for the generic competencies (the mean of the means given in Table 1) was 1.8, whereas the average for the specialty competencies was 2.1. The average amount of variability in the two areas was 0.82 and 0.96, respectively. In other words, respondents rated themselves as more competent according to the generic competencies than in regard to the specialty competencies, which would be expected as these represent a less intensive level of knowledge and skill. Most of the respondents considered themselves to be "somewhat competent" in each of the areas addressed but to need more training if they were to become "very competent" in each area. The low amount of variability in responses to the self-assessment may be indicative of the current state of knowledge of counselors nationwide.

Gerontological Counseling: A Look to the Future

About one third of all counselor preparation programs now offer coursework to train counselors to work with older persons (Myers, 1989; Myers, Loesch, & Sweeney, 1991). Many of these programs offer a specialization in this area as well. The numbers of student dissertations and theses and the numbers of articles in the professional literature related to older persons have increased dramatically in the last decade and may be expected to continue. With courses, standards, competencies, and a certification, it is clear that gerontological counseling is well established as a specialty within the counseling profession.

Nevertheless, it cannot be assumed that the gerontological counseling specialty will be self-perpetuating. If past history can be used to predict the future, strong leadership from the national level and active advocacy at all levels will be required to maintain and enhance this specialty. National preparation standards are available, and specialty accreditation of training programs is possible. Counselor education programs need both encouragement and assistance in the specialty accreditation process, if the new accreditation is to receive support. National certification is available. Students and practitioners need to be encouraged to seek the NCGC credential. In addition, current and future NCGCs need to have access to training opportunities to maintain their certification. Because certification will require continuing education for maintenance of the NCGC credential, counselor educators

TABLE 1. Gerontological competencies for counselors.

A. *Minimum Essential Gerontological Copetencies for all Counselors (Generic)*
   1. Exhibits positive, wellness-enhancing attitudes toward older persons, including respect for the intellectual, emotional, social, vocational, physical, and spiritual needs of older individuals and the older population as a whole.
   2. Exhibits sensitivity to sensory and physical limitations of older persons through appropriate environmental modifications to facilitate helping relationships.
   3. Demonstrates knowledge of the unique considerations in establishing and maintaining helping relationships with older persons.
   4. Demonstrates knowledge of human development for older persons, including major psychological theories of aging, physiological aspects of "normal" aging, and dysfunctional behaviors of older persons.
   5. Demonstrates knowledge of social and cultural foundations for older persons, including common positive and negative societal attitudes, major causes of stress, needs of family caregivers and the implications of major demographic characteristics of the older population (e.g., numbers of women, widows, increasing numbers of older minorities).
   6. Demonstrates knowledge of special considerations and techniques for group work with older persons.
   7. Demonstrates knowledge of lifestyle and career development concerns of older persons, including the effects of age-related physical, psychological, and social changes on vocational development, factors affecting the retirement transition, and alternative careers and lifestyles for later life.
   8. Demonstrates knowledge of the unique aspects of appraisal with older persons, including psychological, social, and physical factors which may affect assessment, and ethical implications of using assessment techniques.
   9. Demonstrates knowledge of sources of literature reporting research about older persons and ethical issues in research with older subjects.
   10. Demonstrates knowledge of formal and informal referral networks for helping older persons and ethical behavior in working with other professionals to assist older persons.

B. *Minimum Essential Competencies for Gerontological Counseling Specialists (Specialty)*
   1. Demonstrates and actively advocates for positive, respectful, wellness-enhancing attitudes toward older persons and a concern for empowerment of persons throughout the lifespan.
   2. Demonstrates skill in applying extensive knowledge of human development for older persons, including major theories of aging, the relationship between physical and mental health and aging, the difference between normal and pathological aging processes, gender-related developmental differences, and coping skills for life transitions and loss.

3. Demonstrates skill in applying extensive knowledge of social and cultural foundations for older persons, including characteristics and needs of older minority subgroups, factors affecting substance and medication misuse and abuse, recognition and treatment of elder abuse, and knowledge of social service programs.
4. Demonstrates the ability to function in the multiple roles required to facilitate helping relationships with older persons (e.g., advocate, family consultant) and to mobilize available resources for functioning effectively in each role.
5. Demonstrates skill in recruiting, selecting, planning, and implementing groups with older persons.
6. Demonstrates skill in applying extensive knowledge of career and lifestyle options for older persons, age-related assets and barriers to effective choices, and resources for maximizing exploration of career and lifestyle options.
7. Demonstrates skill in appraisal of older persons, including identifying characteristics of suitable appraisal instruments and techniques and in using assessment results in developing treatment plans.
8. Demonstrates skill in applying extensive knowledge of current research related to older persons and the implications of research findings for helping relationships.
9. Demonstrates skill in applying extensive knowledge of the intellectual, physical, social, emotional, vocational, and spiritual needs of older persons and strategies for helping to meet those needs.
10. Demonstrates skill in applying appropriate intervention techniques, in collaboration with medical and other care providers, for physical and mental impairments common to older persons, such as acute, chronic, and terminal illness, depression, suicide, and organic brain syndromes.
11. Demonstrates extensive knowledge of the formal and informal aging networks, public policy, and legislation affecting older persons, and knowledge of a continuum of care which will allow older persons to maintain their highest level of independence.
12. Demonstrates skill in applying appropriate intervention techniques for situational and developmental crises commonly experienced by older persons, such as bereavement, isolation, divorce, relocation, sexual concerns, illness, transportation, crime, abuse, and relationships with adult children and caregivers.
13. Demonstrates skill in the use of a wide variety of specialized therapies to assist older persons in coping with both developmental and non-normative issues such as creative arts therapies, pet therapy, peer counseling, and family counseling.
14. Demonstrates skill in applying extensive knowledge of ethical issues in counseling older persons, their families, and care providers.
15. Demonstrates the ability to act as a consultant to individuals and organizations on issues related to older persons and their families.
16. Demonstrates skill in program development for the older population, including needs assessment, program planning, implementation, and evaluation.

TABLE 2. Self assessment of competence in gerontological issues

Competency	M	SD
Generic Competency		
Wellness attitudes	1.2	0.56
Sensitivity to limitations	1.5	0.77
Helping relationships	1.5	0.72
Human development	1.8	0.82
Social and cultural foundations	1.7	0.79
Group procedures	2.2	0.94
Lifestyle and career	1.9	0.88
Appraisal	2.3	0.96
Research	2.3	0.94
Referral network, ethics	2.0	0.91
Specialty Competencies		
Empowerment	1.4	0.72
Human development	1.9	0.90
Social and cultural foundations	2.1	0.94
Multiple roles	1.9	0.91
Group procedures	2.4	1.03
Lifestyle and career	2.1	1.00
Appraisal	2.5	1.00
Research	2.4	1.01
Knowledge of needs	1.9	0.89
Interventions for physical & mental impairment	2.2	1.05
Policy and legislation	2.2	1.00
Situational & developmental interventions	2.0	0.96
Specialized therapies	2.3	1.01
Ethical issues	2.0	0.97
Consultation	2.0	1.01
Program development	2.3	1.06

Note. Scale ranges from 1 = *very competent* to 5 = *not able to judge competence.* Refer to Table 1 for a complete listing of competencies.

need to be prepared to provide in-service education in gerontological counseling.

The results of the gerontological counseling certification survey, in combination with the history of ACA's aging projects, have implications for the future development of the specialty of gerontological counseling. After 15 years of curriculum development and training, the most obvious implication is the continued need for training to raise the level of competence of counselors in gerontological issues. Even those who consider themselves to be qualified gerontological counseling practitioners would like additional training to better serve their older clients.

It also appears that advanced training is needed for those with some experience and competence in working with older people who want to develop higher levels of skill. With the gerontological counseling specialty in place, training must become a priority.

If the counseling profession is to prepare students in the gerontological counseling specialty and encourage practitioners to seek this additional specialty certification, the issue of jobs for trained gerontological counselors must also be addressed. Additional studies need to be conducted to determine available positions. ACA's advocacy efforts need to include attention to jobs in which mental health services for older persons are included and that currently are filled by social workers, psychologists, and other mental health care providers. The classifications for these positions need to be expanded to include counselors as possible employees. For example, legislation in most states mandates that social workers be hired in long-term care facilities. At present, no states require that counselors be hired in these settings. The Association for Gerontology in Higher Education is advocating with the Administration on Aging (AoA) and the federal congress to have all jobs funded through the AoA filled with persons with an associate, bachelor's, master's, or doctoral degree in gerontology. ACA also needs to work with the AoA, if counselors are to be included in AoA-funded positions.

The growth of interest in gerontological counseling, which has evolved over a relatively short time, is encouraging because ultimately it will benefit all of us as we grow older. The ultimate proof of interest and need lies not in the results of any one survey, the development of training standards, or the development of a specialty credential. Only time will reveal changes in the level of competence of counselors in gerontological issues and the quality of counseling services provided to older persons. Outcome research, particularly studies that compare the effectiveness of trained gerontological practitioners with those without such training, is needed. A strong foundation for this specialty has been laid, but one cannot afford to sit back and assume it has enough momentum to carry forward on its own. As a profession, counselors continue to be challenged by the need to build a structure on that foundation with which we can live and grow comfortably. We must actively promote training, standards, certification, competence, and especially jobs for counselors if the mental health needs of older people are to be adequately met.

Finally, although the specialty is "in place," the need to train all counselors to respond to the mental health needs of older persons and their families remains a critical challenge. Indeed, if the infusion model discussed here and elsewhere were to be fully implemented in counselor training, perhaps the need for a gerontological counseling specialty would not be so great as it is now. Perhaps, as counselors continue to espouse a developmental perspective that views aging as a part of rather than apart from the life span, the need for a specialty will quietly disappear. Given a choice, I would argue for *all* counselors having some training to work with older people and their families, rather than just a few specializing in this area.

References

American Association of Retired Persons. (1995). *A profile of older Americans.* Washington, DC: Author.

Blake, R., & Kaplan, L. S. (1975). Counseling the elderly: An emerging area for counselor education and supervision. *Counselor Education and Supervision, 15,* 156–157.

Brammer, L. (1985). Counseling and quality of life for older adults: Beating the odds. *Educational Perspectives, 23,* 3–16.

Burns, B. J., & Taube, C. A. (1990). Mental health services in general medical care and in nursing homes. In B. S. Fogel, A. Furino, & G. Gottlieb (Eds.), *Protecting minds at risk* (pp. 321–330). Washington, DC: American Psychiatric Association.

Burnside, I. (1984). *Working with the elderly: Group processes and techniques.* Monterey, CA: Wadsworth.

Cohen, G. (1977). Mental health services and the elderly: Needs and options. In S. Steury & M. L. Black (Eds.), *Readings in psychotherapy with older people* (pp. 68–72). Rockville, MD: National Institute of Mental Health.

Council for Accreditation of Counseling and Related Educational Programs. (1994). *CACREP accreditation standards and procedures manual.* Alexandria, VA: Author.

Flemming, A. S., Rickards, L. D., Santos, J. F., & West, P. R. (1986). *Report of a survey of community mental health centers* (Vol. I). Washington, DC: White House Conference on Aging.

Ganikos, M. L. (1979). *Counseling the aged: A training syllabus for educators.* Alexandria, VA: American Association for Counseling and Development.

Ganikos, M. L., & Grady, K. A., Olson, J. B., Blake, R., Fitzgerald, P., & Lawrence, P. C. (1979). *A handbook for conducting workshops on the counseling needs of older persons.* Alexandria, VA: American Association for Counseling and Development.

Herr, J. J., & Weakland, J. H. (1979). *Counseling elders and their families.* New York: Springer.

Howard-Jasper, J. (1981). APGA's involvement in aging. In J. E. Myers, P. Finnerty-Fried, & C. Graves (Eds.), *Counseling older persons: Vol. I. Guidelines for a team approach to training* (pp. 187–192) . Alexandria, VA: American Counseling Association.

Knight, B. G. (1989). *Outreach with the elderly: Community education, assessment, and therapy.* New York: New York University Press.

Kunkel, M. A., & Williams, C. (1991). Age and expectations about counseling: Two methodological perspectives. *Journal of Counseling and Development, 70,* 314–320.

Myers, J. E. (1981). *Counseling older persons: Vol. III. A trainer's manual for basic helping skills.* Alexandria, VA: American Association for Counseling and Development.

Myers, J. E. (1989). *Infusing gerontological counseling into counselor preparation: Curriculum guide.* Alexandria, VA: American Association for Counseling and Development.

Myers, J. E., & Blake, R. (1986). Professional preparation of gerontological counselors: Issues and guidelines. *Counselor Education and Supervision, 26,* 137–145.

Myers, J. E., Finnerty-Fried, P. F., & Graves, C. (1981). *Counseling older persons: Vol. I. Guidelines for a team approach to training.* Alexandria, VA: American Association for Counseling and Development.

Myers, J. E., & Ganikos, M. L. (1981). *Counseling older persons: Vol. II. Basic helping skills for service providers.* Alexandria, VA: American Association for Counseling and Development.

Myers, J. E., Loesch, T. J., & Sweeney, T. J. (1991). Trends in gerontological counselor preparation. *Counselor Education and Supervision, 30,* 194–204.

Myers, J. E., & Sweeney, T. J. (1990). *Gerontological competencies for counselors and human development professionals.* Alexandria, VA: American Association for Counseling and Development.

Palmo, A. J., Weikel, W. J., & Brooks D. K. (Eds.). (1995). *Foundations of mental health counseling* (2nd ed.). St. Louis, MO: Charles C Thomas.

Piggrem, G. W., & Schmidt, L. (1982). Counseling the elderly. *Counseling and Human Development, 14*, 1–12.

Poggi, R. G., & Berland, D. I. (1985). The therapists' reactions to the elderly. *The Gerontologist, 25*, 508–513.

Salisbury, H. (1975). Counseling the elderly: A neglected area in counselor education and supervision. *Counselor Education and Supervision 14*, 237–238.

Special Committee on Aging, U.S. Senate. (1983). *Developments in aging, 1983*. Washington, DC: U.S. Government Printing Office.

Sweeney, T. J., & Myers, J. E. (1989). *Infusing gerontological counseling into counselor preparation: Video resources* (Parts 1–4). Alexandria, VA: American Association for Counseling and Development.

Sweeney, T. J., & Myers, J. E. (1990). *Infusing gerontological counseling into counselor preparation: Video resources* (Parts 5–7). Athens, OH: New Hope Enterprises.

Thompson, L. (1987). Comparative effectiveness of psychotherapy for depressed elders. *Journal of Consulting and Clinical Psychology, 55*, 385–390.

Waters, E. (1984). Building on what you know: Individual and group counseling for older people. *The Counseling Psychologist, 12*, 52–64.

Waters, E., Reiter, S., White, B., & Dates, B. (1979). The role of the paraprofessional peer counselor in working with older people. In M. L. Ganikos (Ed.), *Counseling the aged: A training syllabus for educators* (pp. 227–264). Alexandria, VA: America Counseling Association.

2

The Gerontological Counselor: Attitudes and Actions

Minimum Essential Competency #1 for a Gerontological Counseling Specialist: *demonstrates and actively advocates for positive, respectful, wellness-enhancing attitudes toward older persons and a concern for empowerment of persons throughout the life span.*

Older persons may be viewed as members of a minority group, albeit a large minority group. Stereotyping members of minority groups, which is prevalent in our society, results in widespread beliefs that commonly are both pervasive and negative. Gerontological counselors need to understand negative societal beliefs about older people, have accurate knowledge to combat these beliefs, and be willing and able to work proactively to overcome negative perceptions that limit the quality of life for the older population. In this chapter, attitudes toward older persons are explored, and common myths and stereotypes are examined. Gerontological counselors are challenged to examine their own beliefs and to develop strategies for proactive intervention on behalf of persons across the life span.

Attitudes Toward Older Persons

In his Pulitzer-Prize winning book, *Why Survive? Being Old in America*, Butler (1975) first coined the term *ageism* to describe the discrimination toward older persons that is so prevalent in our society today. Similar in nature to racism, sexism, or handicappism, ageism is a tendency to view all older persons in a similar and negative fashion. Numerous studies conducted in the United States over the last 20 years support the assertion that attitudes toward older persons are universally negative (Barbado & Feezel, 1987; Beaver, 1991; Myers, 1989, 1990). These studies have examined the attitudes of a variety of professionals, such as physicians, nurses, psychiatrists, psychologists, and rehabilitation counselors, as well as children, adolescents, and older persons themselves.

Old age is universally viewed as a time of physical and emotional declines and losses, and hence is seen as undesirable (Beaver, 1991; Butler, 1975). Many of the negative stereotypes of older persons result from overgeneralized reactions to the characteristics of some older individuals, and as a consequence may be viewed as reactions based on fear. Fear of personal aging, fear of loss of physical stamina, fear of loss of independence, fear of loss of older friends and relatives, fear of becoming a caregiver, and fear of one's own death are common beliefs that precipitate negative views of the aging process and aging persons (Myers, 1990).

The most pervasive, persistent, and untrue myths and stereotypes of older persons include the following: Old people are all alike; they are all sick; they are all poor. All older people are depressed. Old people all live alone; all old people want to live with their adult children. All old people live in institutions. All old people are senile. It is commonly and falsely believed that intelligence declines with age, that old people are unable to learn new things, and that older persons are incapable of or uninterested in sexuality.

There are more than 28,000,000 older persons in America (American Association of Retired Persons, 1993), and they represent perhaps the most heterogeneous subgroup of our population. It is true that 86% of all older persons experience one or more physical conditions that limit their ability to complete daily living activities, but it is also true that most persons with impairments are able to continue living independently. This is evidenced by the fact that only 4%–5% of older persons are living in long-term-care settings at any given point in time, while over 80% are able to live independently in the community. Between 10% and 15% are largely homebound due to physical and/or mental limitations and disabilities (see Brody & Ruff, 1986).

The effects of ageism are felt in all life arenas, including employment, consumerism, and socialization. Employers are subject to negative biases, and often conclude, erroneously, that older persons make poor employees. Numerous studies have shown older persons to be good employees, with low absentee rates, high motivation, and a greater sense of loyalty to their employers than is found among younger employees (Myers, 1994). Advertisements often are targeted toward young persons, with older people depicted in stereotypical negative ways. Socially, older persons often find themselves excluded from activities dominated by younger individuals, and report that persons of younger generations simply do not have time for them.

One of the most important lessons concerning the effect of negative societal perceptions was first identified through theories of minority identity development. These theories postulated that persons who belong to minority groups tend to internalize the dominant societal views concerning their particular minority group (Pedersen, 1991; Sue & Sue, 1990). This means that older individuals, being a part of society, tend to internalize negative societal perceptions, myths, and stereotypes of older people. Two outcomes of this internalization process are likely, neither of which is positive.

First, when older persons internalize a generalized dislike of all older people, they tend to dislike and not want to socialize with other older people. As a consequence, they may fail to develop satisfying peer relationships. This in turn can contribute to a sense of social isolation and may contribute to social withdrawal.

Second, when older persons internalize the negative societal perceptions of them, at some point they will personalize these perceptions. Examples of things they might say to themselves, consciously or unconsciously, are: "If old people are devalued, and I am an old person, then I am devalued. If old people are sick, lonely, and depressed, and I am an old person, then I am likely to be sick, lonely, and depressed." Thus, the negative perceptions held by society can become self-fulfilling prophecies for older persons who are made vulnerable by the arbitrary criterion of chronological age. Older persons who fail to identify themselves as "old" may in fact experience a more positive adjustment to aging and maintain a higher sense of self-esteem and worth than those who ascribe the descriptor "old" to themselves (Barbado & Feezel, 1987).

Counselor: Know Thyself

Negative societal views also affect those who provide services to older people. In the mental health fields, as in the medical fields, negative

myths and perceptions affect the nature and quality of services provided to older individuals. For example, many older persons are not
treated for depression because depression is viewed as a "normal"
aspect of aging. Difficult or painful subjects, circumstances, or memories are not explored with older clients because service providers are
not sure the former are "strong" enough to deal with the issues. Bad
news is withheld from older individuals, who are perceived as frail and
lacking the emotional strength to cope with personal and family
problems.

Unfortunately, as is true of all stereotypes of aging, there is a kernel
of truth in the examples here, at least for some older people some of
the time. Older persons who are "frail," those whose physical and/or
mental health is poor and fluctuating, may in fact be unable to cope
with the stress of bad news. We err, however, when we assume that all
older clients are "frail." Again, less than 20% may fit this definition,
and will likely be those older persons who live either in long-term care
or in an assisted community environment. For other older persons, it
can be a sign of respect for their abilities when we are willing to share
all of the news, just as would be done with younger persons (or with
those older persons themselves when they were younger). To make
decisions based on the arbitrary criterion of chronological age can be
a serious mistake when working with older individuals; it denies their
individuality and communicates a lack of respect for their abilities.

It is necessary for counselors working with older people to take
the time to examine our motivations for wanting to work with this
population. If the motivation is to help "those old people," then we
must ask ourselves if we truly view aging as *a part of* the normal life
span. Are we seeing older persons as somehow fundamentally different
from ourselves, and in need of assistance, or are we seeing them as an
extension of ourselves? From the latter perspective, it is likely that we
will recognize that older people experience the same nature and type
of concerns experienced by persons of any age. What differs is the
degree of need they experience, not the type of need.

If our motivation is to help older people because we view them as
being unable to help themselves, then again we should question our
motivation. As counselors, our goal should be to work ourselves out of
a job—to help people become as independent as possible within any
limitations they may have. Our resources are the assets that our clients

possess, combined with the assets we can help them create through the techniques and strategies we employ. If our goal is to help people help themselves, then we are on the right track.

Relatedly, we need to continually question our own assumptions and stereotypes about older persons. It is important to remember that our impressions are formed from the people we encounter. If we spend a lot of time with older persons who are unhealthy, poor, and frail, we may generalize these characteristics to "all" of the older population. Similarly, if most of our interactions are with healthy, vital, independent, involved older persons, we may assume that most older people are like those we know. If we find ourselves interacting with a healthy, happy, vibrant older person, and find ourselves thinking or saying how unique that person is, then we truly need to stop and ask ourselves what we really think about older people.

Counselors also need to be aware of their "comfort zones" in talking with older persons. For example, attitudes about older adult sexuality, or lack of knowlege of age-related changes in sexual functioning, may cause a counselor to be reluctant to talk with an older person about sexuality issues. Continuing education through reading or seminars, peer consultation, or referral are appropriate courses of action to deal with issues such as this.

Developing Positive, Respectful, Empowering Attitudes

We can begin to develop or enhance our positive attitudes toward aging by first confronting our own attitudes toward aging and older persons. If we plan to work with older people, some of the questions we need to ask are:

Why do I want to work with older people?
What have been my experiences with older people in my family?
What are the characteristics of older persons I consider to be desirable?
How do I view the aging of my parents?
Have I come to terms with the eventual death of my parents?
How do I feel about my own eventual death?
What signs of aging have I seen in myself physically, psychologically, and socially?

How do other people react toward me as a result of these signs or changes?

How do I feel about the reactions of other people toward my aging?

Having answered these questions, we have begun the lifelong process of examining and reexamining our attitudes toward and perceptions of older people. It is only through self-awareness and development of our own positive attitudes that we can begin to be effective advocates for older individuals.

Whatever our attitudes may be, they will be communicated in some manner to our older clients. We will be unable to hide our negative or positive attitudes. Negative attitudes can only lead to self-fulfilling prophecies: Our clients will become what we perceive them to be. Alternately, if we truly have positive attitudes, our respect for the capabilities of our older clients will, in and of themselves, assist them in reaching their full potential. In chapter 10 (this volume), strategies for enhancing wellness in later life are explored. These strategies are most effective when employed by counselors who truly believe they will work. It is important to realize that our attitudes can be a source of empowerment for others—perhaps an even greater source than any of our actions.

Summary

Attitudes toward older persons in society are generally negative and contribute to a loss of status as well as a lack of personal power for older individuals. To help overcome negative myths and stereotypes and facilitate the empowerment of individual older persons, counselors first need to examine their own perceptions and beliefs about aging. Coming to terms with personal attitudes and values related to the aging process is an important part of self-awareness for counselors. When we experience a positive sense of valuing of older persons, our efforts to help them deal with the circumstances of later life will be most effective.

Case Studies

Following are two case studies that allow the reader to apply the knowledge and skills learned in this chapter concerning the attitudes and actions required of a competent gerontological counselor. Read each case study and think about how you would help the client. Then read the comments for further insights into each situation.

Case One

Mr. S. retired at the age of 65. He is now 71 and has found his retirement income to be inadequate. In addition, he is lonely, feels somewhat useless, and is looking for ways to fill his time. He wants to return to work and has applied for many positions. He believes that employers will not hire him because of his age and has come to you for assistance in finding satisfying work. What are some ways you might help him overcome the effects of ageism in employment?

Comments on Case One

Whatever other issues may be contributing to his inability to find work, it is almost a given that age discrimination is one factor. Mr. S. is not protected by the Age Discrimination in Employment Act because this federal legislation only protects persons ages 40–70. In chapter 7 (this volume), career and lifestyle options for older workers are explored. In this chapter, the focus is on attitudes and ageism. Given this focus, it might be helpful to explore with Mr. S. the basis for his concern that employers will not hire him because of his age. What are some of the things that have been said to him, verbally or nonverbally, that have communicated a concern with his age? How does he feel about these issues?

Another area to explore is Mr. S.'s perceptions of the characteristics of older workers that may work against their being hired. To what extent may these characteristics be true of him? What can he do to advocate with potential employers to overcome their negative perceptions? What can he tell them about himself that will emphasize his positive characteristics?

Case Two

Wendy W. is a young counselor in your peer supervision group who has just had an appointment with an older client. She jokes about her client in negative terms, commenting on her inappropriate dress and obvious hearing problem. She wonders why the client is so anxious about things that happened a long time ago, yet is unable to provide any details about her current life circumstances. She indicates that the client seems too set in her ways to change, and thus she does not see any value in working with her. How do you respond?

Comments on Case Two

We often are confronted with the negative perceptions of our coworkers with regard to older clients. We can choose to ignore them, challenge them, or try to educate them. In this case, the latter choice may be appropriate, but it can be difficult because you do not want to be perceived as reprimanding or criticizing your colleague. Rather, it is important to validate your peer and emphasize the positive actions he or she may have taken. After all, we all want to believe we are doing the "right" thing, and that we are good and effective counselors. At the same time, you want to open opportunities for the older client to receive help.

One option is to state your own preference for working with this type and client, and ask if the colleague would refer her to you. A possibility is to say something like, "What a difficult case! You surely sound like you had a hard session. I have been reading about this type of client, and wonder if I might have a try with her."

Another option is to "disclose" your own knowledge and concerns about working with older clients, followed by either a request for assistance or a referral. You could say something like,

> Older people really can be challenging clients. I learned about problems similar to these in one of my classes. Many older people, especially those living alone who are not involved in community activities, live a daily existence which is not very full of activities. They really don't have much to talk about. At the same time, they are going through a pretty normal process that Erikson calls life review (see chaps. 4 and 15), and as part of this process they tell stories about things that may have happened a long time ago. I'd be glad to share some of my information about this process and how it can be used therapeutically, if you like. If you really don't want to work with this client, would you mind if I tried?

By normalizing the client's interactions, you can provide information to your colleague about what older people "really" are like, thus helping to overcome negative stereotypes.

Discussion Questions

1. What are some of the negative myths and stereotypes of aging that you have heard? What evidence do you have to disprove these statements?
2. What are some ways you can show respect for older persons?
3. What are some examples of positive, wellness-enhancing attitudes toward older persons?

References

American Association of Retired Persons. (1993). *A profile of older Americans, 1993*. Washington, DC: Author.

Barbado, C.A., & Feezel, J.D. (1987). The language of aging in different groups. *The Gerontologist, 27*(4), 527–531.

Beaver, J.L. (1991). *Aged stereotypes and their effects on older persons' self-esteem*. (MF01/PC03). Master's paper, Ohio University, Athens, OH. (ERIC Document Reproduction Service No. ED 334 492)

Brody, S.J., & Ruff, G.E. (Eds.). (1986). *Aging and rehabilitation: Advances in the state of the art*. New York: Springer.

Butler, R.N. (1975). *Why survive? Being old in America*. New York: Harper & Row.

Myers, J.E. (1989). *Infusing gerontological counseling into counselor preparation: Curriculum guide*. Alexandria, VA: American Counseling Association.

Myers, J.E. (1990). *Adult children and aging parents*. Alexandria, VA: American Counseling Association.

Myers, J.E. (1994). Understanding the older worker: Physical and emotional factors. *Career Planning and Adult Development Journal, 10*(2), 4–9.

Pedersen, P. (1991). Multiculturalism as a fourth force in counseling [Special Issue]. *Journal of Counseling and Development, 20*.

Sue, D., & Sue, S. (1990). *Counseling the culturally different* (2nd ed.). Englewood Cliffs, NJ: Prentice-Hall.

3

Development and Transition in Later Life

Minimum Essential Competency #2 for a Gerontological Counseling Specialist: *demonstrates skill in applying extensive knowledge of human development for older persons, including major theories of aging, the relationship between physical and mental health and aging, the difference between normal and pathological aging processes, gender-related developmental differences, and coping skills for life transitions and losses.*

T he needs that older persons have for counseling include personal growth as well as remediation of problem situations. Knowledge of normal aspects of later life development is essential if counselors are to effectively meet needs in both of these areas. In addition, counselors need to be able to distinguish normal from pathological age-related changes. This information is essential when working with older persons and their families as they attempt to cope with the many changes that occur in later life. Knowledge of human development across the life span is a necessary theoretical base for facilitating life satisfaction at all ages, and particularly in later life.

In this chapter, theories of aging are discussed. The relationship between physical and mental health in later life is explored, followed by a consideration of differences between normal and pathological aging processes. Gender differences in aging are briefly considered, followed by a discussion of later life transitions and coping strategies.

Later Life Development and Theories of Aging

Theories of later life development and aging attempt to explain how people generally or "normally" behave as they grow older. These theories may be based in biological, psychological, or social sciences. Theories based in the social sciences are of most use to counselors. These theories usually identify factors that discriminate between older persons who experience a sense of life satisfaction and those who are not satisfied with life in their later years.

Theories of Later Life Development

Erikson's Theory of Life Span Development. Erikson (1963) proposed the first life span developmental theory, according to which persons experience a series of eight psychosocial crises across the course of their life span. These crises are sequential and hierarchical, in that the successful resolution of subsequent crises is dependent on the successful resolution of each earlier crisis. Resolution is not "either–or," but a matter of degree. Thus, by the time persons reach old age, they will have resolved, to some degree of success or nonsuccess, each of Erikson's first seven psychosocial crises. In addition to helping older persons resolve the eighth crisis, the central crisis of later life, counselors may find themselves needing to assist clients in resolving earlier crises.

The life stages or crises posited by Erikson include: trust versus mistrust, autonomy versus shame and doubt, initiative versus guilt, industry versus inferiority, identity versus role confusion, intimacy versus isolation, generativity versus stagnation, and ego integrity versus despair. Although some older adults may be expected to struggle with the first four stages, almost all will experience recurring problems with the last four life stages as a result of the challenges and changes of later life. For example, retirement is a time for reexamination of one's identity and a need to answer the question, "Who am I?" Widowhood forces an examination of needs for intimacy, while loss of friends due to death or geographic moves requires older persons to reestablish support networks to avoid feeling a sense of isolation. Grandparenthood, or lack of grandparenthood status, may stimulate concerns about generativity. Similarly, developing satisfying uses of free time after retirement may stimulate older persons to seek ways to contribute their skills and talents through volunteer activities or community service.

The central psychosocial crisis of later life is the search for ego integrity. The process of life review is an essential means of achieving integrity, or the sense that the life one lived is the best one could have lived (see chap. 14, this volume, for suggestions on how to use life review as a therapeutic process for helping older persons achieve ego integrity). A failure to achieve this sense of well-being leads to despair because it is too late to make the changes that might have resulted in a sense of satisfaction with one's life.

Havighurst's Theory of Aging and Education. Other authors, notably Havighurst (1972), have attempted to define life tasks that must be met if older persons are to age successfully and happily. These include: (a) adjusting to decreasing physical strength and health, (b) adjusting to retirement and reduced income, (c) adjusting to the death of a spouse, (d) establishing an explicit affiliation with one's age group, (e) adopting and adapting social roles in a flexible way, and (f) establishing satisfactory living arrangements. These and other tasks imply the need to make significant life changes if the later years are to be lived with a sense of well-being.

Riker and Myers' Theory of Later Life Development. By adopting a perspective of the human life span as composed of a series of developmental stages, counselors can help older persons understand that each stage includes a series of developmental tasks that must be accomplished successfully if the individual is to move onto the next life stage. Riker and Myers (1989) suggested that a close study of the decades of life beginning at age 60 could reveal a series of life stages and tasks that had not yet been identified. In conducting such a study, they noted two key points: (a) Life changes are frequent at all ages and adaptation to change is thus a continuing task, and (b) some tasks are repeated during the various life stages. Some tasks are important for persons of various ages to consider and accomplish, rather than being specific to a particular age. This becomes increasingly true in later life. Successful resolution or achievement of a task is not an end in itself, but a means to continued successful coping with similar or even identical tasks in later years.

Riker and Myers suggested three basic assumptions about developmental tasks in later life: (a) life tasks should be positive, (b) participation in activities represents a healthy approach to growing older, and (c) in our lives there tends to be an evolution from a concern about relationships with other persons to a concern about relationships to oneself and to one's God. The developmental tasks for later life posited by Riker and Myers all concern reacting to change and building positive life concepts. These tasks include consideration of growth in five life arenas during each decade of later life: career, family, leisure, intimacy, and inner life.

The 50s are often a time for questioning work and leisure values and redefining personal roles in the various life arenas. There is renewed emphasis on relationships with others. In the 60s, persons engage in a careful look at their life habits, replacing busyness for its own sake with personal involvement in helping others, developing one's own capacities, and seeking new life meanings. The 70s are a time when leisure becomes more important than work, family and friendships grow in significance, and the search for life's meaning intensifies. The 80s provide opportunities for aging persons to strengthen their sense of self and their feelings of personal power. These opportunities may be found through continuing to develop family and friendship circles, expanding creative activities, coping with physical changes, taking more time for reflection, and achieving inner peace. In the 90s, individuals build their sense of spiritual wholeness. This is a time when past problems may become inconsequential, when present relationships and activities may be enjoyed for themselves, and when the uncertainties of the future may be faced with a sense of composure. People in their 90s and beyond enjoy their lives by appreciating the events of each day and the people who enter into those days.

Additional Developmental Theories. Most theories of human development offer similar perspectives (Fry, 1992). The later years of life are a time for changes in lifestyle, greater inner-directness, slowing down, and evaluating the totality of one's life span. Erikson wrote at a time when people did not live as long as they do today, leaving him to define the period of later adulthood as that over age 50. Because people now live one fourth to one third or more of their lives as older persons, some reexamination of Erikson's theories is timely. In fact, the results of recent research suggest that the search for integrity is largely completed during the sixth decade, leaving older persons with the time, resources, and energy to make significant life changes and to set new goals (Riker & Myers, 1989).

Theories of Aging

Three major theories of aging have been proposed to explain personality and psychological functioning in later life: Disengagement, Activity, and Continuity. Each theory has some support in the literature (Fry, 1992), thus each may be useful in explaining the behavior of some older persons at some point in time. As a consequence, each of these theories may prove useful at some time for counselors working with older clients.

Disengagement Theory.   The Disengagement Theory, developed by Cumming and Henry (1961), was the first theory specifically developed to explain psychological aspects of the aging process. The theory posited that older persons withdraw from society and society withdraws from older persons in a mutually desired and mutually beneficial process. The withdrawal accommodates both the older person's declining energies and society's need to integrate younger persons into the mainstream of events. Needless to say, the preponderance of comments in the literature concerning this theory are negative.

Activity Theory.   The Activity Theory, proposed by Neugarten, Havighurst, and Tobin (1968), was developed in response to the Disengagement Theory. According to this theory, older persons are similar to persons of middle age, with the exception of biological and health changes. The reduced social interactions observed in older persons are due to society and the effects of ageism, not to factors inherent in older persons themselves. To age successfully, older adults will remain active as long as possible, continuing the activities of middle age, and resist the shrinkage of their social world.

Continuity Theory.   Continuity Theory (Rosow, 1963) suggests that personality remains stable in later life. The unique patterns of personality traits and behaviors of individuals are consistent across the life span and mediate the aging process. At the same time, established personality traits may become more pronounced as persons respond to the stresses of later life. Continuity Theory is operationalized in the statement often made by the authors of this book: "As persons become older, they become more and more like themselves and less and less like anyone else." Fry (1992) noted that Continuity Theory continues to be expanded and studied as a desirable explanation of personality development in later life.

Physical and Mental Health and Aging

Aging is accompanied by changes and declines in virtually every body system (Saxon & Etten, 1992), yet most changes are so gradual that older persons cope with and adapt to them without serious disruption to their daily living activities. What seems to change with age and contributes to declines in overall functioning is the extent of interaction between biological, psychological, and social factors (Kemp, 1986). These three aspects of functioning are universal, and their interaction at all points in the life span is significant. Two aspects of age-related changes in these three areas are noteworthy: the interaction of these aspects of functioning, and the direction of subsequent functional changes.

Throughout the life span, biological, psychological, and social aspects of functioning in all persons overlap and interact so that changes in one area affect or contribute to changes in other areas. As persons grow older, the amount of overlap increases significantly. As a result, even small changes in one area of functioning can create major changes or disturbances in other areas. Medication mismanagement, which can occur if older persons "forget" whether they took their medication and take a second dose, or "remember" that they already took their medication and take no dose, can result in acute onset of confusion or impaired mental functioning. Lack of prompt and accurate diagnosis and treatment can lead to chronic impairment. Short- and long-range changes in the social sphere, such as the loss of a job due to retirement or an argument with an adult child, can lead to agitation, anxiety, or depression. These symptoms may result in older persons failing to eat properly or take medications as prescribed, leading to physical as well as psychological symptoms.

The direction of change need not be negative; changes can be in the direction of increased as well as decreased functioning. For example, use of medications to treat serious depression can result in more positive moods, better social relationships, and a more positive sense of self. Increased appetites stimulated by medications can contribute to improved physical functioning. Part-time employment or volunteer activities can restore a sense of meaning and purpose in the life of an older person who is feeling the negative effects of job and role loss due to retirement. Grandparenting can have a positive effect on older persons, who may once again feel needed and valued in their families. Family counseling can help older persons and their adult children develop more satisfying relationships, which in turn will contribute to an overall increase in functioning for the older adults.

The Social Breakdown Theory is helpful in understanding the relationships among social, psychological, and biological changes in later life, and the impact these changes have on the physical and mental health of older persons. Kuypers and Bengtson (1973) described the Social Breakdown Syndrome as an explanation of negative adjustment in later life, developing the corollary Social Reconstruction Model to explain how the syndrome can be reversed.

According to the Social Breakdown Model, being old in our society creates a predisposition toward vulnerability. The negative messages that older persons hear—from the media, employers, physicians, relatives, and even friends—are almost unavoidably internalized; older persons begin to experience a loss of self-esteem, as well as question their capabilities in later life as opposed to their earlier years. Suggestions that they "act their age," not do certain things because of their age, and so forth exacerbate internal doubts. In effect, if people in positions of authority or loved ones continually suggest that a person is less capable than previously, it is difficult not to begin to believe the message.

Once external social messages of incapacity are internalized, decreases in self-esteem are felt and contribute to an enhanced sense of vulnerability. Combined with the actual physical, social, and psychological changes and losses of later life, the sense of vulnerability and loss of self-esteem begin to interact in a negative downward spiral, resulting ultimately in the death of the now-incapacitated older individual.

Part of the Social Breakdown Model's value lies in its usefulness in helping counselors understand how the circumstances of later life contribute to mental health problems. Ultimately, however, this model is useful because it allows for social reconstruction to occur, in which the negative cycle is slowed, stopped, or even reversed. The impact of social breakdown may be changed at any point in the cycle, through a variety of avenues that are targeted at improving older people's daily lives. Better housing, nutrition, and medical care are examples, as are employment and volunteer opportunities for older persons. Counseling interventions are an important means of empowering older persons to take action on their own behalf to interrupt and reverse social breakdown.

Normal Versus Pathological Aging

Although physical changes and declines are a normal part of the aging process, significant impairment of function is not normal. It is important that counselors be able to discriminate between normal and pathological aspects of the aging process, and that they be able to communicate this information to older persons and their families. The changing relationship among physical, psychological, and social functioning described earlier is an important key to understanding age-related changes. What is seen in terms of the functioning of an older person may be due to multiple causes; some may be remediated, whereas others may require management and adaptation.

The differential diagnosis of pathology in later life can be a complex and difficult process. Hence, counselors need to function as part of a team of service providers when working with older clients. The services of a geriatric physician will almost always be necessary with frail older persons (especially those who are "old-old," or over 85 years of age). Extensive and accurate history taking is essential for effective diagnosis. Involvement of family members, relatives, neighbors, friends, and/or service providers may sometimes be necessary to achieve accurate information about an older person.

Knowing when to refer an older person for needed services is important. Counselors should be familiar with the array of services available in the "aging network" (see chap. 12, this volume), and be willing to provide referrals as needed. In general, referral for medical evaluation is needed whenever changes appear suddenly. Normal age-related changes are almost always gradual in nature. Sudden changes reflect possible pathology and require thorough evaluation. Of course, sometimes changes that occur gradually over time become evident in a seemingly sudden manner. It is always best to error on the side of more thorough evaluations.

Gender and Aging

It is fairly well known that women live longer than men. As a consequence, most older persons (about 58%) are female, and most of them are single (American Association of Retired Persons, 1993). Less than half of older women are married, whereas over three fourths of older men are married. There are five times as many widows as widowers, and the remarriage rate for older men is more than five times that for older women. The ratio of men to women in the population declines after the age of 25, thus women have decreasing chances of marriage as they get older. Older men are more likely to live in a family environment, whereas older women are more likely to live alone.

Demographics suggest that older women are likely to be at risk for loneliness and isolation. In addition, older women experience the cumulative results of a lifetime of social discrimination, particularly in the job market. A lifetime of limited employment opportunities among today's older women has resulted in lower incomes from pension and security plans compared with older men. In addition, many of today's older women did not work outside the home, were not primary breadwinners, or worked in jobs not covered by Social Security. Hence, they may have no income beyond a pension from their spouse. Widowhood and divorce create additional income stresses. Older women are more likely to live in poverty than older men, with all of the attendant problems that come from not having enough income to meet daily living needs. Women (and men) who were poor all of their lives can expect to experience greater poverty in later life.

Additional problems of older women include a lack of attention and negative stereotyping from the medical profession, and a general devaluing in a society that emphasizes youth, lack of wrinkles, firm and slender bodies, and physical vitality.

At the same time, there are positive aspects of aging that are experienced by many older women. These include good health and longevity, freedom from the conflicts between mothering and careers, freedom from childrearing, and often freedom from spousal care or long-term unsatisfying marriages. Older women possess relatively unexplored potential for creative expression. Today's older women are pioneers, having lived longer than women of previous generations, living in a different and more liberal social structure, and having the freedom to create lives that were denied to prior generations of women as a result of the existing social structure. As increasing numbers of women retire from careers with incomes that can support a variety of activities in retirement, additional lifestyle options may be created. These women can serve as role models of independence and success for women in younger age cohorts. In addition to these advantages, older women represent a powerful group politically if they work together, through organizations such as the Older Women's League (OWL), a national political action organization for older women, or through the American Association of Retired Persons, which has special programs for older women.

Many of the problems that affect older women affect older men as well. The literature on aging describes the problems of aging as largely the problems of women, with older men being given far less attention. Yet it is known that the highest suicide rates in the United States occur for older White males, and suicide rates for men exceed those for women in all age groups (McIntosh, 1988–1989; Osgood, 1985). Although it is true that older persons in general do not respond enthusiastically to opportunities for counseling, failure to seek or accept counseling services when offered is even more common among older men than among older women. After a lifetime in which male relationships were stoic and distant, many older men find themselves deprived of needed emotional support during times of illness and stress.

Later Life Transitions and Coping

Transition theories explain how persons of any age cope and adapt to stressful life circumstances. Schlossberg (1984) considered personal perceptions of events, personal characteristics, and characteristics of the environment to be central to understanding how people cope with change. She defined *transitions* as resulting from anticipated or unanticipated events or nonevents, as well as what she called "chronic hassles." Conflicting and confusing emotions occur during any transition and affect the duration and severity of the experience. Common transitions experienced by older persons include biological changes and declines, adjustment to ageist attitudes, retirement, divorce, grandparenthood, residential relocation, and death.

Schlossberg explained transitions as events (or nonevents) resulting in stress and the need for adaptation. Transitions are influenced by older persons' perceptions of the transition, their personal characteristics, and the characteristics of the environment. Transitions may be anticipated, such as occurs with retirement at a particular age, or nonanticipated, such as occurs with an unplanned, forced retirement. They may consist of chronic hassles, such as an unhappy marital relationship that continues over time and emotionally immobilizes one of the partners, or they may be nonevents, such as the transition to grandparenthood that did not occur because one's children did not marry or chose not to have children of their own. Whatever the source of the transition, it is likely to be a process that occurs over time, is accompanied by a variety of confusing and conflicting emotions, and is an opportunity for growth as well as a time of potential or actual crisis.

Transitions commonly experienced by older persons include widowhood, divorce, job loss as a result of retirement, change in living arrangements, change in physical health and energy, and grandparenthood. Many of these transitions are experienced as negative, unhappy events. Counseling techniques that employ strategies for coping with loss are important, as well as those that emphasize crisis intervention (Kampfe & Kampfe, 1992; Myers, 1990).

Helping older persons cope with later life transitions requires a focus on adult roles, routines, assumptions about self, and relationships (Schlossberg, 1990). Thus, a specific, concrete focus is provided as a basis for mental health interventions. Older persons can be encouraged to talk about how the transition has affected or will affect their life and roles, and how their life will be or has been altered as a result. Coping skills can be taught to deal with the transitions either before (preferably) or after they have occurred. Decision-making skills also can be emphasized during transition times.

Summary

In this chapter, several theories of aging and later life development were discussed. Each of these theories is helpful in explaining the behavior of some older persons some of the time. However, there is as yet no one comprehensive theory that is helpful in understanding the behavior of all older persons most or all of the time. Understanding theoretical perspectives on aging and how older persons may be expected to cope with the transitions common in later life provides a starting point for determining normal age-related developmental changes as opposed to what may be non-normal or even pathological changes. Gender issues, reviewed in this chapter, are important considerations in understanding development in later life.

Case Studies

Following are two case studies that will allow the reader to apply the knowledge and skills learned in this chapter related to development and transitions in later life. Read each case study and think about how you would help the client. Then read the comments for further insights into the role of the gerontological counselor in each situation.

Case One

Mr. B. is an 88-year-old man whose spouse recently died. At about the same time, he was hospitalized for pneumonia, and subsequently moved to a retirement community. He uses a wheelchair to get around and has a hearing impairment that is partially corrected through hearing aids in both ears. He takes medication for hypertension, has a slight speech impediment as a result of a stroke, and wears glasses. He returned to work after retirement in a new career in real estate, and has been completely retired only in the past 3 years. He was referred to you by the activity director of the retirement community, who was concerned that he does not participate in activities and may be depressed. She asked him if he would like a referral to a counselor and he said no, so the activity director has advised you not to identify yourself as a counselor when you meet with him. How would you approach working with Mr. B.?

Comments on Case One

Developmentally, Mr. B. may be dealing with a variety of psychosocial crises and life tasks that have been resolved to varying degrees. He probably has dealt with the crisis of ego integrity versus despair; however, the loss of his wife likely has caused integrity as well as identity issues to resurface, along with concerns about intimacy. Family roles and relationships with his adult children are likely to be important. Spiritual issues may surface as well because he is likely to be considering issues related to death and the meaning of life. He has experienced a number of significant transitions that may be fully or partially resolved. You will need to obtain an accurate history of how Mr. B. has dealt with transitions and losses in the past to get an idea of his typical way of coping with stress and change.

You may need to begin by explaining that you are a helper who was asked by the activity director to talk with Mr. B. You may explain that you wish to find out if he has any specific concerns that need to be addressed. Because he has indicated that he does not want the services of a professional counselor, he is unlikely to accept your services at first if you present yourself in this manner. This is not at all unusual when working with older persons, especially older men. As you get to know him, he is likely to be less concerned when you tell him, which eventually you will, that you have been trained as a counselor and that counseling is nothing more than helping "normal" people talk about "normal" situations and concerns.

Building trust with Mr. B. is an important consideration. This takes time, and requires you to establish and maintain a regular schedule of visits. Understanding that most older men lack a feeling vocabulary is important; you should not expect or demand expressions of feelings. Communicating respect and a desire to understand is important, as are approaches that emphasize empowerment (see chaps. 10, 13, and 14, this volume).

Case Two

Mrs. L. was referred by her daughter, who is concerned that her mother is depressed and obsessed with her vision problems. Mrs. L. is 82, widowed, and lives alone. She says she went to a new eye doctor who put drops in her eyes and ruined her vision. She talks constantly about her need to see someone who can help her see again. She has macular degeneration leading to progressive blindness, and her vision is not correctable beyond the current prescription.

Comments on Case Two

Mrs. L. needs someone to take the time to listen to her concerns and help her understand her visual condition. It is important to recognize that she is attempting to address a new problem with old solutions, and that those old solutions have worked effectively for her for decades. Each time her vision changed during her life, she went to a doctor, got a new prescription for glasses, and was able to see well again. Her expectation was that the same thing would happen now, and she is having a difficult time accepting her diagnosis. In addition, her physician has not taken the time to talk with her.

Mrs. L.'s physical changes are contributing to problems in her social relationships because she finds herself unable to talk about anything except her vision. Further, she is depressed and has frequent crying spells related to being unable to see. A referral to her primary care physician for medication, combined with counseling, may be necessary. Family counseling to help her adult daughter cope more effectively with her fears and concerns about her mother can be helpful. Having both generations together will provide an opportunity to improve their intergenerational communication, so that they can solve future problems more effectively without need for outside assistance.

In addition to dealing with possible depression, this client may be experiencing anxiety, which also needs to be treated. Taking the time to assess the reasons for her behaviors is important to the differential diagnosis.

Discussion Questions

1. Think of an older person you know well. Can you explain this person's behavior using one or more of the theories of aging described in this chapter?
2. Think of an older person you know who is experiencing difficulty in one or more life spheres. How can you use the Social Breakdown Syndrome to explain this individual's current functioning and predict future problems? How might you use the Social Reconstruction Model to effect positive changes for this older person?
3. What are some of the major transitions experienced by older persons? What can you, as a counselor, do to help older people cope effectively with these transitions?

References

American Association of Retired Persons. (1993). *A profile of older Americans, 1993.* Washington, DC: Author.

Cumming, E., & Henry, W.E. (1961). *Growing old: The process of disengagement.* New York: Basic Books.

Erikson, E. (1963). *Childhood and society.* New York: Norton.

Fry, P.S. (1992). Major social theories of aging and their implications for counseling concepts and practice: A critical review. *The Counseling Psychologist, 20*(2), 246–329.

Havighurst, R.J. (1972). *Developmental tasks and education*. New York: McKay.

Kampfe, C.M., & Kampfe, R.L. (1992). Coping strategies used by older upper-middle-class persons making residential relocations. *Arizona Counseling Journal, 17*, 3–9.

Kemp, B. (1986). Psychosocial and mental health issues in rehabilitation of older persons. In S.J. Brody & G.E. Ruff (Eds.), *Aging and rehabilitation: Advances in the state of the art* (pp. 122–158). New York: Springer.

Kuypers, J.A., & Bengtson, V.L. (1973). Competence and social breakdown: A social-psychological view of aging. *Human Development, 16*, 37–49.

McIntosh, J. (1988–1989). Official U.S. elderly suicide data bases: Levels, availability, omissions. *Omega Journal of Death and Dying, 19*(4), 337–350.

Myers, J.E. (1990). *Empowerment for later life*. Greensboro, NC: ERIC/CASS.

Neugarten, B., Havighurst, R.J., & Tobin, S. (1968). Personality and patterns of aging. In B.L. Neugarten (Ed.), *Middle age and aging* (pp. 173–177). Chicago: University of Chicago Press.

Riker, H.C., & Myers, J.E. (1989). *Retirement counseling: A handbook for action*. New York: Hemisphere.

Rosow, I. (1963). Adjustment of the normal aged. In R. Williams, C. Tibbits, & W. Donohue (Eds.), *Process of aging* (Vol. 2, pp. 195–223). New York: Atherton.

Saxon, S., & Etten, M.J. (1992). *Physical change and aging: A guide for the helping professions*. New York: Tiresius Press.

Schlossberg, N. (1984). *Counseling adults in transition*. New York: Springer.

Schlossberg, N.K. (1990). Training counselors to work with older adults. *Generations, XIV*(1), 7–10.

4

Social and Cultural Foundations of Aging

Minimum Essential Competency #3 for a Gerontological Counseling Specialist: *demonstrates skill in applying extensive knowledge of social and cultural foundations for older persons, including characteristics and needs of older minority subgroups, factors affecting substance and medication misuse abuse, recognition and treatment of elder abuse, and knowledge of social service programs.*

I t is important for counselors working with older persons to understand the trends and changes in society and the impact of these changes on the older population. Additionally, if counselors are to be sensitive to the needs of a diverse population of older persons, they must be aware of the cultural context of aging. This chapter provides the gerontological counselor with an overview of the social and cultural foundations of aging in the United States. The topics included here are: demography of aging, demography and diversity, life expectancy, older persons and the economy, older persons and geographic location, older women and society, older men and society, health status of older persons, mental health and older persons, sexuality and older persons, marriage and children, family relationships and caregiving, stress and older persons, elder abuse, and drug misuse and abuse.

Demography of Aging

Demographic changes in the population over age 65 are having a profound impact on American society. In 1992, the number of individuals age 65+ had risen to 12.7% of the U.S. population compared with 4.1% in 1900. By the year 2030, it is projected that 21% of the population will be in this age group. Additionally, by the year 2010, there will be approximately 6.8 million persons over age 85, equaling 2.4% of the total population (U.S. Administration on Aging, 1989). Therefore, the number of older persons in the U.S. population can be seen as increasing not only in numbers but in proportion to the total population.

Demography and Diversity

Demographic projections show that the population of older Americans will also increase in diversity. It is projected that during the next 60 years, the number of African American elders will grow from 8.3% to 14%, and the number of Hispanic elders will increase from 3.6% to 11.5% (U.S. Bureau of the Census, 1990). Non-White older populations continue to grow faster than the White older population because of higher birth rates and more rapid increases in life expectancy.

African American elders are likely to live in urban areas, have a relatively high rate of multiple chronic diseases, and traditionally have problems accessing formal support systems. Thus, they underutilize available services, relying more heavily on their families and informal support networks, such as friends and churches, for assistance (Johnson & Barer, 1990; Pedersen, 1991; Taylor & Chatters, 1986).

Research findings are equivocal as to whether Hispanic elders rely most heavily on their families for care and support. Espino, Neufeld, Mulvihill, and Libow (1988) found that Hispanic elders who had been admitted to a nursing home were younger and had more disabilities than non-Hispanics. This finding suggests that families may not be able to maintain an impaired member at home. Because Hispanic elders also have multiple chronic health problems, poorer mental health, and lower life satisfaction than African Americans and Whites, they may need more coordinated community services (Johnson et al., 1988).

The problems of minority older persons in general include the fact that they are more likely than their White counterparts to live in poverty, receive inadequate health care and resort to folk remedies, be victims of violent crimes, have limited access to transportation, have substandard housing, and experience emotional disorders due to loss of meaningful activity, status, and self-esteem (Exum, 1982). In addition, problems unique to subgroups of older minorities may affect the counseling outcomes. Counselors working with minority older persons need to be familiar with the unique social and cultural difficulties faced by all minority older persons in our society, as well as be familiar with the unique aspects of each culture that may affect the counseling relationship (Lee & Richardson, 1991; Pedersen, 1991; Sue, 1990).

Life Expectancy

Life expectancy for both men and women has increased steadily since 1900. A person born in 1900 could expect to live an average of only 49 years, while a person born in 1991 could expect to live 75.5 years (American Association of Retired Persons, 1993). The longer persons live, the longer they expect to live. Thus, a person who was age 65 in 1991 could expect to live an additional 17.4 years, or to the age of 82.4. Women who were 65 in 1991 could expect to live an additional 19 years, while men could expect to live an additional 15 years. The differential life expectancy for women results in older women outnumbering older men in the U.S. population by a ratio of 147:100. The ratio of older women to older men continues to increase to 258:100 for those over age 85.

Older Persons and the Economy

One in five older persons was poor (12.9%) or near poor (8%) in 1992, including 11% of White older persons, 33% of African American older persons, and 22% of Hispanic older persons. Older persons who reside in rural areas are more likely to live at or below the poverty level than those who live in urban areas. Social Security was the major source of income for older individuals and couples (37%), followed by asset income (25%), earnings (18%), public and private pensions (18%), and other sources (3%), such as Supplemental Security Income (SSI) and veteran's payments (American Association of Retired Persons, 1993). Additionally, most older persons experience a one-half to two-thirds drop in total income upon retirement and live on fixed incomes. In summary, the financial status of older persons in general is not as good as that of the population as a whole.

Older Persons and Geographic Location

The states with the largest total populations are also the states with the largest numbers of older persons. These states, in decreasing order of population, include California, Florida, New York, Pennsylvania, Texas, Illinois, and Ohio. However, this does not mean that these states have the highest proportion of older persons in their total population, with the exception of Florida and Pennsylvania. The states with the highest total proportions of older persons in their population, in decreasing order, are Florida (18.4%), Pennsylvania (15.7%), Iowa (15.4%), Arkansas (14.9%), South Dakota (14.7%), North Dakota (14.6%), Rhode Island (14.2%), and West Virginia (14.2%; American Association of Retired Persons, 1993). It is important to note that, for most of these states, the large proportions of older persons are due to the outmigration of young persons and not the influx of older persons.

Most older persons live in metropolitan areas. In contrast to popular opinion, most older adults live in the same place where they lived in midlife. Those who do move are more likely to be married, not working, well educated, and relatively affluent compared with those who do not move.

Older Women and Society

Approximately 57% of older persons are female, and most of them are single. Over 50% of older women are widows, and most of them live alone. There are five times as many widows as older widowers. Society continues to discourage marriage between older women and younger men, therefore the number of potential partners decreases rapidly for older women. Because women tend to marry older men, and because they tend to outlive men by several years, the average American woman can expect to be a widow for 25 years (Special Committee on Aging, 1983).

Older women are less likely to live in family environments than older men. However, this figure decreases with advancing age for both sexes. Older widowed women are more likely to be invited to live with adult children than older men.

Discrimination against women in society as a whole, and the socialization of older women to be dependent on men, have resulted in limited employment opportunities for older women and decreased earnings. Although the research suggests that older women are valuable workers, they continue to be employed in low-status, unskilled, low-paying jobs. Additionally, until 1973, Social Security discriminated against women: Many jobs held by women were not covered by Social Security, and widows only received 82% of their husbands' benefits even though they had worked in the home, without pay, all of their lives.

Positive aspects of aging for older women include increased longevity and good health. Additionally, many older women are free from the pressures of mothering, marriage, and careers. This gives them the freedom to explore areas of interest and develop their creativity and self-expression. Also, women who were pressured into marriage by society may now be free to experience a preferred lifestyle, such as living alone or with a female partner. Older women are increasingly vocal and are a powerful political group. As such, they can serve as mentors and models of independence and success for younger women.

Older Men and Society

Older men are generally married and living with their spouse. If they lose a spouse, they tend to remarry at higher rates than older women. In addition, older widowed men tend to marry younger women. Among persons over age 55, the remarriage rate for widowers is more than five times that for widows (Cox, 1988).

The problems and experiences of older men have been given less attention in the literature than those of older women. This is largely because women make up the majority of older persons, therefore the problems of aging are closely tied to the problems of older women. This fact is interesting because men have higher suicide rates than women at all ages—a disparity that is more pronounced in the older population than in any other age group. Suicide rates are four times the national average for older men, compared with two times the national average for older women. Older males tend to complete suicide more often than older females, and they tend to use more violent methods than older women (Osgood, 1985).

Health Status of Older Persons

A common misconception related to the health status of older persons is that most older persons are in poor health and live in nursing homes. In fact, most older persons report that their health status is either "excellent" or "good." Only a small percentage of older persons report their health status as "poor." Although chronic illnesses increase with age, the majority of older persons are able to carry out their activities of daily living without assistance (approximately 80%). For most individuals, health status and independent daily functioning are not affected until age 75 or older.

Most older persons receive medical treatment for chronic conditions such as arthritis, hypertension, hearing impairment, heart disease, arteriosclerosis, visual impairment, and diabetes. Even so, most older persons cope with the progression of physical limitations without disruption of their activities. The three leading causes of death for older persons, which result in three fourths of all elderly deaths, include heart disease, stroke, and cancer. These conditions create progressive disabilities in later life.

Mental Health and Older Persons

In general, the incidence of mental health concerns increases with advancing age. Both preventive and remedial assistance are important components of mental health care for older persons. Programs such as preretirement counseling, retirement counseling, and preventive, wellness-oriented counseling are examples of important prevention interventions for older persons. Remedial assistance may be needed by older persons due to multiple losses associated with aging, changing life circumstances, and life adjustments necessitated as people grow older. These stresses may be particularly difficult for older persons because they come at a time when older persons' resource base may be significantly declining.

Depression is the most common mental health concern among older persons. Other mental health concerns associated with aging include: dementia, Alzheimer's disease, complications of substance abuse, grief issues, caregiving issues, and family and relationship issues. Mental health concerns and specific interventions strategies are discussed in depth in chapter 11 (this volume).

Older persons are underserved in community health settings. Community mental health clinics serve only 2%–4% of older persons among their caseloads. Additionally, they are overrepresented in public mental hospitals, where they occupy approximately 60% of available beds (Special Committee on Aging, 1983). For many of these individuals, the institutional environment was their first contact with the mental health system. It is essential that mental health counselors attempt to identify mental health issues among older persons living in the community, and to develop appropriate intervention strategies to maximize client independence and prevent premature institutionalization. Within institutional settings, the dual diagnosis of mental health and other pathology is common.

Sexuality and Older Persons

Sexuality is an important aspect of counseling older persons. Because of the number of myths and negative stereotypes involving older persons and their capacity for sexual activity, it may be difficult for older persons to discuss this aspect of their lives. For example, older men who express an interest in sexuality may be called "dirty old men." Older women who express their sexual needs may be viewed as "silly old women looking for love." Adult children as well as caregivers may be unwilling to allow older persons the freedom to express or achieve satisfaction of their sexual needs and concerns. Counselors need to be sensitive to the attitudes and values of older persons regarding their sexuality. In addition, it is important for counselors to be knowledgeable regarding age-related changes in sexuality, and to be able to dispel any myths that older persons may have concerning their sexual potential.

Physiological changes related to aging occur in both men and women. Changes for men include both delayed onset of and prolonged duration of erection, and reduced frequency of orgasm. Vaginal atrophy, decreased lubrication, and other conditions may cause discomfort for older women during intercourse. Many of these conditions can be relieved through medical intervention. Positive aspects associated with these physiological changes for women may be increased enjoyment of sexual intercourse and perhaps the experiencing of orgasm for the first time as a result of prolonged duration of male erection and lack of fear of pregnancy. The most likely cause for decreased sexual activity among older women is lack of access to suitable partners, rather than lack of desire (Butler & Lewis, 1991).

Marriage and Children

Marriage and children have been correlated with overall life satisfaction for both men and women. For older women, Flanagan (1982) found the most important determinant of life satisfaction across the life span was children, followed by the presence of a spouse. For older men, it was the presence of a spouse, followed by having children.

Only a small percentage of today's older persons never married (5%–7%). Those who marry and stay married tend to spend more years together in the postparental period than in the childrearing years. There is some research to indicate that adjustment to retirement is a critical period for marriages. Adjustment is tied to occupational identity for older men. Further, the onset of the "empty nest" period is a potentially more critical time for older women (Cox, 1988). In general, older persons who never marry report lower life satisfaction due to: the difficulties of being single in a marriage-oriented society, and the lack of the gratifications of marriage, such as companionship.

Family Relationships and Caregiving

Family relationships in the United States are not characterized by the classical extended family. Instead, adult children and older parents may live great distances from one another. However, research indicates that, in general, interactions between adult children and aging parents are frequent and reciprocal, with financial support and gift-giving flowing in both directions (Hoffman, McManus, & Brackbill, 1987).

Significant disruption in family relationships may occur due to increasing dependence and frailty of older persons. Additionally, relationships may be disrupted as older persons attempt to resolve the tasks of later life, which involve an external focus aimed at righting perceived wrongs and obtaining a general sense of a life well lived and worthwhile. This may cause difficulties with adult children who are attempting to resolve the tasks of midlife, which involve an internal focus aimed at reassessing goals, utilizing new found freedoms as children leave the nest, and formulating new goals. Difficulties may arise when aging parents request family time and involvement from adult children at a time when the adult children are refocusing on their own resources and goals from an internal, rather than external, other-oriented perspective.

Approximately one fifth of all older persons are impaired to the extent that they require some form of supportive services (Brotman, 1982). Although approximately 5% of impaired older persons are cared for in institutions, most impaired older persons remain in the community with assistance from caring family members (U.S. Administration on Aging, 1989).

Family caregiving accounts for an estimated 80% of all care provided to impaired older persons. The caregiving relationship is differentiated from typical family exchanges and is defined by the existence of some degree of impairment on the part of the older person, which limits independence and necessitates ongoing assistance (Horowitz, 1985). Furthermore, although the family system is often referred to in the literature as providing care, research has documented that one family member usually occupies the role of primary caregiver and is the primary provider of direct assistance (Horowitz, 1985). The identity of the primary caregiver follows a hierarchical pattern: a spouse if there is one available and capable, and an adult child (usually a daughter) if there is not (Cantor, 1983). Techniques for counseling older persons and their families are found in several current texts (Myers, 1989, 1990; Schwiebert & Myers, in press), as well as in chapters 11, 13, and 14 (this volume).

Stress and Older Persons

Five major sources of stress for older persons include: loss of income, loss of role and status, loss of spouse, isolation caused by disability, and loss of cognitive functioning (Cox, 1988). Life events experienced during the aging process, such as retirement and loss of occupational roles, biological changes and declines, and age-related changes, may cause stress for older persons in each of the life arenas including social, psychological, physiological, vocational, and emotional aspects. Fortunately, most older persons are able to adapt and adjust to these age-related stresses without mental health intervention, as was discussed in chapter 3 (this volume).

Elder Abuse

Elder abuse, an increasing social problem, affects approximately 10% of the aging population yearly and is reported less than child abuse. In 1985, only 26 states had adult protective services laws, and even these states were not able to deal effectively with this growing problem. Forms of elder abuse include physical abuse, psychological abuse, basic neglect of human needs, and material abuse. Additionally, self-neglect is a major and frequently occurring category of abuse among older persons.

Older victims of abuse tend to be women over the age of 75 who are in a dependent position, middle class, and White. The incidence of abuse increases if the impairment is mental, emotional, or functional (such as incontinence). Abusers are most likely family members (the primary caregivers)—either a spouse or children. Most cases of abuse are not reported, and abusers and older persons are not likely to seek treatment. Counselors must be familiar with the signs of elder abuse, as well as community resources and interventions aimed at reducing family stress and impacting the cycle of violence. Specific strategies for counselors may be found in Myers and Shelton (1987) and Costa (1984).

Drug Misuse and Abuse

Most older persons have one or more chronic impairments. Therefore, it is not surprising that they are large consumers of both prescription and nonprescription medications. Many older persons take several different drugs, prescribed by different physicians, and filled at different pharmacies. The probability of drug interactions, overdose, and over-medication increases as a result of these commonly occurring practices.

It is estimated that more than two thirds of older persons consume drugs. They average two prescriptions per person, and take two prescription and two over-the-counter drugs daily, in addition to consuming two social drugs (e.g., alcohol, nicotine). Total consumption includes 7.5 drugs per day for older males and 4.7 drugs per day for older females (Wolfe, Fugate, Hulstrand, & Kamimoto, 1988).

Alcohol misuse and abuse is also a common problem among older persons. Many older persons begin to drink later in life as a result of boredom, loneliness, retirement, and losses associated with aging. Other older persons may have begun to drink early in life and continue to do so in later life. Alcohol is a particularly dangerous problem for older persons as a result of their reduced tolerance for alcohol, slower metabolism, and the potential negative interactions with other drugs. Alcohol misuse and abuse among older persons and specific counselor intervention strategies are discussed in detail in chapter 12 (this volume).

Summary

Counselors working with older persons need to understand the trends and changes in society that will affect the older population. Demographic changes such as gender inequities and changes in the number of ethnic minority individuals have implications for persons as they age, as well as for society in general. Older persons may have problems finding marital partners because there are more older women than older men. Both men and women may experience problems in achieveing satisfying sexual lives. Counselors need to be flexible in responding to needs in these areas. In addition, they must be knowledgeable of problems such as elder substance misuse and abuse. Multicultural training is essential if gerontological counselors are to be effective in dealing with the diverse array of older persons and problems that they will encounter in working with the older population.

Case Studies

Following are two case studies that will allow the reader to apply the knowledge and skills learned in this chapter related to social and cultural foundations of aging. Read each case study and think about how you would help the client. Then read the comments for further insights into the role of the gerontological counselor in each situation.

Case One

You are a counselor in a local retirement center for older persons. A 72-year-old woman who was widowed 3 months ago comes to you asking for help with a problem related to her desire to get remarried. It seems that another resident of the retirement center, whom she has known for 10 years and who is a widower, has asked her to marry him. They have both decided that they wish to be married and that they are too old to waste time "waiting" until the socially acceptable period between widowhood and remarriage has elapsed. Her problem is that her adult son and daughter are horrified at this possibility and have absolutely forbid her to remarry. She feels torn between her children and her wish to remarry. What strategies would you use when working with this client?

Comments on Case One

After establishing rapport with the client, the counselor should work with the client to clarify her values and priorities. The counselor should help the client explore both the positive and negative consequences of remarriage for herself and the impact that remarriage will have on her adult children. Most important, the counselor should encourage the client to examine the meaning and importance of her children's reaction to her. That is, not that the children do not support the marriage and would be upset, but what impact would their being upset have on the client? Could she accept their disapproval, or would she allow their disapproval to negatively affect her marriage and happiness? It is important for the counselor to advocate for the client's feelings, values, and priorities, and to provide emotional support to the client regardless of her decision.

Other strategies that the counselor might consider would include counseling sessions with the client and her partner, and/or counseling sessions with the client and her children. The focus of these sessions would be on increasing communication, sharing feelings, and working toward resolution. The counselor may also encourage the client to talk to her children and try to help them understand her feelings regarding the remarriage. In addition, the client should be encouraged to help her children express their fears and feelings of anger and disapproval. It may be that her children are afraid that their mother is being taken advantage of financially, and that a prenuptial agreement might be an option. Referral to an attorney specializing in work with older persons, or to a senior law center, to draw up a prenuptial agreement could provide assurance to the client as well as her children.

It may also be that, even though they are adults, her children feel that if she remarries she somehow loved their father less. These fears may be resolved through a discussion with their mother. Effective communication strategies are essential to all counseling approaches with this client.

Case Two

A 65-year-old Hispanic male comes to your office with sexuality concerns. He states he has been married for 35 years and has always had a satisfying sex life with his wife. Recently, he has been unable to become sexually aroused or to maintain an erection. He states that he seems to have lost interest in sexual activity, and that he is very concerned that this may mean the end of his sex life. What factors do you, as the counselor, need to consider in working with this client?

Comments on Case Two

First, it would be important to talk with the client to ascertain if he has recently been ill, taken new medications, or experienced any other unusual events. It would also be important for the counselor to explore the client's past medical history regarding any chronic physical or psychological problems, alcohol use, and date of last physical examination. A recent physical examination is imperative. It is not uncommon for some medications to cause sexual dysfunction and/or it may be a result of a prostate problem, a chronic condition such as Parkinson's disease or diabetes, and/or complications of alcohol abuse. If, in consultation with the client's physician, all medical conditions are ruled out, the counselor can then begin to discuss other factors that may be contributing to the sexual difficulties, such as relationship issues, fatigue, depression, and other causes of sexual dysfunction.

Couples counseling with the client and his wife may be helpful. The counselor needs to be prepared to address religious and value issues related to sexuality and sexual functioning for this couple.

Discussion Questions

1. What are the social implications of the demographic changes in the aging population?
2. Discuss the differences in roles between older men and older women in today's society.
3. What are the major sources of stress for older persons?
4. Discuss the differences and similarities among groups of ethnic older persons and White older persons.
5. What are the characteristics of older persons with substance abuse problems?

References

American Association of Retired Persons. (1993). *A profile of older Americans*. Washington, DC: Author.

Brotman, H. (1982). *Every ninth American*. (Committee Pub. No. 97-332). Washington, DC: U.S. House of Representatives.

Butler, R.N., & Lewis, M.I. (1991). *Aging and mental health: Positive psychosocial and biomedical approaches.* St. Louis: C.V. Mosby.

Cantor, M. (1983). Strain among caregivers: A study of experience in the United States. *Gerontologist, 23,* 597–604.

Costa, J.J. (1984). *Abuse of the elderly: A guide to resources and services.* Lexington, MA: Lexington Books.

Cox, H.G. (1988). *Later life: The realities of aging* (2nd ed.). Englewood Cliffs, NJ: Prentice-Hall.

Espino, D., Neufeld, R., Mulvihill, M., & Libow, L. (1988). Hispanic and non-Hispanic elderly on admission to the nursing home: A pilot study. *The Gerontologist, 28*(6), 821–824.

Exum, H.A. (1982). The most invisible minority: The culturally diverse elderly. *The School Counselor, 30*(1), 15–24.

Flanagan, J.C. (1982). *New insights to improve the quality of life at age 70.* Palo Alto, CA: American Institutes for Research in the Behavioral Sciences.

Hoffman, L.W., McManus, K.A., & Brackbill, Y. (1987). The value of children to young and elderly parents. *International Journal of Aging and Human Development, 25*(4), 309–322.

Horowitz, A. (1985). Family caregiving to the frail elderly. In C. Eisdorfer (Ed.), *Annual review of gerontology and geriatrics* (pp. 194–246). New York: Springer.

Johnson, C., & Barer, R. (1990). Families and networks among older inner-city Blacks. *The Gerontologist, 30*(6), 726–733.

Johnson, F., Foxall, M., Kelleher, E., Kentopp, E., Mannlein, E., & Cook, E. (1988). Comparison of mental health and life satisfaction of five elderly ethnic groups. *Western Journal of Nursing Research, 10*(5), 613–628.

Lee, C., & Richardson, B. (Eds.). (1991). *Multicultural issues in counseling: New approaches to diversity.* Alexandria, VA: American Counseling Association.

Myers, J.E. (1989). *Adult children and aging parents.* Alexandria, VA: American Association for Counseling and Development.

Myers, J.E. (1990). *Empowerment for later life.* Greensboro, NC: ERIC/ CASS.

Myers, J.E., & Shelton, B. (1987). Abuse and older persons: Issues and implications for counselors. *Journal of Counseling and Development, 65*(7), 376–380.

Osgood, N. (1985). *Suicide in the elderly.* Rockville, MD: Aspen Systems.

Pedersen, P.B. (Ed.). (1991). Multiculturalism as a fourth force in counseling [Special Issue]. *Journal of Counseling and Development, 70*(1).

Schwiebert, V., & Myers, J.E. (in press). A psychoeducational intervention for midlife adults with parent-care responsibilities. *Journal of Counseling and Development*.

Special Committee on Aging. (1983). *Developments in aging: 1983* (Vol. 1). Washington, DC: U.S. Government Printing Office.

Sue, D.W. (1990). Culture-specific strategies in counseling: A conceptual framework. *Professional Psychology: Research and Practice, 21*(6), 424–433.

Taylor, R., & Chatters, L. (1986). Church-based informal support among elderly Blacks. *The Gerontologist, 26*(6), 637–642.

U.S. Administration on Aging. (1989). *A profile of older Americans.* Washington, DC: Author.

U.S. Bureau of the Census. (1990). *Government Publication C 3.223/18, 990-CPH.*

Wolfe, S.M., Fugate, L., Hulstrand, E.P., & Kamimoto, L.E. (1988). *Worst pills, best pills: The older adult's guide to avoiding drug induced death or illness.* Washington, DC: Public Citizen Health Research Group.

Roles for Gerontological Counselors

Minimum Essential Competency #4 for a Gerontological Counseling Specialist: *demonstrates the ability to function in the multiple roles required to facilitate helping relationships with older persons (e.g., advocate, family consultant), and to mobilize available resources for functioning effectively in each role.*

E
ffective gerontological counselors are professionals with a broad range of knowledge and skills that can be mobilized on behalf of older clients. These include all of the skills required to be a professional counselor, as well as the additional skills and knowledge required for the gerontological specialty. In this chapter, the requirements for training as a professional counselor are reviewed, followed by the hallmarks of a gerontological counseling specialist: training and certification in gerontological counseling. The multiple roles and functions of gerontological counselors are discussed.

The Professional Counselor

Professional counselors possess a minimum of a master's degree in counseling, preferably from an accredited training program (American Counseling Association, 1993). The Council for Accreditation of Counseling and Related Educational Programs (CACREP) is the accrediting body for counseling training. The professional preparation standards for counselors, published by CACREP, require a variety of curricular experiences and supervised training as part of the professional preparation program.

The CACREP standards (Council for Accreditation of Counseling and Related Educational Programs, 1994) require curricular experiences in eight core areas of counselor preparation: human growth and development, social and cultural foundations, helping relationships, group procedures, lifestyle and career, appraisal, research, and professional orientation. In addition, counselors in training must complete a 100-clock hour practicum and a 600-hour internship, both under supervision of qualified professional counselors.

In addition to the core curricular areas of counselor preparation, each accredited training program must offer one or more counseling specialties. These specialties include: school counseling, student affairs practice in higher education, community counseling, gerontological counseling, and career counseling, all of which require a minimum of 48 semester hours. Two additional specialties may be accredited for a minimum of 60 semester hours. These include: mental health counseling and marriage and family counseling. The gerontological counseling specialty was approved in the spring of 1993, and was published as part of the 1994 standards (Council for Accreditation of Counseling and Related Educational Programs, 1994).

After receipt of the master's degree, counselors must document 2 years of supervised counseling experiences to be eligible to become National Certified Counselors (NCCs). Application to the National Board for Certified Counselors (NBCC) must be accompanied by three professional references. The NCC is awarded upon successful completion of a national examination, which is given twice each year. Graduates of CACREP-accredited entry-level programs may choose to sit for the National Counseling Examination during their last term of enrollment in their academic program; counselors who graduate from nonaccredited programs must document 2 years of experience prior to taking the examination. CACREP program graduates who complete the examination successfully become "board-eligible," and may receive the NCC upon successful completion of 2 years of postmaster's degree supervised counseling experience.

Professional counselors who have earned the NCC may elect to add a specialty certification in one of five areas: school counseling, career counseling, gerontological counseling, mental health counseling, and/or substance abuse counseling. The development of the gerontological counseling specialty certification was described in chapter 1 (this volume). This specialty was approved by the NBCC in 1991.

The Professional Gerontological Counselor: Training and Certification

As noted in chapter 1, the Association for Adult Development and Aging submitted a proposal to CACREP for specialty training standards in gerontological counseling. The subsequent standards that were approved and are available through CACREP are based on the Minimum Essential Competencies for Gerontological Counseling Specialists. These are the same competencies upon which this book is based.

Counselor education training programs that apply for accreditation of gerontological counseling training programs must first meet the core curricular experiences for training of professional counselors; then they must document curricular experiences in four additional areas of the specialty: foundations of gerontological counseling, contextual dimensions of gerontological counseling, knowledge and skills for the practice of gerontological counseling, and clinical instruction.

Foundations of gerontological counseling include the history of this specialty and many of the topics in the current chapter. Contextual dimensions include studies that provide an understanding of social service needs and the network of services available to assist older persons, as well as roles of gerontological counselors as members of service provision teams. Knowledge and skills for the practice of gerontological counseling include: normative experiences of aging, older persons with impairments, needs and services for older persons, needs of subgroups of the older population, and specialized counseling techniques for working with older persons.

Clinical instruction includes a 600-hour supervised internship, in which students are able to work directly with older clients. Opportunities should be provided in the internship for assessment, treatment planning, intervention, and termination, as well as the opportunity to work cooperatively with members of other professions in the development and implementation of treatment plans.

The National Certified Gerontological Counselor (NCGC) credential is available through the NBCC for professional counselors who have attained the NCC and wish to add a specialty certification in gerontological counseling. The NCGC is a competency-based credential. The competencies are the 16 Minimum Essential Competencies for Gerontological Counselors described earlier and in each chapter of this book. Applicants for the NCGC must complete a self-assessment of competence in these 16 areas, and submit assessments from three professional references. A minimum of three graduate courses dealing with competencies in gerontological counseling is a prerequisite for this credential, or 120 hours of continuing education if approved by the NBCC. Supervised experience with and on behalf of older persons must be documented as well. Supervision may be provided by a qualified mental health professional, as defined by the NBCC. (For up-to-date information and an application, interested persons may write directly to the NBCC, 3-D Terrace Way, Greensboro, NC 27406.)

Roles and Functions of Gerontological Counselors

A variety of roles are possible for gerontological counselors. These roles, which may be preventive or remedial, are somewhat dependent on the setting in which services are provided. These settings may be anywhere that an older person resides, visits, or uses to obtain needed services. The results of two major studies of gerontological counselor roles are discussed in this section.

Johnson and Riker (1982) identified 21 possible roles for counselors who work with older persons. These roles, listed in Table 5.1, illustrate the tremendous variety of roles required to meet older persons' needs.

Johnson and Riker asked a sample of experts in gerontological counseling to rate each of the roles on a 7-point scale according to its value for counselors working with older persons. The mean ratings

Table 5.1 Roles for Counselors Working with Older Persons

Service provider to older persons living alone	Services coordinator/services enhancer/client advocate
Bereavement counselor	Change agent
Personal counselor	Employment counselor
Specialist in psychological education	Financial counselor and manager
In-service counselor educator	Leisure time counselor
Marital and sex counselor	Outreach agent to minorities
Service provider to nursing home and housing complex residents	Preretirement counselor and educator
Counselor of terminally ill	Public relations worker
Gerontological researcher	Family counselor
Educational counselor	Consultant
Medical support outreach counselor	

were uniformly high, again indicating the variety of roles that are both possible and important in working with older persons.

These authors asked counselors to rank order the 21 roles in terms of their importance in working with older persons, and asked a sample of directors of area agencies on aging to do the same. What they found was a discrepancy between the perceived importance of the roles to counselors and to those who work directly in social services with older individuals. Gerontological counselors rated their most important roles as preretirement counselor and educator, bereavement counselor, family counselor, and in-service counselor educator. Area agencies on aging directors rated the most important roles for counselors as service provider to older persons living alone, services coordinator/services enhancer/client advocate, and employment counselor. Clearly, the training and roles of counselors are not well understood by persons working in the aging network. This will negatively affect both the viability of counselors as job applicants in direct service positions and the possibility for older persons to receive needed mental health and counseling interventions.

Robison, Comas, Blass, Kirk, and Freeman (1985) conducted a study of gerontological counselors in the workplace, examining the activities performed in various settings. The most frequently reported services these counselors provided to older persons were psychological counseling, social and recreational programming, and vocational counseling, which was a distant third. The services least frequently provided were linking clients with social services, screening clients for eligibility for social services, advocacy and political activities, and direct health care.

These studies underscore the need for counselors working with older persons, regardless of setting, to be prepared to perform a variety of roles as needed by their older clients. Role flexibility is an important consideration for anyone preparing to be a gerontological counselor. The roles mentioned here are those most commonly performed, however, many surprises await those who dedicate themselves to meeting the needs of the diverse population of older persons and their families.

Clearly, counselors are not the only mental health providers trained to work with older persons. In many settings, particularly medical settings, counselors must compete for jobs with established professionals who have ready acceptance in that setting. Licensed clinical social workers are able to obtain jobs in hospitals and nursing homes, and often jobs in these settings specify social work training, certification, or licensure as a precondition for hire. This does not mean that counselors cannot ever be hired in these settings. Rather, this is evidence in many instances of a lack of awareness of the training and competencies of professional counselors. As counselors emphasize practica and internships in medical and long-term-care settings, we can increasingly "prove" both the validity of and need for our skills in working with older persons and their families. Counselors can learn the language and gain the experience necessary to make placements in medical settings increasingly easier through working in these settings.

Summary

Professional gerontological counselors are first trained as professional counselors, then seek specialized training and credentialing for work with older persons. Specialized training is available through counselor education programs accredited by CACREP. Certification as an NCGC is available through the NBCC. Whether a counselor seeks an accredited training program or national certification is voluntary. Many professional counselors provide services to older persons without being certified. These counselors may benefit from continuing education opportunities designed to enhance their knowledge of the needs of older persons and effective interventions with this population.

Counselors working with older persons will be called on to provide a variety of services and to function in a variety of roles. The needs of older persons are varied, the service network in local communities varies considerably, and, as a consequence, the needs of any given older client are unique. Gerontological counselors need to develop considerable role flexibility to be of service to a broad range of clientele.

Case Studies

Following are two case studies that will allow the reader to apply the knowledge and skills learned in this chapter related to roles for gerontological counselors. Read each case study and think about how you would help the client. Then read the comments for further insights into credentialing processes for gerontological counselors.

Case One

You are a professional counselor with a master's degree from a non-CACREP accredited training program. You have achieved the NCC credential after working 5 years in the field, and now would like to add a specialty in gerontological counseling. How will you go about getting this specialty training, and how will you find a job in this field?

Comments on Case One

The CACREP maintains a list of accredited training programs. Your first step might be to contact them (5999 Stevenson Avenue, Alexandria VA, 22304) to determine if there are accredited training programs in your area. Of course, you want a program accredited in gerontological counseling. The Association for Adult Development and Aging may be able to help you, or you can contact the Association for Counselor Education and Supervision and contact the counselor educator who is the current chair of their Adult Development, Aging, and Counseling Interest Network.

You need to know what counselor education training programs offer beyond the entry-level degree for persons seeking to add a specialty. Some programs have no provision for additional training, some offer a sixth year or advanced certificate, some offer an educational specialist (Ed.S.) degree, and some offer a certificate program in gerontological counseling. Geographic location, cost, and availability of summer or intensive workshop programs may be factors to consider.

Once you have obtained the necessary training, supervision, and credentials, you may find Case Two of interest. In addition, chapter 12 (this volume) on the aging network can provide some ideas of settings in which gerontological counselors may be employed.

Case Two

You have just received your NCGC credential and are seeking a position where you can use your skills to assist older persons and their families. You have been selected for an interview at a local agency, and find that you are the only person with a counseling background chosen to interview. During your interview, the agency director asks you what you can bring to the position on behalf of older persons. What do you say?

Comments on Case Two

As counselors, we often make the mistake of thinking that many people in different professions possess the same or similar skills to those we have acquired. We also fail to realize that, although just about everyone knows (or thinks they know) what a psychologist is and does, what a psychiatrist is and does, and what a social worker is and does, just about everyone also thinks they are a counselor. It is up to you to define for the agency director your background and training, and to explain what a professional counselor is and does. You can use the outline of this chapter as a basis for presenting yourself as a professional.

A professional counselor is just that—a highly trained professional. The entry-level degree for our profession is a master's degree, which requires a minimum of 2 years of full-time study at the graduate level. Supervised clinical experiences are a major component of your training. If you are certified, you can document both a higher level of training and a commitment to gerontological work as a specialty. Training and certification in gerontological counseling reflect the knowledge and skills required to function in many roles and settings with and on behalf of older persons.

A related point, not specifically addressed in this chapter, is that counselors are trained to help "normal" people cope with the vast array of situations and problems that arise in the course of living, as well as to help persons who experience more severe mental impairments. The goal of counselors is often to help older people live as independently as possible, through approaches and techniques that emphasize their wellness and empower them to take action on their own behalf. Our developmental, wellness-oriented, preventive philosophy of care is what sets counselors apart from other mental health care providers.

Discussion Questions

1. What are the curricular standards for the gerontological counseling specialty according to CACREP?
2. What are the NBCC requirements for certification as a gerontological counselor?

3. What are some of the roles for gerontological counselors in working with older people?
4. What are possible sources for supervision in your area to help you meet the NCGC requirements?

References

American Counseling Association. (1993). *Government relations/advocacy paper*. Alexandria, VA: Author.

Council for Accreditation of Counseling and Related Educational Programs. (1994). *CACREP accreditation standards and procedures manual*. Alexandria, VA: Author.

Johnson, R.P., & Riker, H.C. (1982). Counselors' goals and roles in assisting older persons. *Journal of Mental Health Counseling*, 4(1), 30–40.

Robison, F.F., Comas, R., Blass, C., Kirk, W., & Freeman, S. (1985, March). *Gerontological counselors in the workplace: Description of professional background, activities, and information needs*. Paper presented at the annual meeting of the American Association for Counseling and Development, Los Angeles, CA.

6

Group Work with Older Persons

Minimum Essential Competency #5 for a Gerontological Counseling Specialist: *demonstrates skill in recruiting, selecting, planning, and implementing groups with older persons.*

C ompetence in group counseling is required of all counselors, both as part of the Council for Accreditation of Counseling and Related Educational Programs (CACREP) standards for accreditation and the National Board for Certified Counselors (NBCC) requirements for certification as a professional counselor. Competence specifically in counseling groups of older persons is required for gerontological counseling specialists. In this chapter, the advantages of using group work with older persons are discussed, followed by a brief consideration of the historical development and efficacy of groups with older persons. Similarities and differences in group work with older and younger persons are considered, followed by special considerations in working with groups of older people. Types of group approaches, theories, and methods that may prove useful with older clients are considered. Principles of group dynamics as applied in groups of older persons are discussed. Recruiting and selecting participants are considered, followed by characteristics of effective leaders of groups with older adults.

Advantages of Group Counseling with Older Persons

Much of the literature on aging suggests that loneliness and isolation are common problems. Among the major developmental tasks of later life described in chapter 3 (this volume), establishing and maintaining social networks and outlets for social interaction seem to be important later life challenges. Group counseling offers an opportunity for increasing social interaction, hence a major benefit of this type of intervention is the possibility of reducing isolation and loneliness for older individuals.

Group counseling has been found to enhance participants' self-esteem, provide them with information and suggestions for solving problems, encourage socialization, provide contact with counselors and other individuals who can serve as role models, and provide an opportunity for older persons to help one another. Increases in motivation to renew former interests and to reengage in life activities are additional benefits. Groups have been found useful in clarifying both the diagnosis and prognosis for older persons with impairments. Groups have also helped older persons develop more effective relationships with friends and family members, and provide channels for expressing a variety of emotions.

The Social Breakdown Syndrome, described in chapter 3 (this volume), provided an overview of the ways in which the processes of aging can contribute to declines in self-esteem and feelings of worth among older persons. Groups oriented toward reminiscing can help provide older individuals with needed ego support by emphasizing past accomplishments and lifelong coping skills. The social contact provided by groups can help counteract loneliness, provide friendships to help overcome feelings of rejection, and provide peer support to help combat feelings of isolation.

Groups are known to stimulate activity among depressed older persons, which can help alleviate depression, and they provide a supportive climate in which older persons can openly grieve the losses of aging. Groups encourage the learning of new coping skills to adjust to the changing life circumstances that accompany old age (Zimpfer, 1987).

Group activities are the norm in most community programs for older persons, including senior citizens clubs, senior centers, and adult activities programs. As a consequence, group experiences may be more readily accepted by older persons, in contrast to personal counseling, which, as shown in chapter 3, may be rejected. Peer groups, described in more detail in chapter 13 (this volume), may be especially effective because older persons are able to share universal experiences, enhance interpersonal communication skills, and deal with newly acquired social roles such as grandparent, retiree, or widow/widower. Groups also can be effective in institutional settings, helping older persons overcome depression and isolation while developing effective peer relationships.

In general, groups are cost-effective, time-effective methods for providing counseling assistance to many persons at one time. Given the lack of trained gerontological counselors, this is an especially important consideration. In light of the many advantages of group counseling discussed in this section, this may be the treatment of choice for practicing gerontological counselors.

Historical Development and Efficacy of Groups with Older Persons

Capuzzi and Gross (1980) reviewed the literature on group counseling and determined that little attention had been paid to using groups with older persons prior to that time. Fry (1986) noted that group treatment strategies for use with this population were abundant in the literature of other professional groups, notably social work, gerontology, and nursing, beginning in the early 1970s. As counselors began to study these strategies, an increasing emphasis on using groups with older persons has emerged (Waters, McCarroll, & Penman, 1987).

Zimpfer (1987) reviewed 19 studies of the effectiveness of groups for aging persons conducted over a 10-year period. He found that treatment efficacy was more closely related to accurate assessment and diagnosis than to the type of counseling approach employed. However, this author also concluded that the use of groups with older persons was an exciting and potentially effective method.

Similarities and Differences in Group Work with Older Persons

Group processes, principles, and group dynamics are basically the same for persons of all ages. As Yalom (1985) indicated, both the advantages and limitations of group work are relevant without respect to client age. What differs with older persons is the need to apply specialized knowledge of this population in order for group approaches to be effective.

Burnside (1994) suggested that modifications in the group counselor's approach may be required in working with groups of older persons. These reflect differences in the group leader's roles and style, common themes that may be expected to emerge in groups with older persons, and differences in selection criteria and types of groups, all of which are considered in subsequent sections of this chapter.

One of the major differences that has been found in working with groups of older persons is that the development of trust tends to take longer. This reflects a predominant value of today's older cohort of independence in meeting life tasks and "not airing one's dirty laundry in public." As a consequence, leaders may need to use a greater number of introductory and "ice-breaking" activities, and rely more on structured activities in the early stages of the group.

A final difference in working with older persons is that they will be more inclined to reminisce than persons of younger ages. This universal tendency of older persons can be used to establish and conduct reminiscence groups. This can be an important means of facilitating the process of achieving ego integrity in later life. Reexamination of one's life in a therapeutic group setting can help older persons regain or reestablish a sense of identity, resolve unfinished business, and develop strategies for improving relationships with family and friends. Older persons also may use groups to explore or renew a sense of ethnic identity, and to relive and reexamine the dreams of their youth (Burnside, 1994).

Group Approaches, Theories, and Methods with Older Persons

Various types of groups have been found to be effective with older clients, including structured and unstructured, topic-specific and member-specific. Structured groups tend to be more successful with today's older persons because they tend to have less experience with counseling services, and hence are less apt to function spontaneously in the role of "client." Other types of groups that may be effective are self-help and peer support groups, described more fully in chapter 14 (this volume). In general, groups that provide information and allow time for discussion (i.e., questions and answers) tend to be successful with older clients.

Topic-specific groups focus on a particular concern, commonly experienced issue, or difficult transition. For example, a group could focus on grandparenting roles, relationships with adult children, widowhood, or retirement. Groups can be conducted on issues related to sexuality, life review or reminiscence, music or art therapies, or health concerns, to name just a few. Personal growth and life enrichment groups can be effective, as well as groups dealing with assertiveness skills, retirement planning, or support groups for adult children of aging parents (or aging parents with adult children). It is important for facilitators of topic-specific groups to have some knowledge or experience with the topic to be most effective.

Member-specific groups, like topic-specific groups, may focus on a particular concern, commonly experienced issue, or difficult transition. These groups differ, however, in that participant selection is accomplished with the intent of creating a homogeneous group membership. All participants will share certain characteristics that provide a common basis for discussion. The group could be composed of older persons recently relocated to a long-term-care setting, allowing them to discuss their relocation and adjustment concerns. The group could be composed of older persons living with relatives and attending an adult day care center. Or, a group could be composed of all widows or widowers. Groups of soon-to-be or recent retirees, residents of low-income housing, or patients under treatment in a cancer center (Cain, Kohorn, Quinlan, Latimer, & Schwartz, 1986) are additional examples of member-specific groups.

Groups can also be organized with the intent of using a specific technique, such as assertiveness training, multimodal group therapy, cognitive group therapy, or behavioral group therapy. Several approaches have been found to be particularly effective with groups of impaired older persons. These approaches, discussed in chapter 14 (this volume), include reality orientation, remotivation, reminiscing, and group psychotherapy.

Special Considerations in Working with Groups of Older People

When working with groups of older persons, consideration should be given to a site that is physically comfortable and safe. There should be no open, glaring windows that affect vision, no throw rugs on which older people may slip, and no extraneous noises that may be distracting, especially to persons wearing hearing aids. Relatedly, because many older persons have hearing impairments, a room with good acoustics and one in which confidentiality may be maintained are important considerations.

Kampfe (1990) provided a variety of helpful suggestions for communicating with persons who are hearing impaired. In addition to attending to the physical environment, she emphasized the importance of respecting clients' preferred method of communication. For persons who are deaf, speechreading, use of interpreters, use of residual hearing, and group work can be effective.

Because older people may have difficulty with homeostatic temperature regulating mechanisms, room temperature and humidity should be closely monitored for comfort. Chairs should have straight backs and be comfortable for older clients. Having a bathroom nearby is a must, as are relatively short sessions, which allow for the physical comfort needs of the clients to be addressed. The availability of refreshments during breaks will be appreciated. Short sessions of 60–90 minutes, with a break halfway through, may be needed to accommodate for fatigue among older clients.

Transportation to sessions can be a problem for many older clients. In the North, it may be impossible to schedule group sessions during the winter months due to the difficulty of obtaining reliable transportation, unless sessions are conducted at a residential facility. Keeping group sizes small—no more than four to six persons—allows each person time to "tell his or her story," and also allows close seating to accommodate for sensory deficits.

Group Dynamics in Group Work with Older Persons

As noted earlier, building trust may take longer in groups with older persons. Self-disclosure may be more difficult for older clients. They may be less willing or able to discuss their feelings, and may lack an effective vocabulary to allow them to do so. Counselors need to pay particular attention to their older clients' values, needs, and communication styles, and will be most effective if they match, rather than mismatch, these styles.

Capuzzi, Gossman, Whiston, and Surdam (1979) proposed guidelines for group process with older people. These guidelines, which are still relevant today, include an emphasis on not underestimating the capacity of older group members to grow, and the importance of realizing that older persons are human beings with the same needs, interests, fears, and desires as persons of other ages. Groups with frail older persons are best conducted with a focus on present concerns, rather than future goals. A future focus may create anxiety for older persons with an uncertain future, and may contribute to fears that they will be unable to carry out any plans they may make.

Group leaders need to handle termination with older persons carefully, so as not to provide their clients with yet another significant loss. Older clients should be encouraged to review the group experience, their changing feelings and perceptions over the course of the group, and should be allowed to express any negative feelings they may have concerning the termination. Validation of the positive aspects of the group experience and of the courage of the older participants are important considerations. Projecting into the future and encouraging other successful group experiences and positive age-peer relationships can be helpful in facilitating the transition out of the group experience.

Recruiting and Selecting Older Group Participants

Selection of group members is important in all counseling groups, including groups of older persons. The setting may be a primary determinant of group composition with older clients, and may be based on any setting in which older persons congregate or reside (e.g., senior centers, low-income housing complexes, retirement communities, long-term-care facilities). Depending on the purpose of the group and the type of group desired, participants may be selected to be homogeneous according to one or more characteristics, or heterogeneous, representing a variety of ages, life stages and concerns, ethnic backgrounds, or social and educational status.

Similar or differing health status can be a selection criterion. Persons who are adapting well to physical limitations can serve as role models for other impaired older persons. They also can be a source of discomfort, which can be determined only through prescreening or careful attention to participant reactions. It is important for the group leader to be flexible and willing to change the composition of a group after it has begun based on the characteristics of one or more group members.

Some persons are inappropriate for groups, and some groups may be inappropriate for older persons. Severely mentally impaired older persons, especially those inclined to wander, may be inappropriate. Older persons who are incontinent, psychotic, severely depressed, or severely hearing impaired may not be appropriate group members. Older persons who do not like to talk in groups also are inappropriate, and individual counseling should be considered as a first alternative for these individuals.

Groups that may be inappropriate for some older clients include relaxation groups for frail older persons or those taking multiple medications. Due to slower reaction times, relaxation exercises may have a different and slower effect than when used with younger persons. Older persons dealing with practical problems will likely not enjoy insight-oriented groups, whereas persons seeking assistance with current problems may not care to participate in life review groups. These same individuals may find reminiscence or early recollections (see chapter 14, this volume) useful as part of individual counseling sessions.

In selecting participants for groups with older clients, careful attention to communication patterns is important. Older persons who are withdrawn will require more effort from the counselor if they are to be active group participants. Older persons who are inclined to talk a lot also can require a great deal of therapist skill in group sessions. Such persons can monopolize the group to the detriment of other group members. If they cannot be helped to develop more effective communication patterns, these persons may need to be scheduled for individual, rather than group, sessions.

Helping older persons learn to listen to one another is an important part of any group session. It is helpful for counselors to reflect on why an older person may talk excessively. Loneliness could be a factor. It seems that many older persons who spend a lot of time alone seem to "gush" with words when they have an audience. Their family and friends learn to cope with them by not listening carefully, thus reinforcing a "stream-of-consciousness" communication style. When counselors listen carefully to these individuals and begin to reflect feelings and meanings, this style of communication typically will change to something more functional and appropriate, at least during group counseling sessions.

An additional benefit derived from helping older persons listen to one another will be more effective and satisfying peer relationships.

Improved relationships with family members and friends outside of the group are likely to result when older persons develop more effective and interactive communication styles.

Characteristics of Effective Group Leaders for Older Adult Groups

Leaders of groups with older persons may need to take a more active-directive role than is necessary with groups of younger persons. Leaders need to be prepared to give information, answer questions, and disclose information about themselves to gain the trust and confidence of older clients. In addition to support, encouragement, and empathy, specialized knowledge of the concerns and issues faced by older persons is important.

Needless to say, a genuine liking and respect for older persons is an essential characteristic of an effective group leader with this population. Group leaders need to examine their own perceptions and biases related to older individuals and the aging process, and to carefully monitor their own reactions to determine the presence of any transference reactions. If a counselor finds him- or herself thinking that an older client reminds him or her of an older relative, the stage is set for a transference reaction, or it may already be occurring. In such instances, it becomes difficult or even impossible to confront clients or to help them deal with difficult issues. Either a referral is necessary, or the counselor needs to seek consultation, or both.

Group leaders need to be prepared to accommodate the physical needs of older clients, and they may need to modify their own styles to ensure that they speak slowly, clearly, distinctly, and without use of slang or cliches, which may not be understood by older group members. Group leaders may be more effective when functioning as facilitators and role models, rather than task-oriented leaders. At the same time, keeping group members on task and helping them avoid prolonged extraneous storytelling can be a constant challenge.

Leaders of groups with older clients need to pay particular attention to the effectiveness of their interventions. Fry (1986) noted that most of the literature on group work has focused on institutionalized populations. As a consequence, facilitators may underestimate the potential of older clients to benefit from a variety of group methods and techniques. Asking participants for feedback and using their input to restructure group experiences are important means of improving the quality of any counselor's group work with this population.

Summary

Group work can be effective with older persons, and often can be more helpful than individual approaches. Counselors need to adhere to basic principles of group process and dynamics in conducting groups with older persons. In addition, they need to modify their approaches to accommodate the unique characteristics of their older clients. Groups may be formed based on common problems or concerns, or may be groups of convenience based on the settings in which older persons are found.

Case Studies

Following are two case studies that will allow the reader to apply the knowledge and skills learned in this chapter related to group work with older persons. Read each case study and think about how you would help the client. Then read the comments for further insights into the role of the gerontological counselor in each situation.

Case One

Mrs. D. is a "live wire." She was referred by the director of the housing complex because she is constantly trying to convert other residents to her religion. She is offending the other residents, and is becoming socially isolated as a result. Almost every statement she makes includes a reference to what God can do. She freely shares that she is a "softee," and that people like Pat Boone and Charleston Heston regularly call her for contributions. Although she exists only on SSI, she always manages to send money when anyone calls her for a religious cause. The director suspects she may be a victim of fraud as well. In the group, you quickly notice that other participants "tune out" each time Mrs. D. begins to speak, and their facial expressions reflect both anger and disgust. What do you do?

Comments on Case One

Mrs. D.'s values and communication style do not match those of other members of the group. She is a disruptive group member, and her presence is keeping other members of the group from moving forward. If the group is to be effective for the other members, it may be necessary to change the composition and take Mrs. D. out of the group.

At the same time, Mrs. D. presents a number of problems that may be amenable to counseling. One is her pattern of communication, which has resulted in social isolation and probably feelings of loneliness. Of course, she denies feelings of loneliness because "God is always with me." Another concern that needs to be evaluated is the possibility that Mrs. D. is a victim of fraud. She could be mentally quite competent and seeking validation of her worth through contributions to others. She also could have an organic memory impairment that is leaving her open to manipulation by others. A thorough assessment is needed, which cannot be conducted in a group environment. Hence, for Mrs. D.'s needs to be met, as well as the needs of other members of the group, referral to individual counseling is a necessary and even desirable action for you to take.

Case Two

You have been hired as a consultant to a retirement home. Most of the residents are highly educated and from high socioeconomic backgrounds. In talking with a few of them, you learn that "counseling" services will quickly be rejected by the residents, however, there are a number of concerns that need to be addressed. Chief among them is a need for incoming residents to be able to talk to someone about their transition. They have just "downsized" from large homes, in which they had a lifetime of accumulation of "things," to a small apartment with one or two bedrooms, no yard to care for, and no garage in which to store things. Many of the residents have health problems that served as the motivation for their move. Other residents are healthy, but concerned with establishing a support network for a spouse should anything happen to them in the future. What can you do to help meet these residents' needs?

Comments on Case Two

In this environment, both member- and topic-specific groups can be helpful. You will not want to call your groups "counseling" or "therapy" groups, but may find that psychoeducational programs will be appreciated. For example, a "newcomer's" group, in which only residents recently moved to the facility are invited, will bring together persons with like concerns. As a facilitator, you may wish to provide information related to services and programs available at the facility as a stimulus for discussion at the first session, using as an "ice breaker" activities that allow participants to reflect on and discuss the activities and feelings they had while preparing for their move. The beginning of each group can include such an ice breaker. You will want to spend time with long-term residents to learn about the issues they faced in order to develop activities that will meet their needs. You also may find these groups to be similar in many ways to stress management groups conducted with persons of other ages; the situations required in moving and learning to live in a commmunity environment can be quite stressful.

Groups oriented to health issues also will be appreciated. Preventive health care can be a focus, and you may wish to engage a health care professional as a resource. Specific health issues, such as coping with high blood pressure or arthritis, may bring together persons with similar concerns.

Be careful not to make assumptions about the willingness of residents to discuss their concerns in a group. Although many may appear for the lecture or informational part of the group session, many older persons may be expected to leave when the discussion starts. This may be viewed as a positive turn of events because it will reduce the size of the remaining group and allow more participation. Refreshments after the group will facilitate needed socialization, and encourage some participants to remain who otherwise might leave.

Discussion Questions

1. What are some types of member-specific groups that can be helpful to older persons?
2. What are some types of topic-specific groups that older persons might find interesting and helpful?
3. How is group work with older persons similar to and different from group work with younger persons?

References

Burnside, I. (1994). *Working with the elderly: Group processes and techniques.* Monterey, CA: Wadsworth.

Cain, E., Kohorn, E., Quinlan, D., Latimer, K., & Schwartz, P. (1986). Psychosocial benefits of a cancer support group. *CANCER, 57*(1), 183–189.

Capuzzi, D., & Gross, D. (1980). Sexuality and the elderly: A group counseling model. *Journal for Specialists in Group Work, 7*(4), 251–259.

Capuzzi, D., Gossman, L., Whiston, S., & Surdam, J. (1979). Group work with the elderly: An overview for counselors. *Personnel and Guidance Journal, 59*(4), 206–211.

Fry, P.S. (1986). *Depression, stress, and adaptations in the elderly.* Rockville, MD: Aspen Publishers.

Kampfe, C. (1990). Communicating with persons who are deaf: Some practical suggestions for rehabilitation specialists. *Journal of Rehabilitation, 56,* 41–45.

Waters, E., McCarroll, J., & Penman, N. (1987). *Training mental health workers for the elderly: An instructor's guide.* Rochester, MI: The Continuum Center.

Yalom, I.D. (1985). *The theory and practice of group psychotherapy* (3rd ed.). New York: Basic Books.

Zimpfer, D. (1987). Groups for the aging: Do they work? *Journal for Specialists in Group Work, 12*(2), 85–92.

7

Career and Lifestyle Options for Older Persons

Minimum Essential Competency #6 for a Gerontological Counseling Specialist: *demonstrates skill in applying extensive knowledge of career and lifestyle options for older persons, age-related assets and barriers to effective choices, and resources for maximizing exploration of career and lifestyle options.*

C areer and lifestyle options for older persons are essential components of a comprehensive wellness approach to counseling older persons. As the retirement age in the United States continues to decrease and the life expectancy of persons continues to increase, individuals are faced with the possibility of 40 or more years of life following retirement. These years can be spent in many ways, including the pursuit of a second career, volunteer work, leisure pursuits, continuing one's education, traveling, and consultation, to list just a few.

Gerontological counselors must be able to assist clients in the development of proactive strategies for coping with the transition from worker to retiree through preretirement planning (Fretz & Merikangas, 1992), retirement planning (Hays, 1994; Riker & Myers, 1990), career counseling (Dalton, Thompson, & Price, 1977; Holloran, 1973; Super, 1953, 1980), and leisure counseling (Riker & Myers, 1989); as many older persons have stated, "You can only fish for so long." In this chapter, career and lifestyle issues for older persons are explored from the perspectives of career and lifestyle planning, role of work, lifestyle and career development theories, transition theories, counseling needs of older workers, preretirement and retirement counseling, and leisure needs and counseling.

Career and Lifestyle Planning

As counselor educators, the authors often ask graduate students what they envision themselves doing when they are 65 years old or when they "retire." Many students answer with activities such as traveling, living on the beach, skiing, and continuing current leisure pursuits. When asked if their current lifestyle will enable them to be physically, emotionally, and financially prepared for these activities, many students look perplexed. Therein lies the rationale for early counselor intervention, including lifestyle and preretirement counseling. If individuals are to pursue the retirement activities that they choose, early prevention activities and planning are essential to help ensure physical, emotional, and financial preparation for satisfying retirement and postretirement lifestyles. For example, if a young woman states she feels she will retire and travel around the world when she is older, what kind of financial resources will she need to accumulate to accomplish this objective? What kinds of preventive activities can she begin now that may allow her to physically attain this goal? The answers can be found through collaborative work with a counselor early in her career. She may need to consider her current lifestyle, which includes smoking and drinking excessive amounts of alcohol, and which does not include any form of exercise. In addition, she is currently considering a career as a nurse's aide and has enrolled in a local community college training program. Will this type of career allow her to build the financial resources she will need to travel when she retires?

Although the focus of this chapter is on counseling interventions that counselors may use with older persons, the previous case illustrates why lifestyle and career counseling, to be most effective, should begin with young people and be a continuous life process. Additionally, this case points out how vital it is for counselors to work with clients using a comprehensive wellness model, such as that described in chapter 10 (this volume), when assisting individuals with career and lifestyle planning and choices. Unfortunately, many clients do not come into counseling until retirement is imminent or until they have retired and begun to feel dissatisfied with their lives. In extreme cases, they may experience feelings of uselessness, depression, and even hopelessness after they have retired. These feelings are related to the salience of the work role in our society.

Role of Work

One of the most fundamental concepts that counselors must understand when working with older persons facing retirement and lifestyle choices revolves around the meaning of work in our lives (Holloran, 1985). When asked to introduce oneself, many people answer something like this: "My name is Sheila and I am an engineer at Grace Chemical." Think about the number of times you have been asked to introduce yourself and the answer you gave. The standard response usually involves your name and what you do; simply put, who you are is directly linked to what you do. If this is the case, when individuals retire, in essence, they may lose their identity and, along with that, their sense of personal worth. In addition, if they are no longer employed and most of their social life centered around friendships made on the job, they may also be faced with losses in their social network as well. Friends who are still working may not have the time to go fishing, take the day off and go to the beach, or engage in extended golfing outings, especially during work days.

An older person may also experience lifestyle changes at home as well. If both spouses are used to working and seeing each other only in the evenings and on weekends, stresses may develop at home when one or both spouses retire. The retired spouse may be bored and demand more attention from the working spouse. However, the working spouse may experience stress from the additional demands for attention from the retired spouse, and expect the home situation to remain as it had been prior to retirement. The relationship must then be renegotiated to accommodate the change in roles.

In summary, it is essential that the counselor recognize and understand the vital role that work plays in the total well-being of an individual and the impact of the loss of that role. Additionally, it is important to note that retirement may be viewed in the same light as job loss at any time in the lifecycle. Lifestyle and career development theories can offer a framework for understanding the impact of this life transition.

Lifestyle and Career Development Theories

Career development theories, like many theories in the counseling field, were developed at a time when an individual's life expectancy and retirement age were much lower than today. The focus of these theories was mostly on school-age persons and young adults. Therefore, career development theories offer little direct structure through which counselors can understand the vocational development and choices of older persons. In recent years, researchers and theorists have begun to recognize the need for expanded theories of career development that incorporate mid- and late-life, and they have begun to break new ground in this area. However, implementation of career development theories addressing life span career counseling has been slow.

Super (1953, 1980) conceptualized career development as a process with defined stages across the life span. These stages include growth, exploration, establishment, maintenance, and decline. The stages can occur across the life span, as a maxicycle, or may occur when one begins a new job, as a minicycle. An understanding of these stages, in combination with Super's nine life roles, may be used in counseling older persons. The nine life roles, which assume more or less importance to the individual throughout his or her lifecycle, include child, student, leisurite, parent, citizen, worker, spouse, homemaker, parent, and pensioner. All of these roles, considered in combination, comprise the individual's career pattern, or life-career rainbow. To avoid limiting roles of older persons to pensioner and leisurite, counselors must be aware of the various life roles and their importance to the individual.

In his theory of vocational choice, Holland (1973) hypothesized that people express their personality through their choice of a vocation. Holland proposed that members of a vocation have similar personalities and vocational satisfaction, stability, and achievement depending on the extent to which their personalities and work environments are congruent. Thus, using Holland's theory, information gained regarding an older person's work history may give the counselor insight into the individual's personality, values, and interests. This information may then be used to assist the older person in developing satisfying career and lifestyle choices.

Dalton, Thompson, and Price (1977) developed a career stage model describing professional development of individuals in organizations. Although this model is limited because it is aimed at professionals in organizations, it may have certain applicability to working with older persons. The model describes four stages. Stage I includes learning the expected work tasks, doing them well, and demonstrating ability and initiative to progress to the next stage—independent contributor. Stage II involves being responsible for projects from conception to completion. Independence and organization are important components of this stage. In Stage III, the individual begins to take responsibility for others' work, assuming more of a leadership role. In this stage, the individual may be seen as an expert, leader, or mentor to individuals in Stage I. Finally, in Stage IV, the individual begins to give up control and delegate responsibility.

The individual is responsible for policymaking and shaping the direction of the organization in the final stage of this model. Information gained using this model may assist counselors in preparing individuals who wish to change careers for obstacles they may encounter, such as moving back to Stage I from Stages II, III, or IV. Additionally, counselors may assist clients in identifying and using the skills gained in their careers in making appropriate career and lifestyle choices following retirement.

Transition Theories

Retirement has become a normative life transition for most individuals in the United States during the last half century. The retirement decision may be voluntary or involuntary, and may be treated as an event as well as a transition (Hays, 1994). As with any life transition, there may be both positive and negative stresses associated with it. An individual may eagerly await retirement, envisioning it as a time when he or she may do anything he or she wishes, or a time when he or she can do all the things he or she has always wanted but never had the time to do. This time in life was once looked forward to by many midlife adults and considered to be the "golden years"—a concept that increasingly has proved to be a myth.

Many individuals find that retirement is not the utopia they had envisioned. Instead, retirees may find themselves with feelings of loss, depression, emptiness, and lower self-esteem. These feelings may stem from the loss of the worker role. In today's society, work is a valued and meaningful activity. It provides individuals with a sense of worth, self-esteem, identity, and social status. In addition, work provides individuals with income, a sense of accomplishment, and a sense of purpose. The psychosocial transition from the work role to the retired role may be difficult for some individuals due to losses associated with the worker role. It is imperative that counselors working with older persons recognize both the positive and negative effects of the retirement transition to assist older persons in positively adjusting to the new role of "retiree."

Counseling Needs of Older Workers

Older persons who retire may choose to continue to work full or part time, in paid or unpaid activities. Some older persons choose to continue to work out of necessity due to a lack of sufficient retirement income. Other older persons choose to continue to work to feel useful and productive, and to maintain social contacts. The type of work that a retiree chooses may be in the same field he or she retired from or in an entirely different area. Those who choose to continue in the same field may share their expertise through mentoring, consulting, volunteering, or teaching. For example, many retired accountants volunteer their time to assist older persons in completing their income tax returns. Another example might be a retired successful businessperson who receives compensation for consulting with beginning companies regarding strategies for success.

Older persons who wish to continue working may face barriers to continued employment. For example, Social Security has established a maximum amount of money a retired person may earn before benefits are reduced. Additionally, older workers may encounter negative attitudes from employers. These attitudes may stem from myths employers hold regarding older persons, such as older workers are inflexible, slow, unable to adjust to change, and unable to meet the physical demands of the job (Myers, 1994). However, these attitudes are beginning to change. For example, corporations such as McDonald's are beginning to realize the benefits of hiring older workers, such as excellent attendance, willingness to work, and an excellent work ethic; in response, they are hiring more older workers.

In addition to changing attitudes regarding older workers, the federal government sponsors programs with incentives for businesses to hire older workers. The 1978 Age Discrimination in Employment Act made it illegal for employers to discriminate in hiring or promoting older workers based on age. This act only provides protection for workers between the ages of 40 and 70. Also, many employers are experimenting with nontraditional employment arrangements, such as job sharing and partial or trial retirement periods.

It is important for counselors to remember that not all older persons want, value, or can afford to participate in volunteer activities. Additionally, not all older persons want or desire to continue working. Therefore, counselors working with older persons must remember to work with the client to develop individualized plans for successful retirement based on the client's needs and values.

Preretirement and Retirement Counseling

Ideally, preparation for retirement should begin early in one's work career. The research literature supports the conclusion that retirement is more readily accepted and results in more positive adjustment when there is prior planning for this life transition. In addition, the literature suggests that the optimal adjustment to retirement occurs when planning has occurred over a period of years, when individuals are allowed to make decisions regarding their retirement, and when retirement is chosen not forced.

In recognition of this information, many companies are now providing retirement planning for their employees. Additionally, the American Association of Retired Persons (AARP) has developed packaged programs for retirement planning that have been sold to more than 1,000 companies nationwide. These programs focus on a holistic approach to retirement counseling, including planning ahead for transitions in each of the following life arenas: finances, housing, lifestyle, nutrition, exercise, relationships, recreation, education, and future employment. The drawback of these programs is that many of them are aimed at older persons who are retiring in the near future, rather than younger persons considering retirement. Thus, they become remedial, rather than preventive, interventions.

Specific counseling techniques to assist individuals in the identification and achievement of a satisfying lifestyle following retirement are provided by several authors. For example, Holloran (1985) emphasized the importance of dealing with identity issues and recognizing that retirement precipitates an identity crisis. Fretz and Merikangas (1992) suggested an outline for a structured preretirement group seminar, which includes attention to a variety of life concerns, including housing and finances as well as leisure and work pursuits. Riker and Myers (1989) suggested a number of strategies for retirement planning and counseling, which are described next.

Some of the techniques that counselors may use when working with clients to develop specific, individualized retirement strategies include: values clarification, goal setting, identification of interests, and assessment of personal strengths and weaknesses. Vocational counseling involving career exploration, identification of vocational interests and abilities, development of job-seeking skills, and exploring career options is an important component of retirement counseling for workers who wish to develop second or even third careers (Olson & Donovan-Rogers, 1986). The most important components of all preretirement and retirement counseling strategies is that they are holistic in nature and designed specifically for the needs of the individual client.

Family or marital counseling may assist individuals who are having difficulty in their relationships with spouses or adult children as they adjust to their new retirement lifestyle. This may occur as the result of increased time spent around the house and getting to know one's spouse again in an intimate capacity. In addition, it may involve the renegotiation of household tasks and the relationship between spouses or between the older person and adult children (Myers, 1989; Sweeney, 1989).

Leisure counseling may also be an important part of the retirement counseling process. Many individuals never learned how to "play," feeling that somehow free time was "useless" and of no value. Counselors may need to work with clients to help them develop an appreciation of leisure and to develop specific leisure time pursuits that are personally satisfying to the client (Riker & Myers, 1989).

Leisure Needs and Counseling

Many older persons have been indoctrinated with the traditional "work ethic" and may not have developed saitsfying leisure pursuits. This may make the development of a "leisure lifestyle" in the retirement years particularly difficult, due to lack of leisure interests and lack of value associated with leisure activities. Counselors must be aware of the importance of assisting clients in developing healthy attitudes toward and participation in leisure activities.

Leisure activities are those activities that are chosen based on an individual's enjoyment of the activity. Leisure activities can be particularly important in providing older persons with opportunities for self-expression, development, and socialization, which may help facilitate positive adjustment to retirement. Virtually any interest or hobby that an older person has, including a desire to work in a particular area, can be developed into a satisfying leisure pursuit.

Leisure counseling can be used to help individuals develop effective and satisfying use of their time and energy. Bolles (1978) underscored the importance of an integration of education, work, and retirement across the life span. This philosophy implies that both past and present needs form part of the assessment of leisure options, including skills developed earlier in life and activities postponed or neglected due to lack of time during the work years. Basic personality characteristics are also important in planning leisure activities. Some persons prefer to spend their time alone in solitary activities, whereas others are unhappy unless they are involved with groups of other individuals.

Summary

Gerontological counselors need to possess a variety of skills related to career and lifestyle options for older persons, in addition to extensive knowledge of lifestyle options. Counselors need to be skilled in assessing clients' assets and skills, which can be transferred from prior work or hobbies to new activities that will bring satisfaction in later life. The use of a variety of career and lifestyle assessment techniques used with persons of younger ages may be adapted for use in lifestyle counseling with older persons. Leisure counseling methods may also be helpful with older persons who choose not to continue working.

Case Studies

Following are three case studies that will allow the reader to apply the knowledge and skills learned in this chapter related to career and lifestyle options for older persons. Read each case study and think about how you would help the client. Then read the comments for further insights into the role of the gerontological counselor in each situation.

Case One

John is a 55-year-old retiree who comes to counseling with feelings of worthlessness, emptiness, and depression. He tells the counselor that he had retired from the army 6 months ago after 35 years of employment as an enlisted man. He states that he was really looking forward to retirement and doing all the things he never had time to do when he was working. He had planned on buying a fishing boat and a house on a lake. He had done both of these things and had spent a large portion of his time fishing since his retirement. He tells the counselor that he cannot understand why he isn't happy. "After all," he asks, "this is what I thought I always wanted to do. I have it all. Why do I feel so depressed and worthless?"

Comments on Case One

The counselor working with John needs to help him understand that the transition from working to retirement can be difficult and frustrating. Additionally, it is important for John to realize that, in a sense, he has suffered a loss. Helping to normalize the feelings of depression and lack of fulfillment is an important step in helping John realize why he is feeling as he is and how he can begin to feel better. Discussing the positive and negative implications of retirement and his feelings regarding work and leisure are essential to helping John achieve positive adjustment.

In addition, the counselor can help John begin to explore all of the options that he has to fill his time and to begin to feel worthwhile again. Some possibilities to explore would be part-time work, developing other leisure pursuits, opportunities for socialization, volunteer work, clubs he might join, and return to school. These opportunities would be based on John's values and interests. The counselor may find that John has always wanted to own a small business. He states that he has thought about opening a small bait and tackle shop near his home on the lake. This would allow him opportunities for socialization, increased income, self-worth, and an opportunity to combine his leisure and business interests.

If John chose to strongly consider this option, it would be important for the counselor to assist him in exploring fully the implications of this venture. The counselor may refer him to the Small Business Bureau for advice on starting a small business. Discussing his financial situation and where to go for advice regarding necessary permits, finances, and so on would be important as well. Most important, the counselor should assist John in the use of effective decision-making strategies by providing emotional support. If, after careful consideration, John decides this is not the best option for him to take, it is important for the counselor to continue to assist him in the development of alternative strategies for adjusting to retirement.

Case Two

Sara is a 45-year-old nurse who has worked in the medical surgical unit at a local community hospital for the past 20 years. You are an employee assistance counselor at the hospital. Sara comes to see you to begin to discuss preretirement and retirement planning issues. She recently received a statement of her projected Social Security earnings following retirement at age 65 based on her projected continued employment. She was shocked to see that her Social Security checks were much smaller than she had expected. She does not have any other savings accounts, and she has not contributed to her retirement fund at work. Therefore, she will only receive Social Security and a small pension. She tells you that she had planned to retire at age 55, and that she had recently bought a new home with a 30-year mortgage. She states she will never be able to afford the mortgage payments on her current retirement income. She also states that she suffers from back problems related to the lifting and standing required from her job as a nurse, and is concerned that she may not be able to continue working past 10 years even if she chose to do so.

Comments on Case Two

As Sara's counselor, you might want to begin by commending her on the recognition that she may need to take some actions now to obtain the kind of lifestyle she would like following retirement, reminding her that she has time to make some changes and formulate goals for the future. In the following sessions, the counselor may want to explore the client's values, interests, and goals for the future. Once Sara and the counselor have a clear view of what she would like her retirement years to be like, they can begin to formulate strategies to achieve those goals. Some possible components of those strategies might include: working with a credit union financial counselor to examine alternate ways to increase her retirement funds (e.g., increased contributions to be matched, starting an IRA), working with her personal physician to establish a fitness program to maintain her physical strength and improve her back condition, looking at alternate ways of using her nursing skills for continued employment following retirement that do not involve walking and standing for long time periods, and looking at the possibility of returning to school to obtain either an advanced degree and/or retraining in another area. Additionally, Sara should be encouraged to develop and maintain a wellness lifestyle, including the development of leisure activities that can be continued into her retirement years.

Case Three

Mr. B. has contacted you about his pending retirement. He is in good health and is excited about all of the things he can do. He wants to plan this time of his life to be as fulfilling as possible. What can you do to help him?

Comments on Case Three

Assessment of Mr. B.'s values, needs, and options is important. Clarification of his past, present, and future needs relative to basic life concerns, such as housing, medical care, family interactions, and socialization, is important. Use of a variety of assessment tools can help Mr. B. develop a plan that uses his skills and allows him to develop new ones to more fully enjoy his later years.

Discussion Questions

1. Briefly discuss the role of work in today's society. How does the role of work impact an individual's adjustment (both positively and negatively) to retirement?
2. List and discuss several career and lifestyle options that older persons may consider.
3. Consider the barriers to employment for older persons in today's workplace. What strategies might you, as the counselor, use to assist older persons wishing to return to employment in obtaining a job?

4. Discuss the retirement transition from the perspective of dealing with a loss. What impacts might retirement have on one's psychosocial adjustment? How do career development and leisure counseling theories assist counselors in formulating effective strategies for assisting older persons in dealing with this transition?
5. Discuss the importance of preretirement planning/counseling. What are some of the issues that a preretirement or retirement planning program must address?

References

Bolles, R. (1978). *The three boxes of life*. Berkeley, CA: Ten Speed Press.

Dalton, G., Thompson, P., & Price, R. (1977). Career stages: A model of professional careers in organizations. *Organizational Dynamics, 6,* 19–42.

Fretz, B., & Merikangas, M. (1992). Pre-retirement programming: Needs and responses. In H. Lea & Z. Leibowitz (Eds.), *Adult career development*. Alexandria, VA: National Career Development Association.

Hays, D.G. (1994). Retirement—Event or transition? *Career Planning and Adult Development Journal, 10*(4), 36–40.

Holland, J. (1973). *Making vocational choices: A theory of careers*. Englewood Cliffs, NJ: Prentice-Hall.

Holloran, D. (1985). The retirement identity crisis—and how to beat it. *Personnel Journal, 64*(5), 38–40.

Myers, J.E. (1994). Understanding the older worker: Physical and emotional factors. *Career Planning and Adult Development Journal, 10*(4), 4–9.

Olson, S.K., & Donovan-Rogers, J. (1986). Resources for career counselors of older adults. *Journal of Career Development, 13*(2), 57–62.

Riker, H.C., & Myers, J.E. (1989). *Retirement counseling: A handbook for action*. New York: Hemisphere.

Super, D. (1953). A theory of vocational development. *American Psychologist, 8,* 185–190.

Super, D. (1980). A life-span, life-space approach to career development. *Journal of Vocational Behavior, 16*(3), 282–298.

8

Appraisal of Older Persons

Minimum Essential Competency #7 for a Gerontological Counseling Specialist: *demonstrates skill in appraisal of older persons, including identifying characteristics of suitable appraisal instruments and techniques and in using assessment results in developing treatment plans.*

Counselors working with older persons will have many opportunities and requests to assess their clients' functioning and needs. Counselors may choose to use available standardized assessment measures, develop their own measures, or forego objective assessments in favor of clinical evaluations. Most likely, a combination of methods will be required, some performed as part of a team approach to determining the range of needs and treatment options for an older individual. Assessment will be a continuous process as clients' needs change over time.

In this chapter, some basic reasons underlying the use of assessment methods and techniques with older persons are discussed. Considerations in test construction and use that are important when assessing older persons are described, followed by a review of issues related to the reliability and validity of instruments when used with the older population. Available tests and alternative appraisal methods are discussed, as well as considerations in interpreting test results and ethical issues in testing older persons. This chapter's focus is on the use of standardized assessment measures; however, a brief section on clinical assessment is included. Two common areas of assessment with older persons—the assessment of life satisfaction and the assessment of depression—are considered.

Purposes of Assessment with Older Persons

Most assessment instruments currently available and accessible to counselors were developed and normed on young persons. When used appropriately, some of these instruments may be useful and valid in working with older adults. Others may be unsuitable for use with this population, for reasons described in later sections of this chapter.

In earlier chapters, differences between older and younger persons were discussed. It is clear that older persons differ from younger persons in some important ways. For example, the mere fact of having lived more years means that they may have a greater variety and number of life experiences and possibly a greater number of mental and physical challenges. Just as counseling with older persons is different in some ways from counseling with younger persons, assessment is different in some ways with this population.

Counselors can anticipate that older persons will benefit from appraisal and testing to the same extent as clients of other age groups. In this regard, it is far better to err on the side of providing more opportunities for appraisal rather than fewer. For example, tests can provide various types of information in a cost-effective manner to assist clients in making satisfying lifestyle and career decisions (these choices were explored in chap. 7, this volume). Older clients who would like to develop a second (or third) career may benefit from interest, aptitude, vocational, or intelligence testing as they consider training opportunities. Older persons who wish to expand their leisure activities may benefit from similar types of testing. Personality testing can be helpful to older individuals and couples who are experiencing relationship difficulties, or who simply desire assistance with self-exploration and personal growth. Older persons who want to participate in adult basic education can benefit from achievement testing. In short, virtually any older person may have needs for testing in a variety of areas (see Wickwire, 1994).

Older persons with impairments may derive significant benefit from detailed and accurate assessments to assist themselves, their families, and caregivers in planning appropriate treatment strategies. Objective information can be an important basis for significant life decisions, such as where to live and how to use one's time and talents. Counselors can expect to be part of a treatment team when working with impaired older persons, and similarly can expect that their assessment will provide only a partial examination of their clients' needs and options. This will be especially true in health care settings, where physicians, nurses, social workers, and a variety of other therapists also conduct systematic assessments of older clients and their support networks.

Counselors need to develop skills in selecting and using tests appropriately, as well as in communicating test results to their older clients. Understanding how test results "fit" with the total picture of a client's needs and goals is important. Assessment results can help older persons enhance their life satisfaction and obtain needed services. Test results can also restrict an older person's right to function independently. Counselors can expect older clients to be less prepared for testing sessions than persons of younger ages, and may find that suggestions for use of assessment methods may be misunderstood or rejected. It is important to recall that testing experiences for older persons may have consisted of classroom achievement tests when they were much younger. They may not understand the range of available assessment instruments, and may require careful explanations of the purpose and type of instruments to be used, as well as the types and uses of scores that result.

Test Construction and Use with Older Persons

Whether developing their own tests or using commercial or other available instruments with older clients, counselors need to be aware of the special needs of older people that affect their ability to achieve valid test scores. Test developers need to consider and accommodate the special characteristics of older persons that make testing with them different from testing persons of younger ages. Older persons with sensory impairments may require different test materials than younger individuals or older persons who do not experience sensory impairments.

The size of test materials, and especially the size and presentation of typefaces, are important. Tests used with older persons should be in large type, preferably 12 point or larger, and are easier to read if items are double spaced rather than single spaced. Good copies are important, with maximum contrast between the color of the page and the type. If standardized bubble answer sheets are used, counselors may want to ask a small sample of older persons to try out an instrument to determine if the bubbles are large enough or distinct enough to facilitate answering the questions. Older persons with multiple disabling conditions, such as arthritis and visual impairments, may be unable to keep their marks within the proper spaces when bubbles are small and/or outlined in light colors.

Although the educational level of the older population is steadily increasing, as many as 40% of today's older persons did not complete high school (American Association of Retired Persons, 1993). Hence, the reading level of assessment instruments, including the instructions and the items, require careful monitoring. The clarity of directions, clarity or ambiguity of items and responses, format of items and responses, or appropriateness of content often cannot be judged adequately by counselors. Having a few older persons complete tests and provide feedback on these issues can be an important way to prevent older clients from experiencing frustration or anger from the administration of inappropriate assessment tools.

Older persons also may tire more easily than younger persons. Testing sessions should be brief, with the length determined individually to meet the needs of each client. Testing sessions that approach or exceed 1 hour may be too long, particularly with frail older clients.

Reliability and Validity Issues in Testing Older Adults

Reliability, the consistency of test scores, and validity—the extent to which a test measures what it is intended to measure—are important considerations in all types of testing; they take on new dimensions when older persons are assessed. Tests and assessment methods that were developed for use with younger persons may be inappropriate for use with older persons. The only way to know for sure is to establish reliability and validity data using older individuals and groups.

Some types of tests and reliability may be inappropriate for use with older clients. Because older persons have slower reaction times than younger persons, timed tests may be frustrating for these clients and provide inaccurate information to the counselor. Split-half reliability with these tests may provide an inaccurate picture of the consistency of scores for older individuals. Careful review of the types of reliability provided in the test manual is an important consideration in choosing any test, and is especially important when choosing tests for use with older clients.

Validity of the test results can be significantly affected by the content of the items, which may be appropriate for younger persons and inappropriate for use with older clients. For example, many vocational instruments ask questions concerning favorite subjects in school and study habits—issues that may be far removed from the present life experiences of older clients. The counselor's credibility will likely be seriously undermined if such tests are used with older clients.

Older persons tend to lack test-taking behaviors, and are typically unfamiliar with standardized tests, both of which can invalidate test results. It is important to recall that the wide variety of tests in use today were not available when today's older persons were in school. Additional factors that may invalidate test scores for older clients include: increased cautiousness, misinterpretation of test questions, lower expectations for test performance, and lack of motivation to take tests.

Types of Tests for Use with Older Persons

Virtually any type of test that is available and used with any other population can be used with older persons. Older persons differ from younger persons in terms of the degree of need they experience, but not in the type of need. The development of local norms using older clients is more of an issue than the type of assessment methods used. When developing local norms, counselors need to maintain a demographic profile of test takers to ensure that additional older persons who might take the same test are compared to an appropriate normative group.

Older persons may be skeptical about taking any type of test, and often may be fearful about how the results will be used. It is important to involve older clients, and sometimes their families, in the process of selecting tests to be used. Having clients assist in the selection process will help overcome resistance, gain cooperation, reduce fears, and help reduce interference resulting from client disabilities.

Interpreting Test Results to Older Persons

Because few tests have been developed specifically for use with older persons, the availability and relevance of norm groups are extremely important in interpreting results. Norms provide a frame of reference for understanding clients. When older persons are compared with younger persons, a different profile and different conclusions may be reached than when they are compared with persons in their own age group. For example, on a speeded test used as a screening exam for school or employment, older persons may perform less well than younger persons, but equally as well as other older persons. If they are compared with younger persons, they may receive feedback that tells them they did not perform well—a situation that is likely to be avoided if other older persons comprise the norm group. Because reaction time is not related to ability to learn and perform, such tests are inappropriate for older individuals. However, they may be used to screen older persons out of some training and employment opportunities.

Counselors who use tests with older persons need to be aware of the tremendous heterogeneity of the older population; counselors should consider the unique life circumstances of each client when using test results. Finding out what the test results mean to the client, and whether the client considers the results to be valid, are important first steps in the interpretation process. Counselors also need to be aware of any physical and/or psychological factors that may affect the test performance of the older person, such as visual, auditory, or tactile impairments. The cumulative effect of stress, particularly loss and grief issues, should be considered. Due to the high incidence of depression in the older population, some consideration should be given to the effect of depression on test scores.

Test results may need to be communicated verbally to a client and his or her family, as well as to employers, social service agencies, and medical personnel. When writing reports, it is important that the test scores be provided as part of the assessment process, and not the focus of the process. The myriad factors that may affect the validity of the test scores should not only be considered by the counselor in interpreting results with the client, but also should be discussed in the assessment report.

Clinical Assessment with Older Persons

Clinical assessment with older persons can be a one-time event or a long-term process that occurs during each counseling session. Clinical diagnosis and assessment may be conducted using a structured interview format or a series of behavioral assessments by the client and others. Whatever the technique, both the strengths and weaknesses of the older client should be considered and reported.

Clinical assessments with older clients may be lengthy and time consuming, and often require multiple sessions for completion. Keeping the client focused can be difficult, especially when structured assessments are used and when the client does not fully understand the purpose of the session. Exploring the older client's assets may require some discussion of earlier life experiences, with a focus on coping skills used to resolve earlier problems.

Team approaches to assessment have proved to be effective with impaired older clients. If conducted through a geriatric assessment center, a geriatric physician may be the team leader. Other members of the team, who may be the leader as well, include nurses, social workers, occupational therapists, physical therapists, vocational evaluators, or psychologists. Team assessments may be comprehensive as well as lengthy, and provide a great deal of information about the client. Physical, psychological, and emotional functioning, as well as social data and resources, family, occupational, and personal history, comprise parts of the assessment. Three commonly used multidimensional functional assessment techniques that include this type of information are: (a) the Older Americans Resources and Services (OARS) questionnaire (Pfeiffer, 1976), (b) the Comprehensive Assessment and Referral Evaluation (CARE; Gurland et al., 1977–1978), and (c) the Multilevel Assessment Instrument (MAI), which was developed based on a conceptual model of well-being among older persons (Lawton, Moss, Fulcomer, & Kleban, 1982).

One of the most widely used assessment methods with older persons is the Mental Status Examination (MSE). There is a variety of MSE forms, having from 3 to 10 or more questions, that are used to determine the orientation of the older person (or lack thereof) to time, place, and person. Although commonly used, this instrument is brief and may result in a misdiagnosis if not used in conjunction with other assessment information.

Assessing Life Satisfaction in Older Persons

Life satisfaction, or sense of well-being, is often considered to be synonymous with successful aging. Older persons who experience a sense of well-being in later life are said to be aging successfully. Several instruments have been developed specifically for use with older persons to assess the extent of their life satisfaction. Each of these instruments is brief and can be used as the basis for counseling interventions.

The most widely used scale to measure life satisfaction is the Life Satisfaction Index (LSIA; Neugarten, Havighurst, & Tobin, 1961). Adams (1969) developed a major revision of this instrument, called the LSIZ, which is slightly shorter and potentially easier to complete than the LSIA. The instrument has been published in articles by these authors cited at the end of this chapter. It is readily accessible, may be typed in one page in large type, and is easy to complete and score. The items are relevant to older persons.

The Lawton Philadelphia Geriatric Center Morale Scale (PGC) is similar to the LSIA and equally accessible (Lawton, 1975). Whether one chooses to use the PGC or the LSIA is a matter of personal preference. Psychometric data for both instruments are available from the authors or through their publications listed later in this chapter.

Salamon and Conte's (1981) Life Satisfaction in the Elderly Scale is slightly longer than either of the two previously mentioned instruments. It assesses life satisfaction in each of eight categories of influence: pleasure in daily activities, meaningfulness of life, mood tone, self-concept, perceived health, financial security, social contact, and the fit between desired and achieved goals.

Assessing Depression in Older Persons

Fry (1986) estimated that 15%–20% of older persons living in the community experience significant, treatable depression. Depression among older persons is frequently a reaction to loss, with multiple losses leading to a situation of "bereavement overload." The diagnosis of depression is difficult with older clients for a variety of reasons. Fry cited the tendency of physicians to diagnose organic, rather than functional, conditions in older persons as a major problem. Bias among mental health professionals, who assume that older persons cannot be helped, is another significant factor. The differential diagnosis of depression is particularly hard because many of the symptoms of depression in older persons mimic the symptoms of other organic conditions, including Alzheimer's disease. As a consequence, accurate assessment of depression is an essential precursor to effective intervention.

Both clinical assessment and standardized instruments have been used effectively to assess depression. Clinical assessment strategies include attention to the symptom clusters important in depression, including behavioral, cognitive, affective, physical, and delusional concerns. The Beck Depression Inventory (BDI; Beck, Ward, Mendelsohn, Monk, & Brhaugh, 1961) is the most widely used formal assessment tool; it is easy to administer and score, and can be used each time the older person is seen for counseling. Fry (1984) developed the Geriatric Scale of Hopelessness, which assesses depression and negative expectations about the future. Myers (1989) reviewed a variety of other instruments for assessing depression.

Ethical Issues in Testing Older Persons

Tests are neutral, and are only tools of the test user. Any test can be used effectively by a qualified professional who understands the psychometric properties of the test, as well as its limitations when used with specific populations. Counselors who want to use tests ethically with older persons must first be confident in their knowledge of psychometrics and their ability to understand the reliability, validity, and normative information that will affect test results. This knowledge is required to interpret test results appropriately.

The purpose of testing is an important consideration with any client, particularly with older clients. The reason for testing can be to help the client become more independent or to "prove" incompetence, and thus lead to adjudication or institutionalization. Counselors need to be aware of who requested the testing (e.g., the client, family members, social service agencies, or medical personnel) and the reasons for the request. Test selection, administration, scoring, interpretation, and report development should be conducted with full awareness of the potential uses of the test results and the client's needs and rights. The uniqueness of the older client and his or her assets, as well as liabilities, need always be part of the final assessment results and report.

Summary

The use of assessment techniques with older persons is an essential competency for gerontological counselors. Clarification of the purpose of assessment, whether using standardized assessment measures or clinical assessment techniques, is an important first step in the assessment process. Selection of instruments requires knowledge of basic psychometric characteristics of tests and measurement devices, and how these devices can be modified for use with older persons, especially those who are impaired.

Specialized strategies are necessary for assessment of impaired older persons. Often a team approach using multidimensional functional assessment measures is required. For many older persons, knowledge of assessment approaches to determine life satisfaction, depression, and the differential diagnosis of organic pathology is important.

Case Studies

Following are two case studies that will allow the reader to apply the knowledge and skills learned in this chapter related to assessment strategies with older persons. Read each case study and think about how you would help the client. Then read the comments for further insights into the role of the gerontological counselor in each situation.

Case One

You have been invited to a long-term-care facility by family members to assess an older client who has just been admitted that day. She has been in the hospital for 2 weeks due to a broken hip, and was transferred to the nursing home. She is in a lot of pain. You sit with the nurse, who is conducting a mental status examination prior to your own assessment. When asked what day it is, the client responds with, "Oh, that is a good question! What day is it?" When asked where she is, the client looks around the room and then says, "I don't know. It looks like a hospital." The nurse looks at you and says, "Alzheimer's." What are you thinking, and what will you do when the nurse leaves?

Comments on Case One

When people are in the hospital, sometimes they do not have access to televisions or newspapers, which are a major means of orientation to month, day, and year. It is possible that the client really does not know the day because she has lost track of time during her hospitalization, just as a younger person may during a 2-week vacation. Severe pain combined with medication may make anyone unaware of his or her environment. The client's response that "this looks like a hospital" reflects a good ability to analyze her surroundings. As a counselor who is looking for positive assets, rather than pathology, you may conclude that extenuating circumstances exist causing a question as to whether the client is experiencing organic impairment or Alzheimer's disease. A more thorough assessment, combined with behavioral observations and family interviews, may be needed to develop an accurate diagnosis and treatment plan.

Case Two

Mr. P. is 83 years old and retired 14 years ago from a job as an accountant. He thinks he wants to return to some type of work, but is not sure what. What he is sure of is that he is bored and wants something to do to feel useful. He does not want to return to accounting because he cannot see well. He is not sure what he can do and wants you to help him. What can or will you do?

Comments on Case Two

Mr. P. can benefit from career and lifestyle planning. Assessment results could be especially useful in providing information to facilitate his decision making and planning. Because he is not likely to be familiar with psychological tests, a thorough explanation of the types of tests available is important. Starting with an interest inventory would be least threatening and would help identify interest areas for further exploration. To involve Mr. P. in the test selection process, you could explain the nature of two or more interest inventories you have available, the types of scores and information each will provide, and some information about the type of items, length, and so forth. Mr. P. can then select which of the tests might best meet his needs. When interpreting the test results, be sure to ask Mr. P. how the results "fit" with his own experiences. It is important to help him conceptualize his interests as areas for both career and leisure pursuits.

Should Mr. P. choose to develop an area of interest that requires additional education, aptitude, achievement, and/or intelligence tests may provide additional information to assist him in planning. Personality tests can be useful to help identify coping resources and assets that may be developed in certain job or leisure environments.

Discussion Questions

1. Describe the unique aspects of assessment with older clients.
2. What techniques do you typically use for clinical assessments? How might these techniques be modified to more fully meet the needs of older clients?
3. What formal assessment tools have you used? Which of these might be suitable for use with older clients?

References

Adams, D. (1969). Correlates of life satisfaction among the elderly. *The Gerontologist, 11*, 64–69.

American Association of Retired Persons. (1993). *A profile of older Americans*. Washington, DC: Author.

Beck, A., Ward, C., Mendelsohn, W., Monk, W., & Brhaugh, J. (1961). An inventory for measuring depression. *Archives of General Psychiatry, 4*, 53–63.

Fry, P.S. (1984). Development of a geriatric scale of hopelessness: Implications for counseling and intervention with the depressed elderly. *Journal of Counseling Psychology, 31*(3), 322–331.

Fry, P.S. (1986). *Depression, stress, and adaptations in the elderly: Psychological assessment and intervention*. Rockville, MD: Aspen.

Gurland, B., Kuriansky, J., Sharpe, L., Simon, R., Stiller, P., & Birkett, P. (1977–1978). The comprehensive assessment and referral evaluation (CARE)—rationale, development, and reliability. *International Journal of Aging and Human Development, 8*, 9–42.

Lawton, M.P. (1975). The Philadelphia Geriatric Center Morale Scale. *Journal of Gerontology, 30*, 80–89,

Lawton, M.P., Moss, M., Fulcomer, M., & Kleban, M.H. (1982). A research and service oriented multilevel assessment instrument. *Journal of Gerontology, 37*(1), 91–99.

Myers, J.E. (1989). *Adult children and aging parents*. Alexandria, VA: American Counseling Association.

Neugarten, B.L., Havighurst, R.J., & Tobin, S. (1961). The measurement of life satisfaction. *Journal of Gerontology, 16*, 134–143.

Pfeiffer, E. (1976). *Multidimensional functional assessment: The OARS methodology.* Durham, NC: Duke University Press.

Salamon, M.J., & Conte, V.A. (1981). *Salamon-Conte life satisfaction in the elderly scale.* Odessa, FL: Psychological Assessment Resources.

Wickwire, P.N. (1994). Assessment of mature workers in career counseling. *Career Planning and Adult Development Journal, 10*(2), 25–34.

9

Research and Aging

Minimum Essential Competency #8 for a Gerontological Counseling Specialist: *demonstrates skill in applying extensive knowledge of current research related to older persons and the implications of research findings for helping relationships.*

C ounselors working with older persons need to generate and use research findings in their work. This research is primarily in two areas: (a) knowledge of the characteristics, needs, and concerns of older persons and subgroups of older persons; and (b) knowledge of which counseling services and techniques are most effective in meeting those needs. Our current state of knowledge is focused on the first of these two areas, and is still not adequate to guide our interventions with older persons. A major reason for this situation is that knowledge about older persons is most readily gained through studies of captive populations. With only 4%–5% of older persons residing in institutional settings, and 10%–15% largely homebound, it is easy to see that 80% or more of the older population is unlikely to be subjects for research. As a consequence, what we think we know about older people is likely to be biased in a negative direction, particularly if subjects in research studies are persons residing in long-term-care settings (i.e., the most frail older persons).

Although the mental health needs of older persons have been documented, as discussed in other chapters, a relative paucity of empirical support for gerontological counseling services remains. Outcome studies that show the effectiveness of counseling services are needed as the basis for developing and implementing effective counseling programs.

Practitioners as well as researchers and educators need to add to our existing base of knowledge. The purpose of this chapter is to identify issues and considerations to guide our research efforts. The topics discussed include: a review of counseling research on older persons, an evaluation of research methodologies and methodological limitations in research on older persons, ethical and legal considerations in research with older persons, and sources of information and support for conducting such research studies. Finally, attention is provided to strategies for being an informed consumer of research information.

Counseling Research on Older Persons

The most recent comprehensive review of research studies on gerontological counseling outcomes was conducted by Wellman and McCormack (1982) and focused on studies in four areas: individual counseling, group counseling, peer–paraprofessional counseling, and programmatic research. These authors found that individual therapies are equally as effective with older as with younger clients. This finding was supported by Knight (1989), who determined that psychotherapy is as effective with older persons as with people of any age group. Thompson (1987) also suggested that age is not a factor in therapy outcomes. There is some support in the literature for the efficacy of both behavioral and cognitive-behavioral approaches with older persons, particularly those with organic impairments (Mosher-Ashley, 1986–1987; Hayslip & Caraway, 1988).

Group counseling has been used with older persons living in the community, as well as with those residing in institutional settings. As noted in research reviewed in chapter 6 (this volume), group procedures are among the most effective strategies for helping a variety of older persons. Recent research on family counseling with older persons, considered in chapter 14 (this volume), suggests that family interventions may be particularly valuable in later life.

Paraprofessional and peer counseling, also discussed in chapter 14, is increasingly accepted and promoted in the literature as an important means of providing helping interventions to a broad spectrum of older adults. Unfortunately, despite the popularity of these programs, little research exists to support the effectiveness of these interventions. Most research support is anecdotal, rather than the result of controlled studies.

A similar situation exists with regard to program evaluations of gerontological counseling programs. In addition to anecdotal evidence, most studies use questionable instrumentation that lacks sound psychometric development. As a consequence, results must be interpreted with caution because they can provide implications for further program development that may or may not be valid.

Research is needed on virtually all aspects of aging and all strategies for counseling older persons. Research involving various subgroups of the older population, such as older minority individuals, older men, and older persons living in rural areas, is needed. Research studies on the dynamics of the counselor–older client relationship are important, as is research on effective interventions for individual and group counseling. Longitudinal studies and long-term follow-up after the termination of counseling services also are needed if we are to determine the effectiveness of gerontological counseling over long- as well as short-term time periods.

Evaluation of Research Methodologies

The results of most studies with older persons have limited generalizability as a result of methodological limitations. Most common are sampling errors, including a lack of random selection and a tendency to use convenience samples. Such samples may reflect characteristics of persons in a particular subculture or geographic location, rather than characteristics of the older population as a whole. However, for counselors working with a particular subgroup, the results of studies with limited samples can be helpful.

Lack of control groups further limits the interpretation of data. It is often not possible to establish a control group due to limited availability of subjects. Ethical concerns in delay or denial of treatment, discussed later in this chapter, are additional problems in research with older subjects.

Researchers seldom involve older individuals in the design and development of their studies, yet these persons can provide useful feedback on research designs. Older persons can assist in the selection of appropriate interventions, and can identify areas where studies fail due to lack of understanding of older clients. They also can help researchers determine the best ways to recruit older subjects, and they can assist in the recruitment process. In institutional settings, it is especially important to involve older persons in the development of research designs. Such involvement will create roles that are not passive and dependent, but rather contribute to a sense of worth and dignity even among severely impaired individuals.

Hayslip and Caraway (1988) noted additional methodological limitations in research with older persons. One such problem is the placebo effect or halo effect, in which researchers get what they expect to find. If positive therapeutic outcomes are expected, this may contribute to receiving them even if no substantial, long-term change is observed in the older subjects. Another area of concern in research with older persons is that of selective sampling. Older persons who volunteer to participate in research studies may be those who are least assertive or those who are least in need of services. Although not wishing to volunteer, nonasssertive older persons may be reluctant to state their preferences to service providers for fear of loss of support. Independent older persons may volunteer out of interest or desire to be of assistance, although they may not be in need of services or care. Attrition can also be a problem with long-term studies of frail older persons. Older persons may quit, become ill and unable to continue, or become ill and die. The use of large, heterogeneous samples can help overcome these problems.

Of course, practicing gerontological counselors studying outcomes with their clients will not have access to large and heterogeneous samples. However, keeping track of what works and what seems ineffective in one's own caseload is an important means of constantly improving one's counseling skills and of generating consistently positive outcomes in counseling.

Ethical and Legal Considerations

Counselors conducting research with older persons need to have a thorough understanding of the aging process and characteristics of older persons. A lack of knowledge can lead to poorly designed studies that yield invalid results. Further, the potential exists to harm older individuals through a lack of knowledge and understanding of their needs. For example, older persons who are placed in uncomfortable environments for research or asked to perform for extended periods of time may perform less well or become irritated or angry as a result. Researchers who conclude from these behaviors that older persons are uncooperative or incompetent may improperly categorize their subjects and prescribe inappropriate treatments. Service providers who have access to this information may be negatively biased toward their older clients.

The ethical issues discussed in chapter 15 (this volume) apply in research as well as in counseling with older persons. Beneficence and respect are important regardless of the client's age or life circumstances. The American Counseling Association's (1988) Ethical Standards can guide research with older subjects as well as persons of younger ages.

Informed consent is particularly important in research with older subjects. Legally, there are three components to informed consent: competence, knowledge, and voluntariness. Competence may be affected by short- and long-term memory impairments, which are common among the older population. Similarly, hearing and vision impairments may affect perceived competence in older persons, leading to inaccurate conclusions and diagnoses with individuals who are mentally and emotionally capable. Knowledge of perceived risks may not be as obvious to older persons as it may be to younger individuals, hence researchers must take care to explain any risks as part of the process of obtaining informed consent. Older persons may become the victims of their own desires to be useful, volunteering for research projects and thus placing themselves in a vulnerable position. It is incumbent upon researchers to ensure that older persons are not taken advantage of, and that they are treated with dignity and respect at all times.

Voluntary participation may be jeopardized when caregivers or administrators are involved in gaining consent. Older persons may feel intimidated and forced to participate, or they may choose to volunteer for research if they think it will please persons they view as important in their lives, including gerontological counselors. Placing clients' needs and desire to do no harm foremost, rather than our own needs for information, will help maintain older clients' welfare.

Sources of Information and Support for Research

A variety of information and support sources for research exist. The suggestions in this section are intended to provide starting points, and are not intended to be exhaustive of the possibilities.

Any research project requires careful consideration of the existing state of knowledge prior to its initiation. Therefore, the first step in any research project is likely to be a thorough search of the literature to determine both what is known and what methods have been used to determine the current state of knowledge. Most libraries have on-line data search capabilities that allow searches by subject, author, title, or year of publication. Computerized databases, such as ERIC/CASS and Psychological Abstracts, can quickly provide a wealth of information on a wide variety of subjects. Working with a librarian or researcher to identify the key words to be used in a search of computer databases is particularly important. Researchers may want to review a directory of key words prior to beginning a search.

The National Institute on Aging funds the National Archive of Computerized Data on Aging (NACDA), an extensive database of resources useful when working with or designing research projects with older persons. This and other databases may be identified and accessed through the Association for Gerontology in Higher Education (AGHE; 1001 Connecticut Avenue, N.W., Suite 140, Washington, DC 20036–5504).

Most national government agencies maintain resource centers and/or lists of publications that may be obtained at low or no cost. These include: the U.S. Administration on Aging (AoA), the National Institutes of Health (NIH), and the National Institutes of Mental Health (NIMH). Professional associations such as the American Counseling Association (ACA) and the Association for Gerontology in Higher Education (AGHE) also have publications that can be useful in designing and conducting research studies. These agencies often fund research projects as well. In addition, many foundations provide funding for research. Directories of these agencies and additional funding sources are available in most public and university libraries in the reference section.

Accessing and Using Research Knowledge

Most practicing gerontological counselors do not have ready access to university libraries, the major resources for professional journals and research reports. However, this should not be a serious limitation in one's ability to access and use research data. What is important is that each counselor devote at least a portion of his or her continuing professional education to the identification of recent, relevant research, which will improve their delivery of counseling services to older persons.

It is especially important for counselors working in the field to belong to professional associations. Major benefits of membership usually include journals and newsletters. Newsletters are an important resource for identifying current events and training opportunities. Journals are a resource for learning new techniques and for accessing research results. Counselors can join ACA and also its division of Adult Development and Aging (AADA), and may choose to join one or more of the gerontology associations listed in chapter 12 (this volume). Each association has a unique purpose and a journal that emphasizes a particular type of information or audience, such as researchers or practitioners.

Summary

Gerontological counselors need to be producers as well as consumers of research on older persons. The current state of knowledge of older persons' needs and effective counseling interventions remains insufficient. In particular, outcome studies are needed to determine which older persons benefit from which interventions and under what circumstances. Counselors can obtain information about current research from a variety of sources discussed in this chapter, including professional associations and government agencies.

Case Studies

Following are two case studies that will allow the reader to apply the knowledge and skills learned in this chapter related to research with and on behalf of older individuals. Read each case study and think about how you would help the client. Then read the comments for further insights into the role of the gerontological counselor in each situation.

Case One

A friend sends you an article describing a new counseling technique that is "sure" to be effective with older clients. You have not heard of the authors, and are not familiar with the source of the publication. What do you do?

Comments on Case One

The first thing to do is to read the article carefully, paying close attention to the methodology used. Ask yourself a number of questions as you read: Was the sample carefully selected? Was a control group used? Is the sample representative of the types of clients in your caseload? What was the size of the sample, and was it large enough to generate useful results? How were subjects recruited? What instruments were used? Are the reliability and validity of the instruments reported? What kinds of data were collected? How were the data analyzed? Were the analyses appropriate? What was the statistical power of the results? Are the implications directly related to the data, or do they seem to be over-generalized?

It is possible that the new technique will be useful in some circumstances with some clients. You may wish to contact the authors directly for more information on how to use the technique. As you begin using it, be sure to keep careful case notes and records so that you can determine if, how, and when it will be most useful and effective in your own work.

Case Two

You are working in an agency that has decided to conduct a study on all of its clients. You are to assist in the data collection with your own caseload. As you read the instrument to be used, you note that many of the questions are "personal" and may be offensive to an older client. What do you do?

Comments on Case Two

Realizing that informed consent is an important aspect of any research project, you may wish to design an informed consent form for use with your own clients. By making them aware of the nature and type of research to be conducted, you can empower them to choose whether to participate.

At the same time, you need to explore with your own supervisor your concerns about the instrument and its use. It may be that the wording of certain items can be changed, or that the agency can be helped to accept that informed clients may choose whether to participate, and may do so without fear of repercussion for their choices.

Discussion Questions

1. What are some of the major methodological flaws or pitfalls in conducting research with older subjects?
2. What are important ethical issues in research with older persons?
3. What professional associations do you belong to, and what publications do they provide? Is information about research with older subjects a part of this information? If not, where might you learn about current research with older people?

References

American Counseling Association. (1988). *Ethical Standards*. Alexandria, VA: Author.

Hayslip, B., & Caraway, M.L. (1988). Cognitive therapy with aged persons: Implications of research design for its implementation and evaluation. *Journal of Cognitive Psychotherapy: An International Quarterly, 3*(4), 255–271.

Knight, B.G. (1989). *Outreach with the elderly: Community education, assessment, and therapy*. New York: New York University Press.

Mosher-Ashley, P. (1986–1987). Procedural and methodological parameters in behavioral-gerontological research: A review. *International Journal of Aging and Human Development, 24*(3), 189–229.

Thompson, L. (1987). Comparative effectiveness of psychotherapy for depressed elders. *Journal of Consulting and Clinical Psychology, 55*(3), 385–390.

Wellman, F.E., & McCormack, J. (1982). Counseling with older persons: A review of outcome research. *The Counseling Psychologist, 12*(2), 81–96.

10

Wellness in Later Life

Minimum Essential Competency #9 for a Gerontological Counseling Specialist: *demonstrates skill in applying extensive knowledge of the intellectual, physical, social, emotional, vocational, and spiritual needs of older persons and strategies for helping meet those needs.*

C ompetency #9 for gerontological counseling specialists may be restated as follows: The competent gerontological counselor demonstrates skill in applying extensive knowledge of wellness theories and methods for helping meet the needs of older persons. In this chapter, wellness is defined, and models of wellness appropriate for counselors are described. The relationship between physical and mental health and how these aspects of functioning affect wellness are examined. How one of these models can be used as the basis for counseling interventions is explored, with a focus on viewing the older person holistically.

Defining Wellness

The concept of wellness evokes conflicting images in the minds of many people, including counselors and other helping professionals. On the one hand, wellness connotes a positive state that is presumably desirable for all individuals, especially *other* people. On the other hand, taken from a personal perspective, wellness is frequently misunderstood and avoided, most likely because (a) people believe themselves to be, in one or more ways, unwell; (b) people believe that to become well they will need to change, and change is always difficult; and (c) some "unwellness" activities are actually enjoyable.

Several common myth perceptions may be identified that lend themselves to avoiding wellness discussions or activities. These include:

1. The belief that wellness means I *must* exercise. And that means that the old adage "no pain, no gain" applies. I have to hurt or I am not being helped by exercise. Most of us can relate to the cartoon by Mike Peters, Mother Goose and Grimm, in which Mother Goose advises Grimm that his body is falling apart and he needs to start exercising. She asks him if he ever thought of toning his muscles—of lifting weights. He replies, "Sure I lift weights. I'm standing, aren't I?" Whatever fits for a particular individual is what he or she should do. There are no hard or fast rules on exercise, and the nature and type of exercise will change over the course of the life span.
2. The belief that I *must* change my diet. The rule here is that "if it tastes good, it must be bad for me." Extensive time, effort, and energy are required if I am to achieve a "healthy" diet. Consider the wellness cartoon in which a 30-year-old man is shown as a small speck on top of the 25,000-pound oat bran muffin he must consume over the next 40 years if he is to significantly reduce his risk of death from high cholesterol. Clearly, a healthy diet is more than oat bran.
3. Wellness means I *must* be under stress if I am ever physically sick. So any illness means I *must* listen to my body and I *must* change my lifestyle. Again, change is difficult, so why bother?
4. If I smoke, I *must* quit. Actually, this one is true! Although the tobacco industry would like to thank you for smoking, the facts on the risks of smoking, either primary or secondary, are indisputable. There are more deaths from smoking each year in the United States than from the combined total of AIDS, heroin, crack cocaine, alcohol, fire, murders, and car accidents. The number of people who die each day in our country from smoking, or inhaling secondary smoke, is equivalent to two jumbo jets crashing with no survivors.

Most of us react negatively to being told what we *should* or *must* do. Most of us react positively to knowledge of what we *can* do. In this context, wellness is both a philosophy and process for what we *can* do to achieve certain outcomes.

Ardell (1988) defined *wellness* as a conscious and deliberate approach to an advanced state of physical and psychological/spiritual health. The integration of body, mind, and spirit that characterizes the healthy person does not just happen—clearly it is a choice or a series of choices. Each wellness choice strengthens the ability to make increasingly more lifestyle choices that are within one's own best self-interest. So wellness, as a lifestyle, is empowering. Wellness helps people achieve a more meaningful and better human existence—for themselves and also for others. How this occurs may be understood within the context of wellness models.

Wellness Models

Several wellness models are described in the literature. Each model is based on the belief that we function as an integrated whole, such that each aspect of wellness is related to every other. Change in one area contributes to or causes changes in other areas. These changes may be for better or worse.

An example of a widely known model is Hettler's (1984) six-dimensional model of wellness. The six areas of this model are: emotional, intellectual, physical, social, occupational, and spiritual. Hettler's model is widely used on college campuses, and is the basis for two assessment instruments: the Lifestyle Assessment Questionnaire and Testwell. These instruments assess wellness in each of the model's six areas.

Witmer and Sweeney (1992) presented a holistic model for wellness and prevention that is especially useful for counselors. This model incorporates theoretical concepts from a variety of disciplines, including psychology, anthropology, sociology, religion, and education (see Fig. 10.1). The model provides an integrated paradigm that can serve as a basis for theory building, clinical interventions, education, advocacy, and consciousness raising. It is the basis for the Wellness Evaluation of Lifestyle, an assessment instrument that can be used by counselors to measure each dimension of wellness in the model (Witmer, Sweeney, & Myers, 1994).

In the Witmer and Sweeney model, the characteristics of healthy persons are described under five life tasks, which are symbolized in a

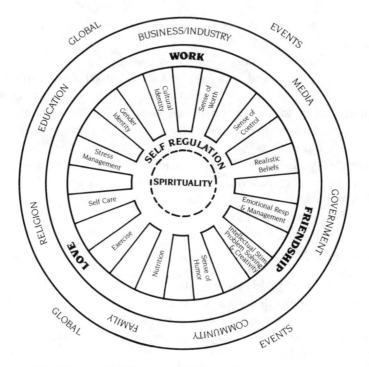

Figure 10.1 Wheel of Wellness and Prevention.
From "A Holistic Model for Wellness and Prevention Over the Life Span," by
J.M. Witmer and T.J. Sweeney, 1992, *Journal of Counseling & Development, 71,*
140–148.

wheel of wellness. Spirituality is the core of the wellness wheel and
one of five major life tasks. The four additional tasks are self-regulation,
work, love, and friendship. The five life tasks interact dynamically with
several life forces, including family, community, religion, education,
government, media, and business/industry. These life forces and life
tasks interact with and are affected by global events, both natural and
human, positive as well as negative. Although we discuss the life tasks
independently, it is important to remember that, in a healthy person,
all life tasks are interconnected and interact for the well-being or detriment of the individual.

Spirituality

The first life task, spirituality, is the center of the wellness wheel. *Spirituality* refers to a sense of meaning or purpose in life—a sense of

values. A major component of spirituality is a desire to experience a sense of oneness with the universe—a sense of wholeness in which one also experiences a sense of inner peace. To be spiritual means to experience a sense of a being or power in the universe greater than oneself. An additional dimension of spirituality is a sense of purposiveness, hope, or optimism about future events. A set of moral and ethical principles or values arise from a sense of spirituality and guide our behavior toward the preservation of human rights and dignity.

Self-Regulation

The second life task, self-regulation, surrounds the spiritual self and provides the spokes in the wellness wheel that connect the core with the remaining life tasks. There are 12 components of self-regulation that strengthen the wellness wheel, similar to the action of the spokes in a bicycle wheel: sense of worth; sense of control; realistic beliefs; spontaneity and emotional responsiveness; intellectual stimulation, problem solving, and creativity; sense of humor; nutrition; exercise; self-care; stress management; gender identity; and cultural identity. Without the spokes, a bicycle wheel does not work properly. Without the spokes in the wellness wheel, the self does not connect in a healthy manner with others in the major life tasks of work, friendship, and love.

Sense of Worth. Sense of worth, or self-esteem, has been identified as the single greatest factor that affects individual growth and behavior (Frey & Carlock, 1989). Satisfaction with and acceptance of oneself with both assets and imperfections are important components of a sense of self-worth. A number of studies have reported that persons with higher self-esteem have better mental and physical health (see Witmer & Sweeney, 1992).

Sense of Control. *Control*, sometimes defined as a sense of competence, refers to feelings of mastery and confidence. Persons with a strong sense of personal control also have a belief in their own self-efficacy, or ability to affect outcomes of events in their lives. This is also defined as having an internal locus of control—a belief that events are contingent on one's own actions.

Realistic Beliefs. Healthy persons are able to see reality as it is, not as they would want it to be. They are able to recognize both rational and logical ideas, and those that are distorted or represent wishful thinking. Persons with a positive outlook and realistic belief system tend to be less anxious and have fewer physical complaints or symptoms.

Spontaneity and Emotional Responsiveness. Healthy persons are able to be spontaneous in their interactions with others and to express, appropriately, the emotions they feel inside. They are sensitive to others and are assertive in finding ways to meet their own emotional needs in relationships while respecting and supporting the needs of others. Being able to have a childlike simplicity and authenticity in emotional responses to events characterizes wellness in this regard.

Intellectual Stimulation, Problem Solving, and Creativity. Being mentally active is important for longevity and also enriches quality of life (Pelletier, 1981). The ability to think soundly and logically, and to solve problems is necessary for effective, independent living in society. In addition, having a sense of wonder and curiosity, and creativity in approaching problems, is important for mastery of the environment and contributes to satisfaction in life. As persons grow older, it is true that "if you don't use it, you're likely to lose it." Intellectual stimulation is thus an important consideration for wellness over the life span.

Sense of Humor. Humor, especially when accompanied by laughter, is important for health. Humor overrides negative emotions, relaxes, energizes, provides flexibility for problem solving, reduces stress, and improves communication. Persons who are the most well adjusted have been shown to use humor as an antidote for distress more than do persons who are less well adjusted.

Nutrition. One should eat a variety of foods that include major portions of fresh fruits and vegetables, whole grain and enriched breads, cereals, and other grain products; a moderate amount of dairy products, meat, poultry, fish, beans, eggs, and nuts; and fats, oils, sweets, and salt sparingly. Good eating habits for most persons include eating three meals a day with little or no snacking and eating breakfast every day. Caloric intake should be such as to maintain normal weight and avoid overeating. "Junk foods" and "fast foods" need to be limited, food fads (eating nothing but _____) avoided, and use of food as a pain reliever and stress reducer checked. In addition, recent research suggests the importance of vitamins C, E, and A (in the form of Beta Carotine) as antioxidants, which help to delay or reverse the aging process.

Exercise.   This is the component most often associated with the concept of wellness, and the area that receives the most attention in the media and among individuals. One's exercise (or job) should include enough physical activity to keep a person in good physical condition. Moderate exercise three or four times a week for a minimum of 20 minutes is recommended (e.g., swimming, tennis, brisk walking, racketball, basketball, jogging/running, aerobics). These activities build endurance and condition the heart and lungs. Additionally, one's work or exercise routine should include the gentle stretching of the major muscles of the body on a regular basis. Such flexibility movements lengthen, stretch, and flex the muscles, thereby keeping the body relaxed and mobile. A third type of exercise, strength developing (e.g., weight training), strengthens the muscles. Regularity in the exercise and not overdoing the activity are important guidelines.

Self-Care.   Good health and longevity require one to take responsibility for all aspects of well-being. Included are the self-care and safety habits that are preventive in nature. Such habits include appropriate and timely medical care when needed. Consultation is made with a physician regarding matters of particular concern to persons your age and gender, including blood pressure, cholesterol level, triglycerides, and blood sugar. Other preventive and safety habits include wearing a seat belt, limiting the use of prescription drugs and avoiding all illegal drugs, seeking consultation for a serious mental or emotional condition, choosing an environment relatively free of pollution, and protecting oneself from the sun's harmful rays.

The relationship among positive health habits, wellness, and life expectancy has been well documented. The most important habits to cultivate bear repeating: eating three meals a day at regular times and not snacking at other times, eating breakfast every day, getting moderate exercise two to three times a week for 20–30 minutes, getting adequate sleep (7–8 hours per night), maintaining a moderate weight, drinking alcohol in moderation or not at all, and not smoking (Belloc & Breslow, 1972).

Stress Management. Stress management refers to one's ability to engage in one's own self-regulation. An important aspect of self-regulation is the ability to see change as an opportunity for growth, rather than as a threat to one's security. This process involves ongoing self-monitoring and assessment of one's coping resources, as well as the ability to organize and manage resources such as one's time and energy. It includes the need to set limits and the need for structure in one's life.

Gender Identity. Gender identity refers to acceptance of those qualities in oneself that one sees or would like to see in a person of your gender. These are not necessarily qualities or roles associated with one's gender by society or culture. A strong sense of gender identity reflects satisfaction with the physical, psychological, and social attributes and roles that one has carved out for oneself as a male or female. Healthy persons have a positive affiliation with others of their gender, and are comfortable with important personal attributes of others without regard to whether they are male or female.

Cultural Identity. Cultural identity reflects the extent to which one is aware and accepting of one's unique cultural heritage. For many healthy individuals, cultural identity is a source of strength and pride. It contributes to a feeling of belonging. Acceptance of one's ethnic, racial, or cultural heritage and viewing one's cultural reference group as having desirable beliefs, values, and behaviors are important aspects of cultural identity. A characteristic of a healthy person is the ability to be comfortable interacting with persons who are culturally different from oneself.

Work

The third life task, work, provides economic, psychological, and social benefits. *Work* refers to meaningful activity engaged in for personal sustenance and to contribute to the sustenance of others. It includes work within the home as well as without, community service, and many other activities in addition to paid employment. Persons who engage in work activities earn income necessary to meet the demands of daily living, such as food, shelter, transportation, and entertainment. Work provides a sense of personal satisfaction and self-esteem, and fosters a sense of control. Socially, work provides a sense of status as a contributing member of society.

Friendship

The fourth life task, friendship, refers to social relationships with others that involve interpersonal connections, but do not involve marital, sexual, or family commitments. Friendships satisfy emotional needs for closeness and interaction with others, and provide social support, including emotional support, tangible assistance, and informational support through advice and feedback. The presence of friendships affects life satisfaction as well as longevity. Persons who lack a social support network, including friendships, experience more illness, a reduced life expectancy, and less satisfaction with life (Cohen, 1988).

Love

The fifth life task, love, refers to the ability to be intimate, trusting, self-disclosing, and committed over time in relationships with others. Love includes friendship and sexual intimacy, as well as altruism. Being able to love others is associated with health—both physical and mental—and longevity. Part of this life task involves the ability to be loved, to receive love from others, and to give love.

Interrelationship of Wellness Dimensions

The five life tasks in the Witmer and Sweeney model are not static, but dynamic. Although the wellness wheel may be drawn in one dimension, in actuality one dimension is only a cross-section of the characteristics of healthy persons. If it were shown in two dimensions, the model would be depicted as a sphere. In three dimensions, it actually would be more in the shape of a tube, with the longitudinal dimension being time or the life span. Healthy people function in each of the five life tasks over time across the life span. As the components or tasks interact over time, changes may be for better or worse. The goal of wellness, of course, is to make changes in positive directions.

If you can imagine movement of the wheel in the third dimension, it may be seen as spinning toward a goal of greater well-being. As the individual chooses healthy behaviors to meet each of the five life tasks, the momentum increases and movement is toward increasing health and wellness. The development of each of the five life tasks is influenced by forces within the individual as well as outside.

The Relationship Between Physical and Mental Health and Wellness

As a group, older persons, especially those 65 years of age and older, are known to experience the greatest amount and type of disabling conditions and to require proportionately more care services than persons of other ages. For example, older persons represent only 13% of the total population, yet they account for 36% of total personal health care expenditures, with an average of four times more dollars spent for each person over 65 than for each person under that age. Older persons average more contact with physicians and account for 34% of all hospital stays and 45% of all days of care in hospitals. Among the more than 26,000,000 older Americans, at least 86% experience one or more chronic physical conditions that limit their daily living activities (Brotman, 1982).

In addition to extensive physical concerns, older persons have a variety of mental and emotional challenges to face. *Aging* has been defined as a period of loss: loss of health, loss of stamina, loss of gainful paid work activity, loss of social roles that accompany retirement, loss of friends through death and geographic moves, loss of loved ones through death, and so forth. Coping with loss requires an active process of grieving, leading eventually to resolution, acceptance, and replacement of the functions served by who or what was lost. Older persons experience multiple losses, often failing to complete one grief process before needing to grieve another loss. Just as stimulus overload occurs when we experience too much stress, bereavement overload occurs for many older persons who experience multiple losses. They need time out to grieve, and often become immobilized, as reflected in the high incidence of depression among the older population.

Functioning at all times and also in later life is affected by both physical and mental changes, neither of which occur in isolation. Rather, biological processes are known to interact with psychological and social factors. This interaction, or interdependence, occurs at all ages, but is known to increase significantly with advancing age. The interaction between physical and mental health problems, in particular, leads to substantial comorbidity among older adults. That is to say, physical problems can lead to mental and emotional disturbance, emotional distress can exacerbate physical symptoms, and the combination of both can lead to significant clinical impairments combined with difficulty, or impossibility, of health care management. How the interaction of these components is reflected in a negative cycle of decreased functioning was described in the Social Breakdown Syndrome (see chap. 3, this volume). This model is well worth studying and understanding because knowledge of how social breakdown occurs can lead directly to strategies for how it can be reversed to promote healthy functioning in later life (i.e., Social Reconstruction). The same model can be used to explain a positive cycle of increased functioning, as reflected in the wellness wheel as it evolves over time.

Using the Wellness Model in Counseling

When using the wellness wheel in counseling, any or all of the dimensions may be the focus of helping interventions. Gerontological counselors may begin with an assessment of the older person's functioning in each of the model's areas, using the Wellness Evaluation of Lifestyle instrument (Witmer, Sweeney, & Myers, 1994) or clinical interviews. Use of the instrument may be less time-consuming, and it may be easier to conduct an assessment in all areas of the model using this method.

Interventions may be structured to address wellness in one or more of the model's dimensions. The creativity of the counselor is the major limitation in developing interventions. It is important to have the client determine which area he or she would like to change prior to initiating a treatment plan. Use of the assessment instrument over time, combined with completion of a workbook (see Myers, Witmer, & Sweeney, 1995), may be helpful to older clients.

For example, to assist clients in exploring spirituality issues, bibliotherapy could be helpful (see chap. 14, this volume). You could invite clients to read one of the books listed in the supplemental reading section of this book, and then discuss what the themes of the book mean to them. Discussion of the clients' sense of meaning and purpose in life is another means of exploring spirituality issues. Friendship issues can be discussed by having clients define what a "best friend" means to them, then talk about the best friends they have had in their lives or have right now. Love issues may be explored in a similar manner. Work issues and strategies for helping clients in this area are explored more fully in chapter 7 (this volume). The life task of self-regulation contains a variety of components, each of which may be explored in counseling by having clients talk about what that issue means to them and how it affects their lives. Exploration of each of these areas can be facilitated through an accurate assessment of the clients' functioning and priorities.

Summary

Wellness is defined in this chapter as a process of striving for optimum human functioning in all areas. Several models of wellness were discussed, with an emphasis on Witmer and Sweeney's (1991) wellness wheel. This model, which is based on Adlerian theory, includes identification of five major life tasks—spirituality, self-regulation, work, friendship, and love—that interact in a manner that contributes to total wellness. These life tasks and related subtasks form the basis for the Wellness Evaluation of Lifestyle (WEL)—an instrument that can be used to assess wellness in the various dimensions of the model. Strategies for using the wellness model and the WEL in counseling with older persons were also discussed.

Case Studies

Following are two case studies that will allow the reader to apply the knowledge and skills learned in this chapter related to wellness in later life. Read each case study and think about how you would help the client. Then read the comments for further insights into the role of the gerontological counselor in each situation.

Case One

Mrs. G. is a 72-year-old widow who was self-referred. She states she is basically content with her life, but wants to use her free time and talents to develop herself more fully. She is not sure how to proceed to develop a healthier lifestyle.

Comments on Case One

Mrs. G. is an excellent candidate for a wellness assessment. You could talk to her about taking a holistic paper-and-pencil instrument like the Wellness Evaluation of Lifestyle (WEL), described earlier in this chapter. If she chooses to take the instrument, her scores may be used as the basis for developing a plan for optimizing her development in each of the areas of the model. She can use the WEL Workbook (Myers, Witmer, & Sweeney, 1995) on her own and/or work with you to explore each area of wellness.

Case Two

Mr. K. is a 75-year-old widower who has periodic bouts of depression related to his retirement and loss of his spouse. His depressive episodes are accompanied by feelings of hopelessness. He has not mentioned suicidal ideation, but you know it is a possibility with older men experiencing similar circumstances. What can you do to help?

Comments on Case Two

In addition to the many counseling techniques you could employ to assist Mr. K. in developing new interests and activities to enhance his life and help overcome feelings of depression, you could approach working with him from a wellness perspective. Rather than focusing on his losses, you could help him identify his strengths and areas of wellness. An assessment of his current wellness in multiple dimensions could provide clues to his strengths, as well as areas where he might place emphasis and develop strategies for improving his overall functioning. The wellness approach could result in a positive asset search and the use of his positive coping skills to help overcome the problems he is experiencing.

Discussion Questions

1. What are the five life tasks in the Witmer and Sweeney wellness wheel? What effect do they have on one another?
2. Describe the relationship between physical and mental health. How can this relationship be used to help improve the quality of life for older persons?

3. What are some strategies for enhancing wellness in each dimension of the model presented earlier?

References

Ardell, D.B. (1988). The history and future of the wellness movement. In J.P. Opatz (Ed.), *Wellness promotion strategies: Selected proceedings of the eighth annual National Wellness Conference.* Dubuque, IA: Kendall/Hunt.

Belloc, N.B., & Breslow, L. (1972). Relationship of physical health status and health practices. *Preventive Medicine, 1,* 409–421.

Brotman, H. (1982). *Every ninth American.* (Committee Pub. No. 97–332). Washington, DC: U.S. House of Representatives.

Cohen, S. (1988). Psychosocial models of the role of social support in the etiology of physical disease. *Health Psychology, 7,* 269–297.

Frey, D., & Carlock, C.J. (1989). *Enhancing self-esteem* (2nd ed.). Muncie, IN: Accelerated Development.

Hettler, B. (1984). Wellness: Encouraging a lifetime pursuit of excellence. *Health Values: Achieving High Level Wellness, 8*(4), 13–17.

Myers, J.E., Witmer, J.M., & Sweeney, T.J. (1995). *The WEL workbook.* Palo Alto, CA: Mind Garden.

Pelletier, K. (1981). *Longevity: Fulfilling our biological potential.* New York: Delacorte Press/Seymour Lawrence.

Witmer, J.M., & Sweeney, T.J. (1992). A holistic model for wellness and prevention over the lifespan. *Journal of Counseling and Development, 71*(2), 140–148.

Witmer, J.M., Sweeney, T.J., & Myers, J.E. (1994). *The Wellness Evaluation of Lifestyle.* Greensboro, NC: Authors.

11

Intervention Strategies for Common Later Life Impairments

Minimum Essential Competency #10 for a Gerontological Counseling Specialist: *demonstrates skill in applying appropriate intervention techniques, in collaboration with medical and other care providers, for physical and mental impairments common to older persons, such as acute, chronic, and terminal illness, depression, suicide, and organic brain syndromes.*

Gerontological counselors may be called on to function as a member of a multidisciplinary treatment team in order to provide comprehensive services to older persons with physical and/or mental impairments. Members of the treatment team may include physicians, social workers, physical therapists, occupational therapists, nutritionists, nurses, and home health care providers. It is important for gerontological counselors to be familiar with common later life impairments that older persons may experience and, most important, to know how their unique knowledge and skills can best be utilized by the treatment team. In this chapter, the roles of members of the treatment team are considered, followed by a discussion of older persons' acute and chronic illnesses. Three common problems that occur in working with older persons—depression, suicide, and organic brain disorders—are considered in depth.

Roles of the Treatment Team Members

When working with impaired older persons, a physician is usually the leader of the treatment team. It is his or her job to oversee the medical aspects of treatment. This includes medical treatment, medication prescriptions, prescriptions for physical and occupational therapy, consultations with other medical specialists, and referral for mental health counseling. The physician is also responsible for seeing that all other services provided to the impaired older person are appropriate given the client's physical condition.

A social worker on the team is responsible for assisting impaired older persons in obtaining necessary social services, home health care services, and durable medical equipment, such as an in-home hospital bed or wheelchair. Social workers are familiar with community resources and the necessary admission criteria to enter each program. They may also work with the impaired older person's family to coordinate in-home care or nursing home placement, and to provide family counseling services.

Physical and occupational therapists may also be part of the rehabilitation and/or treatment team. The physical therapist is responsible for helping the impaired older person regain physical strength and stamina. This may involve exercises to help the older person walk, maintain or improve upper body strength, and improve cardiovascular endurance. The occupational therapist is responsible for helping the older person perform activities of daily living, such as feeding oneself, bathing, and dressing.

Home health care providers, including nurses, nurses aides, homemakers, and personal care workers, are often members of the treatment team when the impaired older person returns home. Nurses provide skilled nursing care, such as administration of medication, changing dressings on wounds, and changing catheters. Homemakers are usually unskilled workers whose primary function is to assist older persons in the upkeep of their homes through activities such as vacuuming, washing dishes, dusting, and mopping. Personal care workers are trained in much the same way as nurses aides, providing services such as bathing, dressing, and shaving clients.

As a member of the treatment team, a gerontological counselor works with other service providers as well as with the older person and the older person's family to meet the client's mental health needs. The counselor may provide emotional support, information, and skill development (such as improving communication skills or stress management) through the use of therapeutic counseling interventions.

Clearly, the provision of care for older persons with impairments is complex and requires multiple approaches, expertise, and interventions. Geriatric care management is an emerging profession that was developed in response to the complex needs that can exist in later life. Care managers assess the array of services needed by an older person and assist the individual and his or her family in accessing those services. Care managers may work for community agencies or practice independently.

Acute and Chronic Illnesses

Illnesses among the older population tend to be chronic, progressive, multiple, and interactive. Acute conditions may be caused by existing chronic conditions, or may exacerbate the negative effects of preexisting illnesses. Medical care and attention are usually aimed at providing management of the illnesses and prevention of further decline, rather than prevention or cure. Additionally, age-related changes may cause older persons to be more subject to acute infections, which take longer to heal.

Counselors working with older persons must be aware of any chronic illnesses that may be affecting their clients. Additionally, counselors must be familiar with the effects of such illnesses on older persons, the effects and side effects of medications, and the signs and symptoms of additional decline. The counselor may need to work with older persons to help them accept their chronic conditions, which may become increasingly debilitating. This may involve assisting clients to grieve about changes in body image, physical limitations, and increasing dependence on others.

Counselors may also work with the families of impaired older persons to educate them regarding normal changes associated with the aging process and common effects of particular chronic conditions. This assists family members in distinguishing between normal changes related to the aging process and changes caused by chronic conditions. This is important so that family members can contact the physician regarding changes in the older person's condition, which may prevent further decline and/or the need for institutionalization.

Families may experience a sense of loss and grief as the older person becomes more dependent and impaired. Spouses who are not impaired may have difficulty adjusting their lifestyle and expectations to the needs of the chronically ill spouse. Counselors can help couples experiencing these difficulties by teaching them effective communication skills, providing emotional support, and providing relationship counseling.

Adult children of chronically impaired older persons also may experience difficulties related to the changing roles between themselves and their aging parent. Often, adult children are called on to provide care for their aging parents, and roles may be reversed. That is, the adult child is then, in a sense, parenting his or her parent. Anger, frustration, burden, and burnout are issues that may surface. Counselors can facilitate communication, provide emotional support, and help both the adult child and the aging parent to understand one another's needs (Myers, 1989).

Counselors working with impaired older persons need to be familiar with community resources and how to access needed services. This is imperative if older persons and their families are to provide care for the older person in the best environment possible. Community resources may allow impaired older persons to remain in their own homes. In addition, the use of community resources may allow adult children to care for their impaired parents in their homes, rather than placing the older persons in long-term-care facilities. Community resources such as Meals on Wheels, home health care, personal care, and respite services are available in many communities. Counselors working with terminally ill older persons should also be familiar with area hospice programs and the services they provide. For additional information on community resources and the aging network, see chapter 12 (this volume).

Depression and Older Persons

Depression, "the common cold" of mental disorders, is known to increase in incidence among older persons (Fry, 1986). More specifically, persons age 65 and older are particularly vulnerable to episodic or chronic depression. The incidence of depression in women outnumbers that in men, with the exception of men over age 80, who have higher rates than women. Many researchers explain the increased incidence of depression among older persons as a result of the increased number and variety of losses associated with the aging process. Diagnosis of depression among older persons may be complicated. Because older persons are less likely to seek mental health care than younger persons, the incidence of depression among this population may be even higher than suspected.

Diagnosis of depression among older persons is difficult for a number of reasons. These include underreporting of depression, reluctance of older persons to seek mental health care, biases of mental health and health care professionals that older persons do not benefit from treatment, differences between symptomology of older persons and younger persons with depression, and frequency of reported symptoms. Although a large number of older persons may report dysphoric moods, a much smaller number of older persons actually qualifies for a diagnosis of major depression.

The literature highlights that older persons experience more losses than younger persons. However, because these losses may be perceived as "on time" or an expected part of the aging process, the losses may be better tolerated by older persons. Therefore, although there is a higher incidence of losses, causing a higher incidence of depressive symptoms among older persons, the prognosis for successful treatment is excellent. Only a small number of older persons do not respond to treatment.

Losses experienced by older persons are varied and numerous. These include loss of health, loss of job (retirement), changes in family relationships, deaths, changes in living arrangements, and changes in financial status. Even developmental tasks related to later life may be experienced as losses and contribute to increased feelings of depression (Riker & Myers, 1989). For example, an older person may be faced with the life task of ego integrity versus despair. This may precipitate a life review, and the older person may perceive that he or she has not led a good life and there is not enough time left to do anything about it. As a consequence, feelings of low self-worth, helplessless, and hopelessness may result. The depression and sense of hopelessness, combined with the aging process, may lead the older person to become more isolated and withdrawn. The question then becomes, how do we, as counselors, help the older person to reframe those life events to obtain a sense of self-worth and alleviate the depression and isolation?

Treatment of depression in older persons begins with accurate diagnosis. As can be seen from the previous example, it is important for the counselor to assess both reported symptoms of the depression (e.g., feelings of worthlessness, hopelessness) and factors that contribute to the depression (e.g., social isolation, physical illnesses). Of particular importance to accurate diagnosis is the differential diagnosis between depression and dementia (see Fry, 1986). Dementia may contribute to the development of depression, and the symptoms of depression and dementia may be similar. Additionally, over-the-counter or prescription medications may cause older persons to experience feelings and symptoms of depression as a result of a particular drug or the combination of drugs, and this may further complicate diagnosis.

Primary symptoms of depression include feelings of hopelessness, dysphoric mood, loss of energy, and feelings of worthlessness. Older persons may lack a vocabulary for feelings and report their concerns in terms of physical rather than emotional problems. Physical complaints such as disturbances in sleep and appetite are common and are particularly pronounced among older persons experiencing depression. Older persons experiencing depression report more physical symptoms than do younger persons, such as lack of appetite, constipation, fatigue, headaches, and difficulty breathing. A thorough medical examination is imperative for the accurate diagnosis of depression in older persons complaining of physical symptoms, and to determine if medical treatment of the physical complaints is needed. In addition, referral to a psychiatrist for an evaluation of the need for antidepressant medications may also be indicated if the client's depression seems to be affecting his or her ability to perform activities of daily living.

Suicidal ideation is a pervasive secondary symptom of depression, and one that requires immediate attention when diagnosing and treating depression. Nearly 80% of all suicides in the United States have been linked to depression (Gotlib & Colby, 1987). Therefore, it is critical for counselors to perform a thorough suicide assessment when working with depressed older persons. This involves asking older persons if they have been thinking of hurting or killing themselves. Assessment of a plan to commit suicide, the availability of a weapon, and the lethality of the plan are important to the assessment.

Preventing a suicide takes priority over treating depression. Severely depressed individuals are less likely to have the energy to actually carry out a suicide or suicide attempt. These individuals are most dangerous to themselves as the depression begins to lift and their energy levels increase to a point that they can carry out the suicide plan.

Typically this occurs 2–4 weeks after the onset of medical or phar-
macological treatment.

Cognitive, behavioral, and cognitive-behavioral approaches to
treatment of depression in older persons have proved most successful.
In addition, directive and supportive interventions appear to be best
when working with this population. Treatment goals should be realistic, modest, and measurable in small, easily achieved increments.
Treatment should be aimed at helping older persons identify pleasant
life experiences and encouraging older persons to engage in such events
more frequently. Identification of negative self-talk and replacement of
negative self-talk with positive self-talk are also helpful in treating
depression. Writing in journals may be an effective strategy to help
older persons identify negative self-talk and events. Journaling may
also help older persons assess their progress as they work to identify
more positive and pleasurable experiences and thoughts.

Electroconvulsive shock therapy (ECT) may be used for clients
suffering from severe depression who do not respond to other forms of
therapy or who cannot tolerate medication interventions. With these
clients, ECT is used as a life-saving measure.

The prognosis for older persons with a diagnosis of depression is
best when the depression is identified in its early stages and when
treatment begins early in the course of the depression. Onset of depression for the first time in old age without the presence of organic impairments indicates a better prognosis for successful treatment as well.
Prognosis is also improved if the causes of the depression are psychosocial or linked to medication mismanagement, and if the older person
resides in a supportive environment.

Diagnosis and treatment of depression and suicidal ideation are
essential skills that gerontological counselors must possess. However, a
thorough discussion of the diagnosis of depression, assessment of suicidal ideation, and differential diagnosis of depression and dementia
are too complicated to be covered adequately in this section. Gerontological counselors are encouraged to seek additional training in these
areas from competent instructors and colleagues.

Suicide and Older Persons

Suicide is 1 of the 10 leading causes of death in the United States. As
is true of depression, the incidence of suicide among older persons is

greater than that among the general population, and it increases with age. The number of completed suicides is higher among older persons than younger persons. This is partly because older persons tend not to give warnings prior to attempting suicide. Therefore, it is critical for gerontological counselors and family members of older persons to be aware of risk factors and to intervene before problems become severe.

There are many psychosocial and physical losses and stresses associated with the aging process; these may contribute to suicidal ideation in older persons. Serious physical illnesses that are painful, debilitating, and progressive have been linked with increased suicidal risk. Diagnosis of a terminal illness such as cancer and progressive organic brain impairments such as Alzheimer's disease may also be precursors of suicide in older persons. Depression and substance abuse are linked to increased suicide risk.

Losses associated with aging, grief, and bereavement are linked with increased suicide attempts. Decreased independence, loss of social roles, retirement, and loss of family status may place older persons at increased risk of suicide. Older persons who are forced to move to more supportive housing, such as long-term-care facilities, are also at increased risk for suicide.

Signs that may alert counselors and family members to suicide in older persons include statements such as the following: "I'm going to kill myself," "I'm not worth anything to anyone anymore," and "Everyone would be better off without me." These statements, whether direct or indirect, may sometimes be mistaken for attempts to gain attention or to manipulate others. Although this may indeed be the case, it is essential that all suicide threats be taken seriously. Behavioral signs of an impending suicide attempt include sudden changes in behavior, giving away one's possessions, making funeral plans, and putting one's affairs in order. Additionally, symptoms such as depression combined with anxiety, isolation, loneliness, and increasing dependence and impairment may trigger suicidal ideation.

Unfortunately, the lethality for older persons who attempt suicide is quite high (Osgood, 1985). They tend not to talk about or seek help for their suicide plans. Their rate of successful suicide attempts far exceeds that for younger persons. Counselors need to be especially alert to signs of depression and hopelessness to help prevent suicides among the older population, especially with older men.

Counselors must be prepared to identify older persons who are at risk of suicide and to perform adequate suicide assessments. Counselors must also be able to teach family members how to look for signs of suicide among older family members and how to get help for their loved ones. Individual and family systems approaches may be helpful in dealing with suicide in the older population.

In cases of completed suicide, the counselor may find him- or herself in a highly stressful situation in which family members need help responding to unanswerable questions. Feelings of guilt, anger, fear, and shame need to be expressed and dealt with by family members. In fact, many families deny or fail to report suicides due to shame. Adult children need to be able to express their feelings related to "not having done more" while the person was alive, and to confront their own fears about aging and dying. In addition to counseling, survivors may benefit from a referral to an ongoing support group or an educational program that can help prepare them for the emotions they may experience.

Surviving spouses need to be included in the counseling process. Just because the surviving spouse is old does not mean that he or she is too fragile for family and/or individual counseling. Losing a spouse to natural causes is a difficult adjustment, but losing a spouse to suicide can be devastating.

Organic Brain Syndromes and Older Persons

Organic brain disorders were described and diagnosed as "senile dementia" prior to the 1900s. Other phrases, such as "hardening of the arteries" and "senility," are used by the general population to explain the presence of symptoms of organic brain disorders, such as memory loss, confusion, and bizarre behavior in older persons. It is essential that gerontological counselors be aware of the different causes and symptoms of organic brain syndromes and other possible causes of similar symptoms, such as medication intoxication. It is also important for counselors to recognize the differences between the normal aging process and memory loss due to other factors. This can be an important component in the education of family members, who may have mistakenly blamed an older person's memory loss on "the aging process" and thought it to be untreatable, therefore not seeking interventions that may have been helpful to the older person.

The major symptoms of organic disorders include a disturbance or impairment in memory, impairment of intellectual function and comprehension, impairment of judgment, impairment of orientation, and shallow or labile affect (American Psychiatric Association, 1994). Several conditions can cause the appearance of one or a combination of these symptoms. Causes that may mimic organic brain syndrome symptoms and that are treatable include: medication interactions or intoxication, malnutrition, dehydration, psychological stress and isolation, depression, and substance abuse. Irreversible organic brain disorders include: Alzheimer's disease, Pick's disease, Huntington's disease, Parkinson's dementia, and vascular dementia. Alzheimer's disease is described later. Pick's disease is a degenerative neurological disease with particularly marked frontal-lobe atrophy resulting in a dementia syndrome characterized by difficulty in reasoning and irrational behaviors. Huntington's disease is a degenerative neurological disease characterized by the development of choreiform movements and dementia. Parkinson's disease is also a degenerative neurological condition, with the primary symptom being uncontrolled tremors, especially of the extremities. Vascular dementia, also known as multi-infarct dementia, is caused by repeated cerebral infarctions or mini-strokes. The causes of most of these conditions are unknown, and treatment options are limited. Therefore, it is critical that differential diagnosis is accurate between causes that are reversible and treatable and the more irreversible conditions listed earlier.

Alzheimer's disease is perhaps the best known and most devastating of the organic brain syndromes. Named after Alois Alzheimer, who discovered the disease in 1907, Alzheimer's disease remains a condition about which little is known. Although recent advances have proved promising in diagnosing a predisposition for Alzheimer's disease through eye examinations and saliva testing, the only definitive test for accurate diagnosis of the disease is postmortem examination of the brain for the presence of plaques and tangles.

Alzheimer's disease is diagnosed following extensive neurological testing, including tests such as MRIs, CT scans, and neuropsychological testing. Once all other organic brain syndromes and causes have been ruled out, a diagnosis of Alzheimer's disease is made. Symptoms that distinguish Alzheimer's disease from other conditions include a gradual onset of symptoms, usually after age 65, absence of physical illness and impairment, and a genetic history of Alzheimer's disease. The condition is progressive, with most patients living an estimated 8–10 years following initial onset of symptoms (American Psychiatric Association, 1994).

Alzheimer's disease is particularly difficult for the spouse and family members of an older person. The older person may look healthy but be unable to recognize family members or remember recent or past events. The older person may also wander and become dangerous to him- or herself as the disease progresses and memory loss increases. Institutionalization may become necessary as the disease progresses. This decision may be particularly difficult for the spouse and/or other family members.

Counselors must be prepared to work with patients who have been newly diagnosed with Alzheimer's disease until symptoms progress to a point where therapy is no longer possible. This is especially important because Alzheimer's may be misdiagnosed when symptoms of organic disorder are present. Because there is currently no known cause, cure, or treatment for Alzheimer's, misdiagnosis may result in a lack of treatment when accurate diagnosis could lead to effective treatment strategies. Educating the older person about the nature and course of the disease, and assisting the older person in getting his or her personal affairs in order and expressing his or her wishes before the impairment worsens are important components of counseling with the newly diagnosed Alzheimer's patient. Providing a safe environment for the older person to express fears, anger, and frustration, and offering emotional support are also important aspects of the counseling process.

Gerontological counselors must be prepared to work with family members of the older person. Watching the slow deterioration of a loved one who appears healthy is devastating for spouses and family members. Counselors can provide individual and family counseling, combining education with emotional support. In addition, referral to Alzheimer's support groups and local chapters of the Alzheimer's Disease and Related Disorders Association (ADRDA) may be appropriate and helpful.

Summary

Gerontological counselors may be called on to function as members of multidisciplinary treatment teams to provide comprehensive services to older individuals. Being aware of the common impairments encountered in later life, and how to address them from a multidisciplinary perspective, are important competencies. In particular, counselors need to be sensitive to depression in older persons and be able to accurately assess the nature and type of depression and any potential for suicidal behaviors. Knowledge of Alzheimer's disease and related disorders is important so that counselors can interact effectively with other members of the treatment team, and explain the unique contributions that counselors can make to the mental health and emotional well-being of older persons and their families. Gerontological counselors also may find themselves needing to explain disease processes and treatments when working with older persons and family members; they may need to provide referral for services and support needed by these persons.

Case Studies

Following are three case studies that will allow the reader to apply the knowledge and skills learned in this chapter related to intervention strategies for common later life impairments. Read each case study and think about how you would help the client. Then read the comments for further insights into the role of the gerontological counselor in each situation.

Case One

An 85-year-old, African American man comes to counseling because he is still significantly depressed since losing his wife nearly 2 years ago. He states that he has difficulty sleeping, has frequent and severe headaches, feels as if he can't breathe, is losing weight, and is drinking more heavily. He states he is overwhelmed by feelings of sadness and loneliness, and that he wishes he would just die. He reports several symptoms of 2 years duration and presents as clinically depressed. What interventions should you, as a gerontological counselor, be considering?

Comments on Case One

First, it is important to further assess the question of suicide. Has he thought about hurting or killing himself? Does he have a plan? Is it lethal? When does he plan on hurting himself? Once suicide risks have been assessed and interventions taken to be sure he is not going to harm himself, the counselor must assess the extent of the patient's depression. An accurate diagnosis of depression requires referral to a physician, who will provide a thorough physical examination to rule out evidence of physical impairment and to determine the need for antidepressant medication.

Understanding the unique concerns of African Americans in later life requires counselors to have multicultural counseling knowledge and competencies. In addition, knowledge of the support network that is mobilized in the African American community for elders when they are in need is essential. Perhaps a natural helper in the older person's commmunity will be a helpful adjunct to attempts at helping this man.

The counselor may then begin to formulate a treatment plan. The client can be asked to identify his negative thoughts and behaviors that are causing him pain. He can be encouraged to keep a journal of those activities that are particularly difficult, what triggers his feelings of depression and sadness, and what he does and thinks when he feels sad and depressed. A journal of positive life events is also important; it can serve as the basis for increasing positive thoughts, feelings, and behaviors.

The counselor and client can go over the journal during the counseling session to look for patterns and triggers of negative thoughts and feelings. Positive thoughts and feelings that are identified by the client can be consciously substituted for negative thoughts and feelings. Positive and enjoyable activities are identified, and the client is encouraged to increasingly participate in these activities. In this way, the client's depression may be alleviated, and the client is encouraged to become more engaged in life and less isolated.

It is also important to assess the client's increased use of alcohol and the possibility of substance dependence. The substance abuse may subside as the depression lifts and the client becomes more engaged in outside activities. However, it may be that the substance dependence or abuse may also need to be the focus of treatment interventions.

Case Two

A 70-year-old woman comes to counseling at the request of her 53-year-old daughter. The daughter, who accompanies her mother to the session, states that her mother is becoming increasingly forgetful. She expresses concern that her mother's memory loss and confusion are increasing. Briefly describe what additional information you would obtain and what additional steps you would take as a gerontological counselor attempting to diagnose and treat the client.

The client appears to be pleasant and able to participate appropriately in the counseling session. The client explains that her daughter became worried when the client began to forget where she had parked her car at the local shopping mall. In addition, the client had begun to forget the names of acquaintances, and sometimes forgets items on her shopping list. A distant relative in their family died of Alzheimer's disease, and the daughter is certain her mother is suffering from early signs of the disease. This has frightened the client as well, and she expresses great concern that the memory loss is not normal and due to Alzheimer's disease.

Comments on Case Two

A first step in working with this client would be to gain a history of the onset of memory loss. Was it gradual or sudden? When did it begin? How long has it been going on? Is it getting worse? Does it seem to be short-term memory, long-term memory, or both? Did the onset of memory loss or impairment coincide with medication, illness, or a significant life event or loss?

The counselor would need to determine what medical care has been provided. Has the client had extensive neuropsychological testing and a neurological examination? What was the diagnosis? Is the client in good physical condition otherwise?

A thorough geriatric assessment may be appropriate, and referral to a geriatric physician or geriatric assessment center may be made. After referring the client for a thorough physical and neurological examination, you may learn that there are no signs of neurological or psychopathological impairment. The physician may suspect that the client's memory losses and her daughter's fear that they are related to Alzheimer's disease are causing her to overreact to normal memory loss that may occur as part of the aging process and part of everyday life. In this situation, you may decide to work with the client and the client's daughter to help them understand and express their fears and concerns. In addition, you can work with the client to teach her specific memory strategies to improve her ability to remember, such as keeping a daily log of things to do, keeping a diary or calendar, and so forth.

Case Three

An older couple contacts you after one spouse is diagnosed with chronic cardiac disabilities. They want to find ways to remain active and as healthy as possible, while finding new hobbies they can pursue to enjoy their remaining time together. What can you suggest?

Comments on Case Three

Working with a medical team is essential when cardiac rehabilitation is involved. Your role in the team is an important one. You need to understand cardiac rehabilitation and the physical requirements of various activities. Learning about the couple, what they value and like, and how they like to spend their time can help you help them identify transferable skills as part of learning new activities. Helping them identify and mobilize a social support network also is important.

Discussion Questions

1. Describe a multidisciplinary treatment team, indicating each member of the team and his or her primary role in the older person's care. How does the role of the gerontological counselor enhance the team?
2. Suicide is a growing problem among the older population. Discuss the factors that contribute to the incidence and prevalence of suicide in this population.
3. What interventions might a gerontological counselor use when working with a chronically ill or a terminally ill older client and the client's family?
4. List and discuss common losses associated with depression in the older population. What interventions might the gerontological counselor use in working with depressed older persons?
5. What are some of the conditions that may cause symptoms of dementia? Which of these are treatable and reversible?

References

American Psychiatric Association. (1994). *Diagnostic and statistical manual of mental disorders* (4th ed.). Washington, DC: Author.

Fry, P.S. (1986). *Depression, stress, and adaptations in the elderly*. Rockville, MD: Aspen Publishers.

Gotlib, I.H., & Colby, C.A. (1987). *Treatment of depression*. Elmsford, NY: Pergamon.

Myers, J.E. (1989). *Adult children and aging parents*. Alexandria, VA: American Counseling Association.

Osgood, N. (1985). *Suicide in the elderly*. Rockville, MD: Aspen Systems.

Riker, H.C., & Myers, J.E. (1989). *Retirement counseling: A handbook for action*. New York: Hemisphere.

12

The Aging Network

Minimum Essential Competency #11 for Gerontological Counseling Specialist: *demonstrates extensive knowledge of the formal and informal aging networks, public policy, and legislation affecting older persons, and knowledge of a continuum of care which will allow older persons to maintain their highest level of independence.*

G erontological counselors function as part of a team of service providers to older persons. That team consists of a variety of components known as "the aging network." As discussed in this chapter, this network includes the services and programs from which older persons derive personal and social support, as well as needed personal, medical, and social services. Both the "informal" and "formal" aging networks are described. The formal network is subdivided into government and quasigovernmental agencies, private agencies and organizations, and professional associations. The chapter concludes with a discussion of how each of these entities contributes to a continuum of care for older persons.

The Informal Aging Network

The informal aging network consists of family, friends, and neighbors of older persons. This network is the source of most (i.e., as much as 80%) of the care needed by older persons. Participants in the informal network provide emotional as well as material support. Assistance with transportation, shopping, meal preparation, or household chores and repairs often is provided through this network.

Older persons may belong to local organizations in their community, such as churches, civic organizations, or local clubs. Any of these memberships can place older persons in contact with others who may assist them in meeting their daily needs. When the resources of the informal network become inadequate to meet older persons' needs, or when their health status or circumstances change such that the informal network is unprepared or unable to provide assistance, the formal network must be accessed.

The Formal Aging Network

The formal aging network is a complex structure that consists of services, programs, agencies, and departments that provide services to and on behalf of older persons. Both the public and private sector are included. Within a given community, the range of services can be extensive. Older persons can obtain help finding the specific services they need through an information and referral (I&R) program. In large communities, a telephone number for an I&R program may be found on the cover or inside the phone book, along with the police, fire, and other emergency numbers. In smaller communities, older persons may look to aging services agencies for this assistance.

Government Agencies

At the federal level, both the U.S. House of Representatives and the U.S. Senate have committees on aging. The Select Committee on Aging in the House and the Special Committee on Aging in the Senate are oversight and advocacy committees. They conduct comprehensive studies of older Americans' needs, typically conducting hearings in which older persons and service providers testify. The information from these studies forms the basis for legislative proposals to various other government committees.

In 1961, 1971, and 1981, a White House Conference on Aging was held to determine the needs of older persons from a national perspective. A conference was not held in 1991, but one is planned for 1995, and it will not be as extensive as the earlier conferences. The federal government passed the Older Americans Act in 1965 as a direct outgrowth of the first White House conference. That conference established the need for national policies and legislation to meet the varied needs of older persons. The primary goal of the Older Americans Act is to assist older persons in living as independently as possible, for as long as possible, and with as much dignity as possible, and to prevent or postpone institutionalization.

The Older Americans Act is periodically reauthorized and amended. Counselors may obtain copies of the current act by contacting their local federal congressperson and requesting a copy. Although the act contains a variety of subparts and provisions, not all services listed in the act are available in any given community. This is because funding for the act is limited, and communities set priorities for their own needs. Further, funds for service programs require local matching funds, usually 25%, further limiting the ability of some communities to take advantage of existing funding opportunities.

Federal funds that are authorized through the Older Americans Act are administered by the U.S. Administration on Aging (AoA). In addition to a national office in Washington, there are 10 regional offices of the AoA. The regions interact with 56 state branches and territories to administer federal funds. Each state must prepare an annual State Plan on Aging, which specifies how they will use both federal and state dollars to meet the needs of older persons in their area. Within each state unit on aging (SUA) are Area Agencies on Aging (AAAs). AAAs are single or multicounty agencies charged with planning and administering coordinated service programs for older persons. The AAAs provide funding to local service programs, such as senior centers, transportation programs, congregate meal sites, and Meals on Wheels or home-delivered meals. Other services that may be available in a particular geographic area include recreation and socialization for older persons, escort service for shopping, assistance with home chores and meal preparation, health screening, nutrition counseling, and mental health counseling.

Quasigovernment

Quasigovernment agencies include agencies that receive federal funds for all or part of their services and programs. These include the service programs funded through area agencies and administered through local government or private agencies. Some community mental health services fall under this category. Independent living rehabilitation programs that serve older persons are found in a variety of communities throughout the United States. All of these programs may have private funding as well as government funding, and may require means testing to determine eligibility for services.

Private Agencies and Organizations

A wide variety of private agencies and organizations exist to provide services to older persons. These include health care organizations such as physicians, clinics, hospitals, in-home care providers, and long-term-care facilities. They also include service programs provided by business and industry, and private organizations in the community.

Private organizations may exist at the state and/or national levels, or they may have their own network of contacts at national, state, and/or local levels. An example is the American Association of Retired Persons (AARP), a membership organization composed of more than 35,000,000 older persons worldwide. In addition to direct membership services such as a journal, discounts on medications, and a travel service, AARP advocates with the federal government for the needs of older persons.

Professional Associations

Although they do not directly provide services to older persons, professional organizations affect services to older individuals through efforts to improve the quality of professional preparation of their members. The American Counseling Association (ACA), for example, maintains a division on Adult Development and Aging, which is a focal point for ACA members concerned with adults and older adults. ACA provides advocacy for legislation affecting jobs for counselors and gerontological counselors. Through joining one or more professional associations, counselors can network with other professionals who share their interests in working with older persons, as well as gain knowledge required to work more effectively with older clients.

Continuum of Care

Older persons' needs for assistance can be and often are extensive. These needs may change as persons grow older and experience life changes such as illness, chronic disease and disability, or multiple losses. As a consequence, the services required to meet their needs may be expected to change over time. For these changing needs to be met in a timely manner, a continuum of care is required. This continuum needs to include components that address the multiple and complex needs of the 35,000,000 older Americans. The goal of this continuum is to provide the services needed by older persons that will allow them to live independently in their own homes for as long as possible.

The 80% of older persons who are able to live independently in their own homes may require no or only periodic assistance from their informal support network. Within the continuum of care, individual and family counseling can be an important means of helping older persons maintain their independence. When older persons begin to experience physical or mental impairments, such that their ability to continue living independently is jeopardized, the formal aging network may be mobilized.

Given the goal of helping persons remain in their homes for as long as possible, the first services older persons may require are community services such as socialization, medical support, congregate nutrition, housing renovation or repair, or transportation. As their needs increase, home delivered meals and in-home health services may be necessary. These services may be provided by quasigovernmental or private agencies. Older persons with more serious impairments who are living with caregivers may require adult day care services. These programs provide needed respite for caregivers while providing rehabilitative services for impaired older individuals.

Housing and supportive housing are major concerns for older persons. Although they may live independently in their own homes, apartments, or condominiums, many older persons choose to live in senior housing. Senior housing may or may not include social support services. Similarly, retirement homes may or may not provide support services—it depends on their purpose and available staff. Continuing care retirement communities are those that provide fully independent housing, apartments, assisted living, and health care (long-term care) depending on the needs of the older persons. This differs from life care, in which older persons invest a substantial sum in exchange for needed services for the remainder of their life span.

When older persons can no longer live independently in the community, a move to some type of assisted housing may be required. Long-term-care facilities are not the only choice. Boarding homes, where a small number of older persons live with a caretaker, adult congregate living facilities, and retirement homes and communities are options to consider before nursing home placement. In addition, echo housing, which provides a place for older persons with or near their adult children, is possible.

Summary

Counselors working with older persons need to know the available services in their home community that can be mobilized to meet the needs of older clients. These services collectively comprise what is known as "The Aging Network." This network includes all of the services, programs, and resources required by older persons to live satisfying and fulfilling lives. An informal network of family, friends, and neighbors is supplemented by a formal network of governmental, quasigovernmental, and voluntary agencies that provide services to this population. The network may be conceptualized as providing a continuum of care to meet the needs of older persons, whether they are fully independent, in need of one or more services, or severely impaired and in need of multiple services.

Case Studies

Following are two case studies that will allow the reader to apply the knowledge learned in this chapter related to the aging network. Read each case study and think about how you would help the client. Then read the comments for further insights into the role of the gerontological counselor in each situation.

Case One

You are working with an older person who is having increasing difficulty remaining in her own home independently. What assistance can you provide?

Comments on Case One

It is important for counselors to view themselves as part of a treatment team, thus relieving themselves of the impossible task of trying to be all things to all people. If they do not know where to refer an older person for services, they are limited in their ability to help them.

Counselors need to conduct an assessment of services available in their community (see chap. 17, this volume) and develop a referral network that can be mobilized when needed by older clients.

Case Two

You are contacted by the adult children of an aging parent and asked for help. The aging parent has recently sold her home and relocated to a retirement community. She has become angry, packed her bags, and is waiting to be taken "home." Her home has been sold, at her request, but she does not accept this fact. The retirement home has no social services department or support services. The administrator has contacted the adult children and indicated that their mother is becoming "a problem" for the other residents and may be asked to leave. What assistance can you provide?

Comments on Case Two

The mother in this situation likely displayed indications of an inability to live independently prior to her move to the retirement home. The family members, unwilling to accept their mother's increasing incapacity, took advantage of the time she seemed willing to move and mistakenly thought their problems were solved when the move had been accomplished. They are likely to be confused and angry, and need to express and work through those feelings in a safe environment. They also may feel financially trapped because their mother's money has now been invested in unsuitable housing. If the facility is new and not filled to capacity, the likelihood of getting out of this setting without a major financial loss is small.

The mother needs to have a thorough geriatric assessment as part of the treatment planning process. You can refer the family to a geriatric physician or geriatric assessment center. Even if there is not one in your community, it is worth a drive to obtain a thorough assessment from a trained geriatric treatment team. The family needs an accurate diagnosis and prognosis from which to base their decisions. You can offer to work with the mother in an attempt to diffuse her anger and resentment. But if the retirement home is in a community not geographically near you, this will not be a choice. Knowing how to access other counselors in your state, through your state professional association or the NBCC, will be helpful.

Discussion Questions

1. What services are available in your community to meet the social service needs of older persons?
2. What services are available in your community to meet the mental health needs of older persons and their families?
3. What are the addresses of your state agency on aging, area agency on aging, and local service programs for older persons?

13

Intervention Strategies for Situational and Developmental Crises

Minimum Essential Competency #12 for a Gerontological Counseling Specialist: *demonstrates skill in applying appropriate intervention techniques for situational and developmental crises commonly experienced by older persons, such as bereavement, isolation, divorce, relocation, sexual concerns, illness, transportation, crime, abuse, and relationships with adult children and caregivers.*

Older persons may experience a number of situational and developmental crises that accompany the normal aging process. These may include: bereavement, increasing social isolation, divorce, relocation to more supportive housing, sexuality concerns related to physiological changes, acute and chronic illnesses, difficulties in obtaining transportation, crime, abuse, and changes in relationships with spouses and adult children who may become caregivers. Gerontological counselors must be knowledgeable regarding the situational and developmental transitions that older persons may experience. In addition, gerontological counselors must be able to formulate effective intervention strategies to meet the needs of older persons and their families experiencing such transitions. In this chapter, common situational and developmental crises are considered (some of which have been more extensively explored in other chapters), as well as intervention strategies counselors may use to assist older persons and their families in dealing with these issues.

Bereavement

Bereavement refers to a loss through death. Bereaved persons are expected to grieve. The grief process refers to the survivor's state of distress and is both socially and culturally defined. That is, there are socially expected and acceptable grief reactions, as well as socially accepted time limits on the grieving process. "Abnormal" reactions to the loss of a loved one are those that exceed the social prescription for "normal" grief in some manner.

Normal grief reactions include stages in which the bereaved individual experiences shock, numbness, denial, and, ultimately, acceptance (Kubler-Ross, 1969). Within 2 weeks following a death, feelings such as sadness, guilt, hopelessness, and helplessness may occur. In addition, somatic complaints, such as headaches, loss of appetite, exhaustion, and sleeplessness, may occur. Affective and cognitive reactions, including anger, crying, hostility, resentment, agitation, and difficulty thinking or concentrating, may also be present. For any given individual, these stages may not occur in the order stated, and individuals may pass through a given stage more than once. The length of time an individual experiences a given stage also may vary considerably.

The severity and duration of these symptoms depend on several factors, including the suddenness of the loss, preparation for the loss, and significance of the deceased individual to the bereaved person. Normal grief reactions may take as long as 1–2 years to be resolved. A general rule of thumb is for the bereaved individual to avoid making any significant decisions or changes within a year following a significant loss. The grief process is self-limiting and is usually resolved by the individual without outside intervention. However, if grief reactions are unusually strong and of an unusually long duration, counseling intervention may be necessary.

Pathological grief reactions include the presence of severe grief symptoms approximately 8–10 weeks following the loss of a loved one. Severe depression, intrusive thoughts, ill health, psychiatric and psychosomatic disturbances, depression, and inability to perform activities of daily living are all considered extreme reactions to stress, particularly if they persist 10 weeks after one's loss. It is also interesting to note that a significant number of widowed persons die within a year of their loss. Extreme grief reactions always indicate the need for counseling intervention.

In addition to normal and pathological responses to bereavement, individuals may experience anticipatory grief. This involves experiencing the grieving process before the individual has actually died and usually follows the diagnosis of a terminal illness. Anticipatory grief may be helpful because it gives the individual a chance to prepare for the impending loss, and therefore to recover faster following the loss. However, no one is ever fully prepared for the death of a loved one. Older persons may experience more losses than younger persons, and may therefore become chronic grievers.

Gerontological counselors can assist older persons and their family members in coming to terms with death. Before the death of a parent or spouse, counselors can assist older persons in discussing their feelings about death and making necessary arrangements, including preparation of a will and resolution of conflicts with significant others. Counselors also can assist family members of terminally or chronically ill older persons in coming to terms with the impending loss. Both the older person and family members will benefit from exploring and clarifying feelings related to death and dying in a safe and supportive environment. Counselors can also help the older person and family members to view and accept death in a more positive way—as a final stage of life.

Resolving family problems, finishing unfinished business, and/or affirming mutual love and caring can be helpful to all family members when one is dying. Life review can be an especially helpful strategy. In helping older persons and their families review, remember, and recall times spent together, counselors can help all to focus on and enjoy the positive aspects of their lives and relationships, as well as the bonds forged through times of difficulty or stress (Hughston & Cooledge, 1989).

Counselors can assist survivors in coping with their losses, working through the stages of grieving, and reaching the stage of acceptance. It is important for the counselor and bereaved person to remember that acceptance does not mean an end to feelings of sadness; rather, that the individual can accept the loss and go on with his or her life.

There are no real set patterns for the experience of grief or for counseling the bereaved. Catharsis is an essential component of the grieving process that can be facilitated through the counseling relationship. Probably the most important components for counseling individuals who are dying or bereaved include caring, sharing, listening, and reminding the persons that they are not alone.

Isolation

Isolation may be a problem for some older persons. As mobility decreases and impairments increase, older persons may no longer be able to drive and may become increasingly isolated. In some communities, there are bus services that allow older persons to remain mobile. Loss of a driver's license may be particularly difficult for older persons because it may signal the final loss of independence. Sometimes allowing older persons to keep their driver's license, but not have access to a vehicle, can assist them in maintaining a sense of independence. Other times allowing older persons to keep a car, even if they do not drive it, can allow them to maintain a sense of independence, knowing they could go somewhere if they needed to do so. They also may ask others to take them places in their own automobile, thus reducing feelings of dependence.

Older persons who live alone in rural communities, where distances between houses and stores are great, may be even more isolated than those living in urban areas. However, neighbors may form more of a support network for individual older persons in rural than in urban settings. As spouses and friends die, older persons in any area may experience a greater sense of isolation, particularly if adult children or other relatives do not live in surrounding communities. Poor health, difficulty ambulating, and reduced vision and hearing may also contribute to isolation.

Gerontological counselors can assist older persons in overcoming isolation in a number of ways. Older persons can be encouraged to become socially active. This may involve participation in community meal sites, community centers, churches, and other community activities. In addition, many communities have programs designed to send persons into the homes of older individuals to reduce isolation, such as adopt-a-grandparent programs, friendly visitors programs, or telephone reassurance programs, in which older persons receive a daily phone call from a volunteer. Encouraging older persons to wear hearing aids if prescribed, continue to exercise, and maintain their strength can also help them overcome feelings of isolation. Consideration of various alternatives such as a move to a retirement complex or networking among neighbors or friends who have access to transportation may be helpful. Working with older persons to increase social and communication skills can also be helpful in overcoming isolation.

For those who enjoy volunteer activities, a sense of meaning, purpose, and usefulness can be achieved through activities that provide service to others. Not all older persons enjoy volunteering, so such activities need not be seen as a panacea for the problems of isolation and aging.

Divorce

Rising divorce rates in America indicate that a significant proportion of older persons will have experienced divorce in their lifetime. Although divorce rates are highest for individuals who are in their early 20s and have been married only a few years, divorce and remarriage rates are rising among other groups. The possibility that either older persons or their offspring may experience a divorce is significant and may greatly impact family relationships and grandparenting.

Divorce may mean that noncustodial parents find even fewer familial supports available in later years. In addition, midlife and older women who are divorced have a significantly lower potential for remarriage than older divorced men. Therefore, gerontological counselors must be prepared to help older persons experiencing divorce to deal with the significant emotional and social effects of divorce on older persons. In addition to individual counseling, support groups and singles groups may provide support for older persons who experience divorce. Church groups may also be a source of social interaction and support following divorce.

Single living can be a particular challenge for older persons who spent most or all of their lives living with others. For example, many older women lived with family until they married, with husbands and children until children left home, and with husbands until their husbands died; suddenly they may find themselves living alone for the first time in later life. These individuals can benefit from individual and group counseling, as well as support to help them reestablish a sense of identity and purpose as a single individual.

Relocation

Older persons who become increasingly impaired may need to consider a move to more supportive housing. Additionally, older persons who must live on fixed incomes and who cannot financially afford to continue living in their own homes may need to consider a move to more supportive housing. Many times, older persons may need to move to more supportive housing, but are reluctant to do so because they assume this means losing their independence. In addition, many older persons do not want to be a burden to their families, nor do they wish to be placed in a nursing home.

Adult children, spouses, and older persons may all be involved in the decision to move older persons to more supportive housing. Gerontological counselors can facilitate communication and the decision-making process, and offer alternatives that may not have been considered. Encouraging the expression of feelings associated with the move, such as sense of personal control, coping strategies, availability of social support, life satisfaction, and loss, and allowing older persons as much participation in the decision as possible are critical to a successful move. Exploration of all possible alternatives for housing is also a crucial component of a successful transition.

Although nursing homes are one alternative, there are several other housing alternatives that should be considered. These alternatives may vary from community to community. Apartment complexes or retirement highrises, continuum of care communities that provide living arrangements from independent living to nursing home care within one community, adult congregate living facilities that provide group living arrangements for older persons, foster homes that provide supportive care for a few older persons, and living with adult children or peers may all be alternatives to consider. If a nursing home is the chosen option, older persons should be encouraged to visit potential facilities and to have a voice in deciding which facility they would most prefer. Additional resources, such as physicians, community advocacy groups, area agencies on aging, and the better business bureau, can provide more information regarding specific alternatives and sites in their communities.

Above all, it is important for counselors to encourage older persons to participate as much as possible in the decision to move to more supportive housing. Successful transitions are facilitated by allowing

older persons to bring selected personal possessions to their new surroundings. Allowing for a slow transition and continuous orientation
to the new living arrangement is important.

Even when older persons choose to make such a move, regrets,
recrimination, and considerable concern over whether they made a
mistake may be evident. Careful listening, combined with affirmation
of their decision-making skills and the importance of the choices made,
are important in facilitating adjustment.

Sexual Concerns

Sexual concerns related to the normal aging process were discussed in
chapter 4 (this volume). It bears repeating that sexuality is an important aspect of counseling older persons. Because of the number of
myths and negative stereotypes involving older persons and their capacity (or lack thereof) for sexual activity, it may be difficult for older
persons to discuss this aspect of their lives. Counselors need to be
sensitive to the attitudes and values of older persons regarding their
sexuality and discussion of sexuality concerns. In addition, it is important for counselors to be knowledgeable regarding age-related
changes in sexuality, and to be able to dispel any myths that older
persons may mistakenly believe.

Additional concerns related to sexuality in later life may be associated with the increased divorce rate among older persons, illnesses
and medication side effects related to decreased sexual interest and
activity, lack of suitable partners, and restrictions associated with certain types of living facilities. For example, even married individuals
may not share a private room in some nursing homes. Sexual activity
between residents of nursing homes and other supportive housing facilities may be prohibited based on stereotypes and attitudes regarding
sexuality in later life. Prohibitions on sexual activity in these settings
also can reflect a concern for the rights of residents, particularly impaired residents.

As part of a sensitivity to sexual issues in later life, gerontological
counselors must be willing to assist their clients in exploring ways to
meet sexual needs. Touch is an important consideration with older
clients. For many, caring touches from others are less frequent than
when they were younger. Although touch with younger clients may be
avoided due to concerns about sexual harassment, touch with older

clients, if they choose to touch, can be an important means of affirming their dignity and worth. If uncertain about whether to touch, the counselor may simply ask the client if a hug would be okay.

Illness

Illness in later life was discussed in chapter 11 (this volume). Illness among the older population tends to be chronic, progressive, multiple, and interactive. Acute conditions may be a result of existing chronic conditions or may exacerbate the negative effects of preexisting illnesses. Medical care and attention usually are aimed at providing management of the illnesses and prevention of further decline, rather than at prevention or cure. Additionally, age-related changes may cause older persons to be more subject to acute infections, take longer to heal, require more hospital stays, and stay an average of twice as long in acute care settings compared with younger persons. Side effects of medications may cause sexual dysfunction, sleep disturbances, appetite disturbances, and sedation.

Gerontological counselors must be aware of the impact of specific acute and chronic illnesses on older persons and their families. Contact with national organizations and local support groups for conditions such as diabetes, Parkinson's disease, or Alzheimer's disease can provide a wealth of information about particular conditions, as well as access to support for older clients and their families. Interventions aimed at helping older persons accept and successfully manage their illnesses are imperative.

In addition, preventing additional decline is an important aspect of counseling. This may involve working with older persons and their families to manage activities of daily living, medication management, and safety proofing living facilities. Such interventions may consist of obtaining grab bars for bathrooms, removing throw rugs that may cause falls, improving lighting, using medication organizers to help older persons remember their medications, and so forth. Counselors need to work with social workers, rehabilitation counselors, occupational therapists, and other professionals when environmental modifications are required.

In addition, gerontological counselors can create a safe place in the counseling session for older persons and their families to express their fears related to increased dependence, physical changes in appearance and function, and other age- and illness-related changes. Once these fears have been expressed, counselors can work with older persons and their families to develop strategies to overcome these fears. Individual treatment plans and strategies will vary based on the illness, degree of impairment, and resources available to each client.

Transportation

Transportation is indirectly related to isolation and feelings of independence. As discussed earlier, transportation, particularly a driver's license, can be the final avenue of independence for older persons. Once older persons lose the ability to drive, isolation and dependence can greatly increase if alternative transportation is not available. Counselors must help older persons and their families develop strategies to maintain independence through alternative forms of transportation. Not all older persons are unable to drive. There are courses available through the community safety council and the American Association of Retired Persons (AARP) that are specifically designed for older persons; these courses focus on ways that older persons can maintain good driving records. Some insurance companies even offer discounts to older persons who participate in these programs.

Alternative forms of transportation may be available in the community. Public buses, buses for older persons, minivans operated through senior centers and other local agencies, friends, neighbors, walking, and subways are alternative sources of transportation that can be explored. Church and volunteer groups may also have members who are willing to provide transportation on a limited basis. Shepherd's Centers, formed in many communities, are a resource for coordinating volunteers to help older persons with needs such as transportation. Counselors who are familiar with existing community resources can encourage older persons to use these alternative forms of transportation as necessary.

Crime

Although older persons are victimized by crime to a lesser extent than younger persons, their fear of crime is much greater than that of other age groups. In studies of older persons' needs, protection from crime and fear of victimization consistently rate high in both urban and rural environments (Burke & Hayes, 1986; Watson, 1991). Fear of crime may cause older persons to constrict their activities, and thus become more isolated. Activities may be limited to daylight hours and then only within their own neighborhoods. Fear of crime may be due, in part, to feelings of vulnerability caused by physical declines and limitations. Additionally, older persons may spend a great deal of time watching television and reading the newspaper, which focus on negative events and increase their fear of crime.

Many older persons become victims of scams and con artists. These people prey on older persons, who may be isolated and enjoy their company. Additionally, they may use older persons' fear of financial difficulties to get them to buy unnecessary life insurance or make bad investments designed to "make them financially secure." Older persons who are isolated may also spend a great deal of money on home shopping networks or send large sums of money to television religious organizations.

Counselors need to be aware of the fears that many older persons experience related to crime and victimization. In this way, counselors can then help older persons determine what fears are realistic and what fears may be exaggerated. Strategies can then be formulated to help older persons feel more secure and encourage them to be less isolated. Security systems, neighborhood watches, buying a dog, burglar bars, and emergency response systems, which allow them to contact help in an emergency, may all be alternatives. Should a crime occur, counselors may assist in locating crime victim advocates, through the local police department or senior services agencies, who are trained to help older victims through the crisis period.

Abuse

Elder abuse may occur when older persons reside with and are cared for by adult children or other relatives. In addition, instances of abuse can occur in institutional settings and by nonfamily in community settings. Abuse is usually the result of an accumulation of stresses, lack of respite care, inadequate support of caregivers, and lack of access to resources.

Elder abuse includes physical abuse, psychological abuse, material abuse, and violation of personal rights. Physical abuse may involve withholding medication and food, or hitting of older persons. Psychological abuse includes isolating, neglecting and ignoring older persons' needs or pleas, and demeaning older persons' sense of dignity and worth. Material abuse includes theft or misuse of money or other resources. Finally, violation of personal rights includes attempts to seek adjudication of older persons as incompetent when in fact they are quite competent to handle their own affairs.

Counselors must be aware of the signs of elder abuse, which are much the same as those experienced by abused children and spouses. Abuse seems to be directly linked to a lack of information and resulting frustrations and stresses on the part of caregivers. Interventions designed to provide information related to the normal aging process, medication management, community resources, and stress management can be extremely beneficial in preventing abuse. Group therapy and support groups are particularly beneficial; they provide the additional advantages of peer support, learning new strategies through sharing, and experiencing an emotional outlet for frustration, anger, and fear. Individual counseling with the abused older person and/or caregiver may also be beneficial (Myers & Shelton, 1987), along with couples counseling when a spouse is involved. Referral to domestic violence programs in the community can be helpful.

Counselors must be aware of other issues surrounding the reporting and ending of abusive situations. Some older persons are reluctant to report abuse because they are afraid that institutionalization will be worse than the abuse they receive living with an adult child. In addition, counselors must be familiar with state laws regarding mandatory reporting of suspected elder abuse.

Relationships with Adult Children and Caregivers

Relationships with adult children, particularly as caregivers, have been discussed in several places throughout this book. Because many older persons require some form of assistance to remain in the community, and because adult children are usually the providers of this care, gerontological counselors must be familiar with the unique stresses and strains adult children and aging parents face related to the caregiving process (Myers, 1989).

Issues that may be important to consider include previous relationships with adult children, past patterns of family interaction, and ability and willingness of adult children to provide care. Problems with communication and familial interaction that have occurred in the past may resurface as adult children are called on to provide more and more assistance to the aging parent. Unresolved conflicts may also resurface at this time. In addition, problems associated with the role reversal of adult children now caring for the aging parent may also exacerbate the situation.

Counselors must be sensitive to these issues and work with the older person and caregiver to resolve old conflicts and learn new ways of effectively communicating and relating to one another. In addition, stress management techniques and emotional support are important components of the counseling process for both the older person and the caregiver. Information related to the normal aging process is important for the counselor to provide to the caregiver. The counselor may also be called on to provide assistance in contacting community resources and exploring available options for the older person as well as the caregiver.

Summary

Gerontological counselors need to be sensitive to the unique situational and developmental issues likely to be encountered when working with older adults. These include acute and chronic illnesses, crime, elder abuse, and caregiving situations, among others. It is important that counselors work with older adults, their spouses, other family members, or caregivers to resolve these concerns. When working with families, it is always important to consider and help resolve preexisting conflicts, and to help families learn new ways of communicating effectively. Stress management techniques and emotional support are also helpful.

Case Studies

Following are two case studies that will allow the reader to apply the knowledge and skills learned in this chapter related to situational and developmental challenges in later life. Read each case study and think about how you would help the client. Then read the comments for further insights into the role of the gerontological counselor in each situation.

Case One

An older married couple comes to counseling stating that they are aware that they must begin to explore alternatives for future care. Neither spouse has any living relatives or children. They are financially comfortable and currently live in the house they have resided in for the past 20 years. The husband is 70 and the wife is 68. They wish to find a place where they can live and make friends, and yet not some unknown location. They ask your help in exploring possible options, concerned that they may end up "stuck in some state nursing home." An additional concern is their desire for a support network that can be mobilized to assist one spouse, should something happen to the other. What options might you explore with them?

Comments on Case One

It would be important to discuss this couple's preferences, as well as likes and dislikes, related to housing options. Additionally, information related to their financial situation and health status would be important. Concerns about lifestyle and independence need to be addressed.

This couple needs information about living options in their community. You may have access to some such information, and can call the local information and referral service or area agency on aging for additional information. One option may be a continuing care community, in which residents can begin in an independent living situation, move to an apartment-type residence as their needs increase, and finally to a nursing home environment if skilled nursing care is needed. This differs from a life care community, which, while offering all of the same living options, may require a considerable down payment for entry. Continuing care services typically are provided and paid for on an as-needed basis. All of these living arrangements are contained in either setting in one community, which may also provide a church, grocery store, entertainment, and activities center, all within easy walking distance.

After providing information on available alternatives, the clients may be encouraged to visit different facilities to obtain additional information. A follow-up appointment is important to help them sort out the information they have received and make final decisions.

Case Two

One of the first challenges you may face with this client is a language barrier. Additional issues will include her specific cultural values as a member of the Hispanic community, as well as values related to being a woman in her culture. If you are unfamiliar with multicultural or diversity issues, continuing education is essential. For this client, you may find that enlisting the services of a trained multicultural counselor or natural helper in her community is key to success.

A 75-year-old Hispanic woman is referred to you for counseling following the death of her husband a year ago. Since the death of her husband, she has been increasingly isolated. She continues to cry and "choke up" whenever her husband's name is mentioned. She states that she has difficulty eating and sleeping, and just "gets through the day." She states she has three children who live in the area who stop by to see her every day, but she does not go out. She did not have many friends outside her marriage, and her family was everything to her. Although she attended church regularly until the death of her husband, she states she did not feel like she could "face people" and thus has not attended church since her husband's death. She spends most of the time with her children reminiscing about her husband. As a geronto-logical counselor, what do you do?

Comments on Case Two

It is important to begin by exploring her reactions to her husband's death. Assessment of the grieving process is the first step in developing an intervention aimed at reducing grief symptoms. The counselor could begin by helping the client to express her deepest feelings regarding her loss. It is important to have her talk about what her husband meant to her, and to review both the good times they had together as well as any difficult times. Validating her feelings of loss is important, as is helping her begin to consider new roles for herself outside of her marriage relationship.

Eventually, it may be important to teach the client new skills related to managing her household, finances, transportation, and social life. Treatment goals should be small and attainable so that the client can begin to experience success as an independent and capable individual. The counselor should also work with the client to increase her social and communication skills, and to rebuild her self-confidence.

The client can be encouraged to increase her social interaction. This may be accomplished through reinvolvement with her church, attendance at a local community center, which has a large Hispanic population, and possibly networking with neighbors. As the client begins to take control of her own life, learn new skills, and feel competent, her self-esteem will increase and her depression and grief may begin to lift.

Involvement of the family in the counseling process is also essential for success. Culturally, members of the Hispanic community tend to highly value family relationships. It is important to include the client's children in developing and implementing counseling strategies. Family support, combined with counseling efforts, will offer the client maximum possibility for success. Depending on the severity of the depression, a referral to a psychiatrist for evaluation and even medical management may be needed.

Discussion Questions

1. How are the issues of isolation and transportation interrelated with regard to working with older persons?
2. Briefly discuss the similarities and differences between the normal grieving process and pathological grieving.
3. Elder abuse is a growing concern among the older population. What factors are important to consider when formulating counseling interventions for abused older persons and their families?
4. What additional family counseling issues or problems might you encounter when working with older persons (e.g., siblings, adopted children, adult children with developmental disabilities), and how might you address these issues?

References

Burke, M.J., & Hayes, R.L. (1986). Peer counseling for elderly victims of crime and violence. *Journal for Specialists in Group Work, 11*(2), 107–113.

Hughston, G.A., & Cooledge, N.J. (1989). The life review: An underutilized strategy for systemic family intervention. *Journal of Psychotherapy and the Family, 5*(1–2), 47–55.

Kubler-Ross, E. (1969). *On death and dying.* New York: Macmillan.

Myers, J. E. (1989). *Adult children and aging parents.* Alexandria, VA: American Counseling Association.

Myers, J.E., & Shelton, B. (1987). Abuse and older persons: Issues and implications for counselors. *Journal of Counseling and Development, 65*(7), 376–380.

Watson, W. (1991). Ethnicity, crime, and aging: Risk factors and adaptation. *Generations, 15*(4), 53–57.

14

Specialized Therapies for Use with Older Persons

Minimum Essential Competency #13 for a Gerontological Counseling Specialist: *demonstrates skill in the use of a wide variety of specialized therapies to assist older persons in coping with both developmental and non-normative issues, such as creative art therapies, pet therapy, peer counseling, and family counseling.*

Before beginning a discussion of specialized therapies for use with older persons, it is important to point out that almost any counseling technique that can be used with persons of another age may also be used with older persons. In addition, counseling techniques that meet the special needs of older persons also may be utilized. These techniques, which are briefly reviewed in this chapter, include: life review; early recollections; integrative counseling; family and group counseling; paraprofessional and peer counseling; self-help groups; creative art therapies; bibliotherapy; music, movement, and dance therapies; pet therapy; horticulture therapy; imagery and self-hypnosis; and reality orientation, remotivation, and resocialization therapies.

Life Review

The process of life review is a normal occurrence among older persons as they prepare for their eventual death. Looking back, recalling life events and experiences, and "telling stories" about their lives are all part of the life review process, as is internalization and assessment of one's life goals. Although this process may occur spontaneously, counselors can use life review as a counseling strategy as well. The process of life review may be seen as working to resolve Erikson's stage of ego integrity versus despair, which was discussed in detail in chapter 3 (this volume). Erikson (1963) saw the major psychosocial crisis of late adulthood as achieving a sense of ego integrity. Ego integrity is achieved by those who feel they have lived a productive and worthwhile life, coping with successes as well as failures and having few regrets. These persons do not fixate on what they might have done, but rather derive satisfaction from what they have done. They are also able to accept their own mortality. Failure to achieve ego integrity may result in feelings of despair, hopelessness, and guilt. Persons who fail to achieve ego integrity focus on what could have been and do not find satisfaction in the lives they have lived. This realization—that they have wasted their lives—results in a sense of despair.

Life review involves assisting older persons in looking back over their lives and, ideally, coming to the realization that they have lived productive and worthwhile lives, coping with successes as well as failures and having few regrets (i.e., achieving ego integrity; Butler, 1963). Counselors using life review may be able to help older persons identify events that have been remembered negatively, and to reframe those events in a positive manner so that a positive sense of ego integrity may be achieved.

When using life review, counselors may ask clients to reflect on a certain period of life or on specific life events, such as their 20s, 30s, 40s, and so on, or to focus on the Depression years, war years, and other periods. Additionally, common issues such as work, family, and leisure may be the focus of life review. Counselors may then ask clients to use a specific technique or combination of techniques to evoke memories the older persons can discuss and review. Methods and materials that may be used by counselors to facilitate the life review process include written or tape-recorded autobiographies, reunions, genealogies, scrapbooks, diaries, and photographs.

Early Recollections

The technique of early recollections (ERs) is taken from Adlerian theory and may be used by counselors to help older persons structure their reminiscence (Sweeney, 1989). Using this technique, counselors may ask older persons to remember and recount their earliest memories. Themes and patterns from these recollections reflect the older persons' view of themselves, others, and life in general. These themes become guiding principles for living (Sweeney, 1989; Sweeney & Myers, 1991). This technique differs from life review in that recollections of specific early events are not the same as early memories, which may be of types of events rather than specific, one-time occurrences.

Adlerians believe that, by analyzing the older persons' recollections of early events for themes, counselors may be able to help clients identify current views of themselves that may be either positive or negative. Becoming aware of their life scripts, they can then become free to validate or change their underlying themes. In addition to this goal, the use of early recollections may help clients understand the motivations for their behaviors, and may help strengthen the clients' sense of personal power over their lives (Sweeney & Myers, 1991). By helping older persons identify their guiding themes and patterns, counselors can empower their clients to recognize and use, in a deliberate manner, their most fundamental coping resources.

Long-term memory remains intact until the end of life, whereas short-term memory is the area in which most older persons experience declines. Older persons, even those with memory losses, tend to have intact recollections of early life events. Thus, the use of early recollections can be very helpful even with older persons experiencing significant organic impairment.

Integrative Counseling

Integrative counseling is a specific, eclectic approach designed for use with older persons. It was developed based primarily on Eriksonian theory, and uses a social reconstruction model as a basis for counseling interventions. Its overall goal is to achieve ego integrity. This approach stresses a holistic approach, which must be used in order to be effective when working with older persons. Thus, counselors using this model must be willing and prepared to work in all areas of their clients' lives, including mobilizing community resources and dealing with psychological, spirituality, physical, social, and vocational issues, to name a few. Additionally, counselors using this technique should be familiar with holistic wellness models, which may be used as a basis for approaching each of the components of wellness in counseling older persons (see chap. 12, this volume).

Family and Group Counseling

Family and group counseling are particularly valuable for use in addressing the needs of older persons. Family concerns associated with aging may include older persons' decreased independence, resulting in family caregiving or a transition to more supportive housing. Adult children may be called on to provide assistance to their aging parents in the form of financial, emotional, and physical caregiving. When this occurs, issues related to communication, role definition, past history of family relationships among children in the family and between children and parents, proximity of the adult children to the older person, and financial resources may become the focus of counseling interventions. Family counseling may provide an avenue for the counselor to work with the entire family to strengthen communication skills, decrease stress, increase knowledge of the aging process and community resources, and provide emotional support to families faced with changing roles.

Additionally, as older persons begin the process of life review in an attempt to gain a sense of ego integrity, they may realize a need and desire to work on their relationships with their own children and extended families. This is particularly important when older persons feel there is a need to right a past wrong in a relationship. However, the adult children may be experiencing a life stage in which they are focusing on themselves and their own needs to evaluate life goals and develop new goals or adjust old goals. This can create difficulty in terms of priorities between older parents and their adult children. Conflicts may arise when aging parents communicate a desire to spend more time with their adult children and their families at a time when the adult children's priorities may be focused on achieving their own personal goals. Family counseling may help both parties to recognize and appreciate one another's needs.

Group therapy with older persons has several advantages. Older persons may feel more comfortable with this type of approach because they have been exposed to groups in many settings, such as clubs, senior center activities, and adult activity programs. Group therapy is economical in terms of time, cost, and effective use of resources, particularly important considering the lack of sufficiently trained gerontological counselors to work with this population.

Group therapy in which the members of the group are all older persons provides an excellent opportunity for older persons to experience normalization of their experiences and feelings, to improve communication skills, to increase socialization, to decrease isolation, and to learn new social skills. Group therapy has been found to increase self-esteem, provide information and suggestions for problem solving, increase socialization, provide channels for emotional expression, and increase reality orientation. Therapy groups that may be particularly valuable for older persons include reminiscence groups, sensory stimulation groups, grief groups, support groups, personal growth groups, and peer groups (see chap. 4, this volume, for more information).

Paraprofessional and Peer Counseling

Paraprofessional and peer counselors are particularly valuable to the field of gerontological counseling due to the shortage of professional gerontological counselors in the United States. Paraprofessional and peer counselors who are adequately trained (having participated in 8–20 hours of basic listening and communication skills training) and supervised can provide individual and group counseling in many settings, including: nursing homes, senior centers, community mental health agencies, churches, crisis centers, and specialized support groups such as Alzheimer's support groups, Parkinson's support groups, and so on.

Paraprofessional and peer counselors gain the personal satisfaction of feeling productive and worthwhile. Peer counselors may provide older persons with positive role models and help with the normalization of age-related changes. Additionally, peer counselors who have successfully dealt with issues currently being experienced by older persons may be perceived as more credible; they may offer practical suggestions that may not have been thought of previously. In return, peer counselors may gain the therapeutic benefit of feeling as if their struggles with those issues were productive in helping others in that particular situation.

Although paraprofessional and peer counselors may provide valuable services to older persons, they must be adequately trained and supervised to ensure that older persons receive quality experiences. Caution must be taken to select and train those volunteers who have resolved their own issues to a point where they are able to focus on helping others. It is also important to be certain that paraprofessional and peer counselors understand ethical principles such as confidentiality and boundary issues to avoid becoming enmeshed with their clients.

Self-Help Groups

Self-help groups provide individuals with an environment in which they can gain mutual support and assistance with shared concerns. These are groups of older persons that are peer led or led by volunteers who have usually benefited from such groups. Self-help groups may deal with a variety of topics, including areas such as grief and loss, caregiver support groups, substance abuse/misuse, and spirituality. Examples of specific groups that may be found nationally include the widow-to-widow program and Alzheimer's and Parkinson's caregiver support groups. These groups may be led by professionals such as counselors, psychologists, nurses, and social workers, or they may be led by trained paraprofessionals and/or peer counselors.

Creative Art Therapies: Poetry, Writing, and Drama

The use of the arts as a medium for therapy is an interesting approach for counselors. Gerontological counselors can use art mediums, including poetry, writing, and drama, to assist clients in self-expression, personal awareness and insight, and self-exploration. Counselors need not be English or theater majors to use these techniques. Simply providing an environment in which clients are encouraged to express themselves by writing poetry, writing autobiographies, or acting out life events or plays may be beneficial to clients. In all of these approaches, what is central is not the medium or the product that is produced, but rather the meaning of the product to the older persons.

The essential component of these approaches is self-expression through a medium with which the client is comfortable, followed by sharing those expressions with others in a group or with the counselor in individual sessions. The use of creative art therapies provides counselors with additional insight into clients' thoughts, attitudes, life experiences, and feelings. In return, the creative art strategies help clients express thoughts, ideas, or feelings that may not be readily accessed or expressed using other strategies.

Bibliotherapy

Bibliotherapy utilizes books and other written materials as therapeutic aids for clients. Bibliotherapy involves the counselor asking the client to read a specific book, either nonfiction or fiction, written passage, or audiovisual materials. The client may be asked to write a poem or story, keep a log or journal, paint a picture, or model with clay. These are just a few of the limitless resources for use in bibliotherapy (Hynes & Hynes-Berry, 1986).

The importance of bibliotherapy is not in the book or other resource, but in the meaning the client attaches to it. Processing the assignment requires the counselor to ask the client to discuss what meaning the material had for that client. This may involve questions such as: What character did you most identify with? How did the book make you feel? Who did you like best or least in the book? What themes did you see in the book?

The overall goal of bibliotherapy is to assist clients in exploring and gaining new perspectives and insights, problem-solving skills, self-exploration, and coping strategies. In addition, counselors can gain valuable information into the way clients view themselves, their problems, and the world around them by listening to the clients' interpretation of meaning after reading the bibliotherapeutic materials. Therapeutic benefits of bibliotherapy for clients may be gained from the experience of reading the material itself, and may be increased through processing their reactions to the material with the counselor. Bibliotherapy may also be done in groups (Hynes & Wedl, 1990).

It is important to carefully select materials related to clients' needs, concerns, and issues. In addition, counselors must be thoroughly familiar with the materials they assign and sensitive to issues such as client literacy, reading level, and size of type set. Examples of literature that may be particularly helpful when conducting bibliotherapy with older persons, and that may be found in most bookstores (some in the children's section) include:

The Giving Tree (Silverstein, 1961)—a book that evokes discussion of life span development and family relationships, especially relationships with children.

The Velveteen Rabbit (Williams, 1983)—a book that describes, methaphorically, how persons become more special as they grow older.

When I Am An Old Woman, I Shall Wear Purple (Martz, 1987)—a book of poetry and prose written by and about older persons. Any of the selections can be the basis for discussion with an older person.

If I had My Life to Live Over, I Would Pick More Daisies (Martz, 1992)—a book of poetry and prose written by and about older persons. Many show the humor in life.

Music, Movement, and Dance Therapies

Music, movement, and dance therapies also can be used to encourage self-expression and self-exploration in older clients. Additionally, these therapies may result in emotional catharsis and socialization for older clients. Clients may be asked to listen passively to music or to watch dance performances. They may also actively participate in these activities by creating their own music, or expressing themselves through movement and dance. Physical impairments may limit the types of movement and dance older persons are able to participate in. However, this does not mean that some type of movement/dance may not be experienced. Even minimal movement may help reduce pain and stress and allow clients to feel better.

Pet Therapy

Pet therapy provides many advantages for older persons who like pets and are able to care for them. Older persons who like pets but are unable to care for them (e.g., patients in nursing homes) also may benefit from exposure to pets through programs that encourage individuals to bring pets into nursing homes to visit residents. Many residential settings have realized the benefits of pet therapy and have adopted a mascot (usually a dog or cat) who resides in the setting with older persons. Research indicates that people who like pets and are exposed to them experience reduced levels of stress, are happier, and are healthier (Cusack & Smith, 1984).

Pets promote socialization and provide unconditional positive regard and acceptance, and thus help build self-esteem and reduce loneliness. Pets may also give older persons a sense of responsibility and the feeling of being needed. Additionally, older persons who are exposed to pets experience more opportunities for therapeutic touch, sensory stimulation, and affection, which are important for self-esteem and reality orientation.

Counselors should also be aware that, although there are many benefits of pet therapy for older persons, pets can also be a liability. People who do not like or are afraid of pets will not enjoy pet therapy. Some impaired older persons who would benefit substantially from a move to more supportive housing refuse to consider such a move unless their pet is able to move with them. This is often not possible, and therefore older persons may remain in their current living situation in which they may not receive necessary assistance. Further, because people become attached to pets, the loss of a pet can be a major loss to older individuals.

Horticulture Therapy

Horticulture therapy includes any therapeutic intervention that involves the use of plants or activities related to plants. Horticulture therapy may take the form of window box gardening in some nursing homes and retirement centers. In other settings, older persons may work together to create gardens to beautify their surroundings. Planting, growing, and nurturing gardens is beneficial to older persons in many ways. This therapy provides the opportunity for older persons to develop improved physical functioning, reduce stress, increase self-esteem, and promote positive feedback from others. Additionally, horticulture therapy can help older persons feel more productive and worthwhile. Some older persons may experience a need to continue their nurturing roles, and may find that horticulture therapy provides them with an outlet for their nurturing.

Imagery and Self-Hypnosis

Imagery and self-hypnosis may be taught to older persons as methods of reducing stress and anxiety, managing pain, and problem solving. The technique of imagery involves asking older persons to close their eyes and imagine a place where they feel comfortable, safe, warm, at peace, and pain-free. As they imagine this place, they are encouraged to relax and focus on feeling good. As they come back to the present, they are asked to bring with them those feelings of peace, wellness, and so on. They are encouraged to continue to practice imagery, and to use it whenever they are feeling particularly stressed or anxious.

The use of self-hypnosis follows some of the same guidelines. Older persons may be asked to close their eyes and imagine they are on an escalator going down. As they go down, they feel more relaxed, heavy, warm, and at peace. At the bottom of the escalator is a place that is serene, comfortable, and safe. They are asked to stay in that place until they are ready to return. The return may then be guided by the counselor, back up the escalator taking with them all of the good feelings experienced in their resting place. This technique may be used during times of stress or painful procedures.

The previous descriptions are provided only as a brief overview. Counselors should not attempt these techniques without supervision and training from a qualified professional trained in their use. In addition, caution must be used with frail older persons and with those suffering from hypotension as they may be unsteady for a period of time following the use of relaxation techniques.

Reality Orientation, Remotivation, and Resocialization

Reality orientation, remotivation, and resocialization are all techniques that are used in inpatient settings with severely impaired older persons. These techniques require training and coordination of the approaches by all members of the treatment team to be effective. Counselors should not attempt these interventions without specialized training in their use. Descriptions of these techniques are provided next.

Reality orientation is a therapeutic technique that is employed in residential and inpatient settings with confused and/or disoriented patients. As noted earlier, this is a coordinated effort utilized by all staff, the goal of which is to assist clients in remaining oriented to time, place, and person. This may involve the use of calendars throughout the institution, the use of name tags and names on the patient's door, and constant reinforcement of the time, place, and person through interactions with the staff.

Recently, the goal of continually challenging confused patients' reality orientation has come into question. An alternative therapy, validation therapy, asserts that it may be therapeutic for confused older persons to retreat to the past when life was happy and more comfortable for them (Babins, 1988). Therefore, it may not be therapeutic to continually try to orient them to time, place, and person. Rather, the goal of validation therapy is to allow older persons to experience their own reality, which may be more pleasurable than present reality. This approach is also used in an inpatient setting and must be used by all staff in a coordinated approach.

Remotivation therapy involves the use of a highly structured therapy group. The purpose of remotivation therapy is to promote patient discussion of topics relating to the "real" world and to improve interpersonal relationships and communication. The overall goal of this therapy is to help clients who are confused or disoriented to maintain contact with the "real" world and to build relationships with other group members.

Resocialization often follows remotivation therapy. Remotivation therapy assists clients in maintaining contact with reality and in beginning to develop interpersonal relationships. Resocialization therapy focuses on the continued development of interpersonal relationships, social relationships, and expansion of client choices. Again, a group approach is used to facilitate discussion of interpersonal relationships and feelings. This group is similar to psychodynamic group therapy. The leader in a resocialization group takes a less directive and more interpretative role than in the remotivation group.

Summary

In summary, all counseling and therapy techniques that can be used with persons of any age can be used successfully with older persons. In addition, there are specific techniques that can be particularly beneficial for older adults, such as life review, early recollections, bibliotherapy, and validation therapy. Depending on the needs of particular older clients, one or more of these approaches may be selected as the basis of helping interventions.

Case Studies

Following are two case studies that will allow the reader to apply the knowledge and skills learned in this chapter related to specialized therapies for use with older persons. Read each case study and think about how you would help the client. Then read the comments for further insights into the role of the gerontological counselor in each situation.

Case One

Helen is a 74-year-old, widowed, Hispanic woman who lives alone and has become increasingly depressed and withdrawn. Her 45-year-old daughter has become quite concerned that her mother rarely leaves the house, and seems to spend a great deal of time talking about "the old days" and looking at old pictures and memorabilia. Her daughter's most recent concerns were prompted when her mother suddenly gave away many of her possessions. Helen comes to counseling at her daughter's request.

Helen arrives for the counseling session neatly dressed and oriented to time, place, and person. The initial interview ascertains that, following the death of her husband, Helen has been increasingly worried about her own death. She states she feels a need to "make things right" with her family and friends, "does not want to be a burden to her children," and she feels a need to "get things in order." She states that she is not depressed or suicidal, and does not understand why her daughter is so concerned.

Comments on Case One

Possible interventions that a counselor may use when working with Helen include some form of reminiscence therapy, possibly asking Helen to write or record her autobiography. She can then share this with her daughter, who presumably will benefit from learning more about her mother's background and life. A counseling session with mother and daughter to discuss the autobiography can be helpful, especially if ineffective communication patterns exist between the two generations. The counselor also can use the autobiography to conceptualize issues related to life review and the achievement of ego integrity.

Bibliotherapy might also be used with Helen to help her identify and integrate different stages of her life. *The Giving Tree* (Silverstein, 1961) might be used to help her look at the full circle of life, and to help her find meaning and purpose in her life at all stages. Alternately, this book could generate issues related to her adult daughter and their relationship over the life span.

Participation in a group for widows might help Helen work through her grief and loss. Growth groups for older persons also could be helpful, and could help her develop a focus on future goals that can emerge as she puts her affairs in order. Role modeling from other older persons who have resolved similar issues can be particularly beneficial.

Case Two

A 79-year-old man enters your long-term-care facility in a confused state with a diagnosis of Alzheimer's disease. He does not seem to be oriented to the present. He continues to talk as if he were a young man trying to get back home, referring to his home when he was a little boy. As a counselor in the nursing home, what interventions might you use with this client?

Comments on Case Two

After initial development of rapport with the client, therapeutic strategies that may be considered include reality orientation or validation therapy. The therapist might actively engage the client in a discussion of issues such as: What is at home? Why do you want to go home? What will you do at home? What do you remember about home? In this way, themes may emerge that allow the counselor to connect with the client at some level and give the counselor some insight into the client's issues, values, and interests. From this information, the counselor might then add additional strategies to match the client's interests and abilities, such as horticulture therapy, art therapy, and so on.

Validation therapy may also be used with the client and is consistent with the early recollections approach. Validation therapy, as stated previously, would be used to talk with the client as if reality were whatever the client perceived it to be. The counselor would talk about where the client was, what the client was thinking, how old the client was, what needs the client has, and what it is about that particular time and place that is comforting to the client. If validation therapy is used, it is important that all members of the treatment team agree to use this approach. It can be confusing and frustrating to the client if some of the staff work toward reorientation therapy to the present and other members of the staff employ a validation therapy perspective.

Discussion Questions

1. What issues does Helen need to address in counseling? What issues, if any, need to be addressed with Helen's daughter?
2. Based on the issues you identified, what approach or approaches would you choose in working with Helen?
3. Which of the therapies listed previously would you feel comfortable using with older persons? Why?
4. Which of these therapies do you feel you need more training in to comfortably use with older persons?

References

Babins, L. (1988). Conceptual analysis of validation therapy. *International Journal of Aging and Human Development, 26*(3), 161–168.

Butler, R.N. (1963). The life review: An interpretation of reminiscence in the aged. *Psychiatry, 26,* 65–76.

Cusack, O., & Smith, E. (1984). *Pets and the elderly: The therapeutic bond.* New York: Haworth Press.

Erikson, E. (1963). *Childhood and society.* New York: Norton.

Hynes, A.L., & Hynes-Berry, M. (1986). *Bibliotherapy, The interactive process: A handbook.* Boulder, CO: Westview Press.

Hynes, A.L., & Wedl, L.C. (1990). Bibliotherapy: An interactive process in counseling older persons. *Journal of Mental Health Counseling, 12*(3), 288–302.

Martz, S.H. (Ed.). (1987). *If I had my life to live over, I would pick more daisies.* Watsonville, CA: Papier Mache Press.

Martz, S.H. (Ed.). (1987). *When I am an old woman, I shall wear purple.* Watsonville, CA: Papier Mache Press.

Silverstein, S. (1961). *The giving tree.* New York: Random House.

Sweeney, T.J. (1989). *Adlerian counseling: A practical approach for a new decade.* Muncie, IN: Accelerated Development.

Sweeney, T.J., & Myers, J.E. (1991). Early recollections: An Adlerian technique with older people. *The Clinical Gerontologist, 4*(4), 3–12.

Williams, M. (1983). *The velveteen rabbit.* New York: Simon & Shuster.

15

Ethical Issues in Gerontological Counseling

Minimum Essential Competency #14 for a Gerontological Counseling Specialist: *demonstrates skill in applying extensive knowledge of ethical issues in counseling older persons, their families, and care providers.*

Although ethical issues related to counseling all persons are equally relevant to counseling older persons, there are some ethical situations and dilemmas that are unique or particularly important to consider when working with older persons. Counselors working with older persons are required to observe certain ethical standards based on the professional organization(s) to which they belong and/or based on the licensure or certifications they hold. In this chapter, the ethical standards of the American Counseling Association (ACA 1988) are emphasized. Counselors who adhere to additional ethical codes need to consider these as well in working with older clients (see Fitting, 1984), and may expect the principles and guidelines to be similar to those in the ACA code. The topics discussed in this chapter include special ethical considerations for working with older persons. Two specific examples of ethical situations that gerontological counselors are likely to encounter provide a basis for discussion of ethical issues.

Special Ethical Considerations for Working with Older Persons

The ultimate goal of counseling older persons is the same as when working with individuals of all ages: to provide services that are in the best interest of the client, that preserve the dignity of the client, and that promote the integrity of the client. Aspects of the aging process may present special ethical dilemmas. These include coping with issues such as terminal illness, death and dying, multiple losses, grief, suicide, guardianship, competency, elder abuse, and institutionalization. Compounding these issues is the lack of literature related to differences and similarities among older persons in the areas of gender and ethnicity. Such factors may complicate the resolution of these already sensitive ethical issues.

According to Fitting (1986), gerontological counselors work with older persons who have four areas of concern. These include those who are coping with normal developmental issues associated with aging, such as grief, loss, and retirement; those who are coping with chronic illnesses common among the aged, such as vision and hearing impairments; those who have major mental illnesses that may occur in later life, such as Alzheimer's disease and major depression; and those who suffer from a terminal illness, such as cancer or heart disease. Counselors will most likely be faced with clients experiencing difficulties in each of these areas. Ethical dilemmas occur most often when an older person's choices or wishes are significantly different from those choices proposed as the "best option" by the counselor and/or the older person's family or service providers. Two examples of such dilemmas follow.

Examples of Ethical Dilemmas with Older Persons

Example One

A conflict with ethical implications can occur with an older person who has Alzheimer's disease. Suppose the client's disease has progressed to the point where she is a danger to herself. She leaves the stove on and forgets to turn it off. She wanders off late at night and gets lost. Her family and counselor feel it is in the client's best interest to sell her home and move into a nursing home. The client refuses to even consider selling her home and moving to a nursing home. She states she would rather die than go to a nursing home.

At first glance, the decisions to be made in this case seem rather clear cut. If the client is a danger to herself or someone else, the counselor is bound to protect the client (and others) as much as possible. Although the ultimate goal might be for the client to sell her home and move to more supportive housing voluntarily, the counselor may need to work with the family to gain guardianship of the older person if a move is to occur. It may become necessary to work toward a forced move to more supportive housing in the client's best interest. However, these decisions and transitions may be stressful for the client and the client's family.

What makes this situation difficult is that the client's needs and rights have not yet been fully considered. The counselor might ask if the client has truly been diagnosed with Alzheimer's after a thorough assessment, or if this diagnosis was made based on preliminary information and bias on the part of service providers or physicians. It is important to recall that many conditions, such as dehydration, stress, malnutrition, and drug interactions, can cause symptoms similar to those this older woman is experiencing, and the condition underlying these symptoms may be treatable and reversible. A thorough and accurate geriatric assessment is essential prior to making any firm decisions.

The counselor may also experience feelings of being "caught in the middle" of what the client wants and what the family wants, or between what the client wants and what is in the client's best interests. Although many older individuals decline faster and eventually die earlier when placed in institutions such as nursing homes, others find this environment to be healthier and are able to live longer and with better health. It is impossible to tell what the outcome will be with this client, which is an added reason for proceeding with caution in making decisions. The counselor needs to sort out who the client is—the older person, her family, or both—and facilitate decision making that maintains, to the extent possible, the rights and dignity of all those involved.

Example Two

An older man living alone has degenerative arthritis and diabetes. He is thin and frail, and has difficulty with many activities of daily living, including meal preparation and bathing. Despite receiving home health care services and meals on wheels, he continues to lose weight and states that his quality of life is so poor that he would rather die. He is mentally alert and competent, and shows signs of significant depression over his life circumstances. His physician and daughter have indicated that they believe he should move to more supportive housing—either to the daughter's home or to a nursing home. He vehemently states, "I was born in this house and I want to die in this house." Further, he indicates that he would rather take his own life than be forced to move.

The counselor may agree with the physician and the client's daughter that it is in the client's best interests, at least physically, to move to more supportive housing. However, his emotional health and well-being are important as well. The ethical challenge lies in determining where the client's best interests and the client's right to make his own decisions begin and end. In this case, the two are in conflict.

Counselors are ethically bound to keep their values and judgments out of counseling sessions and to support clients in their decision regarding what is right for them based on their own values, so long as they are not a danger to themselves and others. In this case, the client seems to be a danger to himself, in that he is unable to care for his physical needs. The counselor could continue to work with the client to find other community resources to support his decision to remain in his home, and to do so safely. In addition, the counselor might continue to work with the client to help him clarify his values and to determine what other options might be available to him.

Addressing the issue of effective communication between the client and his daughter would also be important. Perhaps through increased communication and conflict-resolution skills, the client and the client's daughter might reach a mutually satisfying decision. The client and the counselor might also attempt to discover creative ways to improve the client's current quality of life, such as engaging in a hobby, learning a new skill, or participating in an Adopt a Grandparent program.

The client's depression and possible suicidal ideation are also of great concern. Treatment for the depression could help the client engage in more effective decision making. Exploring the suicidal thoughts is critical, as is an accurate suicide lethality assessment. If the client is a danger to himself in this regard, hospitalization may be required. Ethically, again, the counselor needs to understand who the client is— whether it be the older person who wants to be allowed to live and die with dignity (from his perspective), or the adult children who want their aging parent to live in a "safe" environment where he can receive the quality of care that will extend the quantity of his life, even if the quality of his life is not optimum.

A Model for Ethical Decision Making

The ethical principles demonstrated in these two cases involve those defined by Fitting (1986) and include fidelity, autonomy, and beneficence. These principles may guide the ethical decision making of the counselor. Fidelity is the ethical principle that addresses the quality of the relationship between the counselor and client. It implies that trust, faithfulness, and loyalty are essential components of the helping relationship. Examples of fidelity in the two previous cases include these questions: Whose side are you on counselor? I thought you were supposed to help me and support my decisions?

Autonomy is the right of older persons to make their own choices regarding matters that affect their lives. This principle implies that counselors respect clients' choices and not force their own values on their clients. This is demonstrated in both previous cases, as the dilemma in what the counselor views as the best option for the client and what the client chooses. In the first case, the counselor cannot fully support the client's choice because the client seems to be a direct danger to herself. In the second case, the counselor may feel that moving is the best option, but is obligated to support the client's decision based on his values. Of course, through mobilizing community resources, this choice can be supported in a safe and healthy manner.

Beneficence is the concept of helping people by preventing harm and actively intervening for a positive outcome. In both cases, this principle comes into play. In the first case, there is a direct danger to the health and welfare of the client that must be prevented and that requires active intervention. In the second case, the options are not so clear. Would it do the client more harm than good to move to more supportive housing against his wishes? Research indicates that many older persons who move decline and have a higher mortality rate than those who do not. Others actually improve when they are in a safe environment with three meals provided per day, along with health care, housekeeping, and opportunity for social interaction with staff and peers. The counselor is faced with developing options that best help the client to meet his needs, and must keep those needs foremost in mind during the process of intervention.

Implications for Counselors

How do counselors and helping professionals decide when to override certain ethical principles in favor of others? They can only do so when there is a strong moral obligation to do so. The ethical guidelines established by the American Counseling Association (1988) can assist professionals in making those decisions. However, the ultimate responsibility for the decisions rests with the counselor. Counselors working with older persons may feel trapped between strict adherence to the ACA Code of Ethics and special considerations presented by elderly clients that may confound ethical decision making.

Examples of these special considerations include the unique life position of elderly clients. Older persons have accumulated a wealth of life experiences that may guide their choices regarding the way in which they choose to live the remainder of their life. They may be well aware that they have limited time left to live, and this fact may be guiding the decisions they make. In addition, many older persons suffer from chronic diseases and disabilities. Therefore, for many older persons, quality of life versus quantity of life is an issue.

Older persons have spent a lifetime developing their own unique priorities and values regarding what constitutes quality of life. These values and priorities may guide their choices even when others consider the choices not in the clients' best interests. For example, in the second case stated earlier, the older man values remaining in his home above moving to more supportive housing, even when the move may have afforded him with "increased quality of life" from the perspective of his children and the counselor. To him, a move meant "decreased quality of life." The value of most importance to him clearly is independence, whereas the values foremost in the minds of his children and possibly the counselor are safety and personal care.

Who is the Client?

Gerontological counselors often have to ask themselves, repeatedly, who is their client? Is it the older person? Is it the family? Is it the older person's children? Is it the physician or referral agency? Often the values and priorities of these groups come into direct conflict. The ethical principles of ACA clearly state that counselors' first duty is to their client, and with older persons they need to clarify who that person is. All too often it begins as an older person and shifts to others when the competence of the older individual comes into question. It is always better to err on the side of the client, but even this "rule" can be a problem when the client seems to be in danger physically or mentally.

The gerontological counselor's ultimate responsibility—to support the client's decisions—does not mean that the counselor is not equally responsible for jointly developing creative strategies to honor the client's autonomy and to increase quality of life in the chosen setting. The counselor must work in conjunction with the family members, the older person, community resources, and other health care professionals to maintain the client in his or her chosen setting with the highest quality of life possible. This may include family conferences in which the counselor acts to facilitate communication and understanding between the older person and the members of his or her family. It may also include referral for home care services. It can include working with health care professionals to develop unique strategies tailored to meet an individual client's needs.

There are myriad community resources designed to assist older persons who wish to remain in their own homes (see chap. 12, this volume). These include programs such as Adopt-a-Grandparent, Habitat for Humanity, Home Health Care, and other programs sponsored by Area Agencies on Aging. It is essential that counselors working with older persons are familiar with all community resources available to both the older person and their families, and/or where to access information about available resources.

Ethical Dilemmas and Societal Values

Further ethical dilemmas that may be encountered by the gerontological counselor occur at a much broader level than with individual clients. Societal values regarding the treatment of older persons may influence the availability and goals of programs designed to assist this population. Some of these values include a societal emphasis on young people, and the attitude that resources should not be "wasted" on old persons with chronic ailments; the attitude that if there is no chance of a "cure," efforts should not be spent on chronic ailments; the attitude that treatment occurs in a fragmented system rather than from a holistic perspective in which the total "well-being" of the person is treated; and, finally, the fact that many families no longer reside near one another, and therefore family caregiving may not be an option. Families also may choose to "save" family resources by not providing needed health care for their older relatives. Such decisions are as likely to be made by an older person as by his or her adult children. Limited resources, such as beds in nursing homes, funds allocated for home health care programs, and the high cost of medical care, also complicate ethical decision making.

Identifying Values and Alternatives

Ethical dilemmas may occur when working with older persons due to several factors. These factors involve differences in values and priorities between the counselor, the family, society, and older persons. Counselors must emphasize the exploration and clarification of values with older clients if these differences are to be resolved. At the same time, counselors must be prepared to explore their own personal values related to aging, death and dying, and quality of life issues.

Once the counselor recognizes the many facets of ethical dilemmas, he or she can begin to work on resolving them in everyone's best interests—but above all in the client's best interests. Many times there is no "ideal" solution that will satisfy all parties involved. Therefore, the counselor must work to develop alternatives for the client and his or her family that cause the least harm to all involved.

Once alternatives have been developed, the counselor may then assist the client, and possibly the client's family, in examining the positive and negative aspects associated with each alternative. This decision-making process is similar to the process that would be used with clients of any age. Care must be taken to respect and address concerns of older persons and their families related to societal myths, such as: All nursing homes are terrible places, or Nursing homes are only places to die. Gerontological counselors may provide older persons and their families with additional information regarding each of the alternatives identified to ensure that the client may make an informed decision based on consideration of all factors and possible outcomes.

Guidelines for Working with Older Persons

Several guidelines may assist counselors in their work with older persons. First, as stated previously, counselors have an obligation to maintain the dignity and autonomy of older persons as much as possible. Second, even when working with cognitively impaired or confused clients, it is essential that input be sought from the clients to the extent that may be possible based on current competencies or past behaviors and attitudes. Family involvement in decision making should also be sought whenever possible. Although freedom of choice and autonomy are important, other factors such as quality of life, benevolence, preservation of life and autonomy, and humaneness must also be considered.

The stress experienced by older persons and their families as older persons' autonomy decreases and dependence increases may result in feelings of frustration, hurt, anger, and helplessness. It is essential that counselors continue to work with older persons and the family members to increase communication, increase client and family control over the situation, and manage the stresses involved in making difficult decisions.

Summary

All counselors find themselves faced at various times with ethical challenges and dilemmas. Although these also occur when working with older persons, the unique circumstances of later life can result in additional ethical challenges. Gerontological counselors will find the ethical principles of fidelity, autonomy, and beneficence to be helpful in determining how best to resolve ethical situations for the benefit of all concerned.

Case Studies

Following are two case studies that will allow the reader to apply the knowledge and skills learned in this chapter related to ethical and legal issues encountered in work with older persons. Read each case study and think about how you would help the client. Then read the comments for further insights into the role of the gerontological counselor in each situation.

Case One

You are working with an older person who has been diagnosed with a terminal illness. The patient's family and physician have chosen not to tell the older person that his or her condition is terminal. The older person senses that something is very wrong. He or she asks you if his or her condition is terminal, and states that he or she "has a right to know." The client is mentally competent. What will you do?

Comments on Case One

The counselor may know the diagnosis, but it is not the counselor's role to communicate this information. Before taking any action, and with the client's permission, the counselor should consult with the family and physician, relaying the client's request and concerns. The client has a right to know, just as the family has a right to protect an older loved one from information they consider to be harmful to his or her well-being.

If the counselor is still unable to resolve the problem by having the physician talk with the older client, the counselor may choose to function as an advocate for his or her client. In the role of advocate, the counselor could assist the client in requesting from the hospital the opportunity to review his or her records—a right to which he or she is entitled by law. In this instance, the counselor should be prepared to provide emotional support and counseling for the client, as appropriate, once the client learns of the diagnosis. In addition, the counselor must be willing to deal with anger on the part of family members for actions taken on behalf of the client.

One might ask what right the counselor has to interfere in affairs of the family, particularly if the family was the source of the referral. Again, the question of who is the client arises and must be addressed and resolved.

As with all situations involving ethical decisions, the counselor's response to this situation requires consideration of the three basic principles of fidelity, autonomy, and beneficence. Fidelity requires that the counselor clarify whether the client is the older person, his or her family, or other service providers, or all three. If the relationship with the client is placed foremost, all decisions will be made in the context of what is best for the client at this point in time. Autonomy means that the client is respected and allowed to make his or her own decisions. Beneficence requires that the counselor do no harm.

Case Two

You have been working with an older, widowed female referred by her physician for depression. The physician, who has treated this woman for many years, believes that social isolation and loneliness are among her greatest problems. The client lives with an adult daughter. You learn that the daughter is requiring her mother to "turn over" her Social Security check at the beginning of each month in exchange for her care. As the client begins to trust you, she increasingly tells you things about her adult daughter that cause you to suspect elder abuse, not just in the form of financial abuse, but also in terms of emotional abuse and neglect. When you voice your concerns in a caring way, the client begins to cry and begs you not to tell anyone. She fears that she will be placed in a nursing home. She also fears retaliation and harm from her daughter. Further, she says she would rather just die because she is not of much use to anyone anyway. How will you proceed?

Comments on Case Two

If your state has a mandatory abuse reporting law, you are required to report the suspected abuse. In some states, mandatory laws apply to abused children, but not to abused adults or older adults. You need to know the laws in your state.

Counselors typically do not "investigate" cases of suspected abuse. It would be wise to consult a social worker, whose training and expertise in the area of adult protective services is critical in this situation. The social worker may take a referral and follow up through his or her agency, or you may be guided in appropriate interview techniques to verify your concerns prior to a referral.

Alternately, you may choose to request a family counseling session with the client and her adult daughter. You may meet with the adult daughter individually and attempt to ascertain her side of the story. It may differ considerably from the client's version of the home situation.

The principle of fidelity is always a concern when the need arises to prevent harm to a client or others. However, the ethical standards are very clear on this point. You need to inform the client of what you are required to do—to report an abusive situation to prevent further harm to your client. The principle of autonomy is an important one. To the extent possible, you need to try to obtain the consent of the client to the actions you must take. Finally, beneficence requires that you consider all alternatives in an attempt to avoid harm to the client.

Follow-up for Case Two

Suppose you refer the client to a social worker, and this person conducts an investigation to determine whether the older person is in fact being abused. The adult daughter denies the abuse and presents convincing evidence to the contrary. Despite the social worker's best efforts, the final report indicates a lack of elder abuse in this situation. What are your options at this point?

Comments on Follow-up for Case Two

This situation is not unlikely. At this point, you have jeopardized your relationship with your client. In addition, it is unlikely that you will be able to establish a relationship with the adult daughter that will result in effective family counseling. Your best option may be to continue to work with the client, if the daughter will allow you to continue, and rebuild rapport while you work on other aspects of the client's depression and isolation. Also help the client develop appropriate assertive behaviors to maintain her independence. Seeking peer consultation from an experienced colleague can help you deal with your own feelings about this client and the circumstances that have resulted. So long as you have kept the client's needs foremost, you have acted in an ethically appropriate manner.

Discussion Questions

1. What ethical issues are you likely to encounter when working with older persons?
2. Examine your own personal values and beliefs regarding aging, death and dying, quality of life, and caregiving issues associated with older persons.
3. Given the ethical guidelines of the professional association(s) to which you belong, what special considerations may occur when working with older clients? Do the ethical guidelines speak directly to the rights and responsibilities associated with counseling older persons?

References

American Counseling Association. (1988). *Ethical standards*. Alexandria, VA: Author.

Fitting, M. (1984). Professional and ethical responsibilities for psychologists working with the elderly. *Counseling Psychologist, 12*(3), 69–78.

Fitting, M. (1986). Ethical dilemmas in counseling elderly adults. *Journal of Counseling and Development, 64*, 325–327.

16

The Gerontological Counselor as Consultant

Minimum Essential Competency #15 for a Gerontological Counseling Specialist: *demonstrates the ability to act as a consultant to individuals and organizations on issues related to older persons and their families.*

Given the increasing number and proportion of older persons in the U.S. population, and the fact that there continues to be a lack of professionally trained gerontological counselors, the gerontological counselor may be called on to provide consultation in a variety of situations and settings. The specialized knowledge and training of the gerontological counselor may be used to assist helping professionals across disciplines in meeting the needs of older persons. In this way, the expertise of gerontological counselors as a resource providing both direct and indirect service to older persons may be maximized. In this chapter, settings for gerontological consultation are discussed, followed by consideration of several specialized roles for the consultant. These roles include educator, trainer, supervisor, professional counselor, and expert witness.

Settings for Gerontological Consultation

Gerontological counselors who establish their professional expertise in the community through professional networking may be called on to provide consultation in a variety of settings. These may include consultations in community mental health agencies, long-term-care facilities, retirement facilities, churches, community organizations, hospitals, and industry, to name a few. Gerontological counselors may also be called on to provide consultation in the form of teaching, workshops, and conferences in a variety of settings. In addition, individual professionals in the community may also request consultation from gerontological counselors regarding specific patients. These professionals may include physicians, nurse practitioners, mental health counselors, psychologists, social workers, and social service providers.

As discussed in chapter 5 (this volume), the roles of gerontological counselors are varied. This is important to note as we begin to consider the specific roles gerontological consultants may play in each of the settings noted earlier. The depth and breadth of the gerontological counselor's training and experience serve as the foundation that allows for consultation in these diverse settings.

Gerontological Consultant as Educator

There are three basic roles that the gerontological counselor may be called on to perform as a consultant: educator, trainer, and counselor. As an educator, the gerontological consultant's major role is to provide information regarding the unique aspects of working with the older population. This information may include any of the areas addressed elsewhere in this text. The specialized knowledge base possessed by gerontological counselors must be presented in such a way as to allow other helping professionals to integrate that knowledge into their particular settings and job functions.

For example, a local in-home care service may request a gerontological counselor to provide in-service education to their homemaking staff regarding normal changes related to the aging process, and how those changes affect the mental health and well-being of persons in later life. The homemaking staff is responsible for providing in-home services to disabled individuals across the life span, including older persons. The homemakers have contact with their clients at least three times per week and may be one of the only consistent individuals who comes into contact with that person. It is important for them to understand the normal changes associated with the aging process in order for them to identify significant changes in the individual's functioning, and to report those to the appropriate supervisor. Additionally, it is important for the homemakers to be familiar with strengths and limitations of older persons in order for them to provide the best services possible to older persons.

In preparation for the consultation, the gerontological counselor must be familiar with the services homemakers provide to in-home clients. The counselor must also consider the level of education and skills that the homemakers currently possess. This is important in designing an educational program that can be readily understood by the participants. In addition, it is particularly important for the counselor to focus on how the information gained during the in-service presentation may be integrated into the performance of the homemakers' duties with their older clients.

Gerontological Consultant as Trainer

The primary goal of the gerontological consultant as trainer is to provide both knowledge and specific skills training to participants. This may involve providing participants with small units of new knowledge related to older persons, specific skills and strategies for working with older persons based on that knowledge, and practice of those skills in a supervised environment. It may also involve training participants to be trainers themselves. That is, to maximize resources, the gerontological consultant may be asked to train representatives of a group with the expectation that those individuals will then train the rest of the members of the group at some future time. Again, it should be stressed that the training program needs to focus on the integration of the skills learned with the current level of participant skill and job responsibilities.

There are several components that must be considered when planning and developing an effective training consultation. First, it is important to understand precisely what specific skills and/or knowledge the person requesting the services expects participants to possess upon completion of the training program. Trainers must also gain information related to the population to receive training. Specific information regarding education level, current skill level, required skill level, job requirements, and expectations of the individual participants is important. The consultant must be able to utilize this information in order to adequately assess the request for training and the realistic limits of such training. Can the training be accomplished in the time provided? Do the participants possess the required prerequisite knowledge or skills on which to build the training program? Most important, does the consultant possess the required knowledge and skill level to teach others the specific skills requested?

Once the consultant has considered each of these components and has decided that the training goals are realistic and attainable, the consultant may begin to plan the actual training session. The development of any training should be based on several principles. The training program should be interesting and utilize as many different types of resources as possible (e.g., lecture, visual aids, handouts, group exercises, role plays). Participants should be actively involved in the learning process. As much as possible, training should be interactive, and participants should be encouraged to share their particular experiences and how they relate to the specific information/skills currently being taught. Information provided in a short, concise format, followed by demonstration of the skill and participant practice sessions, is the most effective format for most training sessions. Participant feedback should be encouraged at all times, and participants should be made aware of the goals of the training session and expected outcomes at the beginning of the training session. Evaluation information is essential for effective development of future programs.

An example of gerontological consultant as trainer follows. A gerontological counselor may be called on by a local church organization to provide a 1-day training session for adult children caring for their aging parents. The church has just formed a support group for adult children caring for aging parents as a result of church member requests. This group consists of approximately 15 members, ages 55–70 years, who have identified themselves as the primary caregivers of aging parents. The group specifically requests training in the improvement of communication and stress management skills. The following workshop is designed by a gerontological consultant based on these requests.

The session would begin with introductions, an overview of topics to be covered and expected outcomes, and discussion of confidentiality and ground rules. This would be followed by a discussion of the myths related to aging, and the presentation of information related to the normal aging process. This information is essential for participants to understand; it is the foundation for effectively coping with the demands of caregiving for an aging parent.

Following the presentation of this information, the focus shifts to improving communication skills within the family. This would be done through a discussion of communication barriers and essential components of communication, followed by communication exercises involving attending behaviors and facilitative responses. Additionally, a discussion of family dynamics initiated by the group leader would be included using stimulus questions, such as: What is the history of the caregiving relationship? Is the caregiver being a caregiver by choice? Do other siblings participate in caregiving? What is the caregiver's relationship with his or her spouse and children?

The next topic to be discussed would be stress and time management. Information presented would include identification of signs of mind, body, and situation stress. This would be followed by experiential exercises using several stress reduction techniques (e.g., thought stopping, imagery, health-enhancing phrases, exercise, counting, Will it really matter in five years?, progressive relaxation, breathing exercises). In addition, time management techniques would be explored by encouraging participants to share what has previously worked for them.

The training session would conclude with a discussion of mid- and later life developmental issues and the impact of these issues on the caregiving relationship. Differences and similarities in tasks faced by both adult children and aging parents would be highlighted. Additionally, information would be presented on available community resources, followed by a wrap-up of the group sessions. Participants would be encouraged to continue meeting together as an informal support group and to discuss the effectiveness of these new skills. It would be stressed that, as with any new skill, it takes time for the participants to notice significant improvements in communication and relaxation skills, and that the effectiveness of these skills increase with practice. Finally, trainers should always request feedback from participants regarding the effectiveness of the workshop. This is essential if trainers are to continue to refine and improve their own training skills.

Gerontological Consultant as Supervisor

When providing training in basic communication and helping skills, it is important that the gerontological counselor be available to provide supervision in the acquisition and development of these skills. When a peer or paraprofessional training program is first designed, consideration of methods of supervision needs to be incorporated into the program. If a trained gerontological or professional counselor is on site where the trainees will be working, that individual may be the designed supervisor. Alternately, the gerontological counselor may need to arrange periodic meetings for follow-up. Topics of discussion will likely include working with difficult clients and recognizing symptoms of emotional disorders that reflect the need for referral for mental health care.

Paraprofessional and peer helpers should never be allowed to feel that they are "on their own"—they may not have the skills to intervene in serious situations. They need to know that they have access to trained professionals for consultation as they encounter difficult, unique, or troublesome situations in their daily work.

Gerontological Consultant as Professional Counselor

The gerontological counselor may also be called on by individual helping professionals to provide consultation related to specific client situations on a case-by-case basis. As previously stated, this may include a variety of professionals, including physicians, nurses, social workers, rehabilitation counselors, psychologists, and social services case workers. Requests for consultations are generally based on the recognition of the specialized expertise of the gerontological counselor in working with older persons.

The individual counselor's reputation in the community and professional networking connections are generally the sources of these consultation requests. Therefore, it is important for gerontological counselors to recognize the importance of building positive community and professional relationships based on mutual respect. It is also important for the gerontological counselor to educate both professionals and members of the public regarding their particular areas of expertise in working with older persons.

Requests for the gerontological counselor to serve as a case consultant may involve participation at different levels. The request may be for the counselor to provide the helping professional with specific information related to community resources for older persons, strategies for dealing with a particular problem being experienced by the older person, or the counselor's clinical opinion related to a particular case. This type of consultation may involve telephone conversations or meetings with the requesting helping professional and may be relatively brief in nature.

The gerontological counselor may also be contacted to serve as a consultant in the role of temporary member of a multidisciplinary treatment team. This may involve working with all the members of the treatment team to develop and implement an effective treatment plan for an older person. This type of consultation usually involves more than one meeting and direct involvement in the client's care. In addition to providing input into the team meetings, the gerontological counselor/consultant may also be asked to meet with the client to implement a portion of the overall treatment plan.

An example of this type of consultation follows. An older man with Parkinson's disease has recently been discharged from the hospital and is currently being followed by a family physician. The client is being seen by several members of the treatment team on an outpatient basis. These members include the physical therapist, in-home nursing provider, social worker, and physician. The team has recently become concerned that the client's wife is showing signs of caregiver burnout, and that the client is becoming increasingly hostile and depressed. The team requests a consultation with you, as a gerontological counselor, to obtain your assessment of the situation and your input regarding treatment strategies.

Following the team's request, you agree to meet with the older man and his wife to assess the situation. In this session, you learn that the client has some unresolved issues related to anger, identity, and his increasing dependence on his wife. You also learn that his wife feels tied to the house, unappreciated, and frustrated at the client's lack of appreciation of her efforts. You meet with the treatment team and propose that the couple receive counseling to discuss the client's feelings related to increasing dependence and the wife's feelings of lack of appreciation. In addition, you suggest that the social worker try to arrange for a local respite service to allow the wife at least 1 day off per week. You may continue to work with the couple as part of a treatment team composed of other helping professionals.

Gerontological Counselor as Expert Witness

One final role that the gerontological counselor may be called on to perform is that of expert witness. Although this is not defined specifically as a consulting function, it may be seen as falling under this general heading. In this role, the gerontological counselor may be called on by an older person's attorney to testify as an expert witness on a number of issues. Examples of cases in which counselors may serve in this capacity involve worker's compensation cases, in which return to the workplace and vocational opportunities may be the focus, elder abuse cases, in which the counselor may be called on to provide information related to the incidence and cycle of violence related to elder abuse, and in cases involving the competency of an older person and the possibility of the appointment of a legal guardian and/or placement in more supportive housing.

Summary

In summary, the gerontological counselor may be called on to serve as a consultant in a variety of settings and roles (see Dougherty, 1990). It is important for the counselor to possess the knowledge and skills necessary to meet the challenges of this critical role. As the number of older persons increases and society begins to recognize the need for the expertise of gerontological counselors, the requests for gerontological counselors to serve as consultants may increase dramatically.

Case Studies

Following are two case studies that will allow the reader to apply the knowledge and skills learned in this chapter related to the gerontological counselor as consultant. Read each case study and think about how you would help the client. Then read the comments for further insights into the role of the gerontological counselor in each situation.

Case One

As a gerontological counselor, you are asked to serve as a consultant to a local company that is developing a retirement program for its employees. You are specifically requested to work with the company's personnel manager to develop an education series for employees who expect to retire within 1 year. What components would you include in the series? What issues should be considered when developing this program?

Comments on Case One

The first step in planning a consultation, which is discussed more fully in chapter 17 (this volume), is to conduct an assessment of the organization's needs. Components that will likely be included in the retirement program include role changes resulting from retirement, such as changes in financial status, changes in relationships with family and friends, and changes in self-worth and identity. Planning one's use of time and leisure activities following retirement is also important. Participants should be encouraged to begin exploring their interests and abilities in order to develop realistic retirement plans. Do they wish to continue working part time or full time? What job-seeking skills will that require? Do they wish to do volunteer work? How will their relationships with friends and spouses change?

The program also should contain a component designed to assist individuals in dealing with the grief issues surrounding the loss of one's job. Issues that would be important to explore might include individuals' personal meaning associated with work, adjustments in self-concept and identity related to work, and adjustments in self-esteem and sense of worth. Finally, the program should include the development of an individualized retirement plan for participants based on their needs, values, and interests.

An evaluation plan should be developed as the program is being conceptualized. Evaluation information is important in the development of revised programs to better meet the needs of the organization and individuals who participate.

Case Two

One of the authors was asked to serve as a trainer and supervisor for paraprofessional helpers in a retirement community. The helpers worked in the assisted living center with severely disabled older persons, were supervised on a daily basis by a registered nurse, and met with you weekly for 1–2 hours. In talking with the nurse 3 weeks after the initiation of the program, she made the following statement: "Your 'counselors' have been working with these people for 3 weeks and I haven't seen any changes yet. I find it hard to believe that we need this service." How would you respond to this situation, which really happened?

Comments on Case Two

A common problem in social and mental health services is a lack of understanding of the training, roles, and functions of other professionals. The nurse in this example, unlike many nurses, did not understand how counselors are trained and what skills they have to offer, nor did she understand that counseling is a process not an event. Unlike medical care, the results of counseling interventions are most often not seen immediately, and may be quite subtle and only become evident over a period of time. Education as to what counselors do is important in this situation. As the nurse comes to understand what you are trying to do, it is quite likely that she will increasingly cooperate and come to value the helping services. In the meantime, relieving her of some of the supervision duties that have been added to her already heavy workload can contribute to more positive relationships, which will benefit your mutual older clients.

Discussion Questions

1. What are the advantages of gerontological counselors serving as consultants?
2. What settings and roles are available for gerontological consultation?
3. What skills and competencies must gerontological counselors possess to be effective consultants?

References

Dougherty, A.M. (1990). *Consultation: Practice and perspectives*. Pacific Grove, CA: Brooks Cole.

17

Planning, Implementing, and Evaluating Programs for Gerontological Counseling

Minimum Essential Competency #16 for a Gerontological Counseling Specialist: *demonstrates skill in program development for the older population, including needs assessment, program planning, implementation, and evaluation.*

P rogram development is a skill that gerontological counselors will find useful in developing and implementing programs that effectively meet the needs of the older population. The development of programs may involve the counselor as a consultant, a member of a planning and treatment team, or a professional counselor. Program development may focus on mental health and counseling needs. However, the older population's complexity of needs may require a broader approach to program development than just mental health concerns.

As seen in previous chapters, many services that are necessary to the health and welfare of older persons are not available in many communities. Counselors working with older persons must be able to ascertain, or to help ascertain, which of their needs are not currently being met. Then, working independently or (most likely) with other professionals, counselors must be able to develop programs targeted at meeting those needs. The basic skills necessary for program development include needs assessment, program planning, implementation, and evaluation.

Needs Assessment

Before counselors can begin to develop programs designed to meet the needs of older persons, it is important to assess accurately exactly which needs are not currently being met by existing programs. Simply put, counselors need to know where they are before they can begin to decide where they want to be, and finally, how they will get there. If the initial needs assessment is not accurate and comprehensive, resulting programs may be only marginally successful.

Additionally, because there are limited resources available for aging programs and services in any community, it is essential that program effectiveness is maximized to obtain the most benefit for older persons. Accurate needs assessment is the first step in maximizing program effectiveness. Although the needs of older persons and the resources available to meet those needs may vary greatly from community to community, the basic process of needs assessment remains the same.

Needs assessment may be defined as a systematic process of collecting information that permits the counselor to analyze the magnitude of needs, frequency of needs, and perceived seriousness of problems. The basic task of needs assessment is to identify what needs of older persons are currently not being met. The gerontological counselor must begin by gathering information related to existing programs in the particular community and the limitations of the available services as related to client needs. Several important sources of information will assist the counselor in determining this information.

Counselors may meet with social service program directors to determine which services are currently being offered by which programs. Counselors may interview individual clients served by these programs to determine their perceptions of the services provided to them, quality of those services, and additional services they feel would be of benefit to them. Additionally, counselors may contact other health care professionals involved in working with the older persons (e.g., local family physicians, social workers, nurses, and physical and occupational therapists.).

Counselors may meet with community leaders, such as members of the city council, the mayor, and local church leaders, to determine their perceptions of the services being provided to older persons and current needs for additional programming. Public meetings may be conducted to ask local residents what services they perceive as most necessary for older persons in their community. Surveys may be developed and distributed to members of the community as well.

There are several other sources of information the counselor may wish to access to comprehensively assess client needs. These include the most recent U.S. Census report, state and community demographic information, and community resources and information hotlines. Local libraries and chambers of commerce are also excellent sources of information.

Inclusion and involvement of all affected persons—from the beginning stages of program development, including needs assessments—is essential to successful program implementation and effectiveness. If individuals or organizations with vested interests in older persons are not involved in all stages of program development, important information related to needs and services may be lost. Moreover, these individual and/or organizations may then actively work against program development efforts, feeling that their opinions and input were not sought or valued.

Once the counselor and other service providers with whom he or she may be working are satisfied that all available information has been gathered, they must begin to analyze the information in a systematic way to identify the specific needs and problems of older persons in the community. Following identification of these needs, some consideration must be given to prioritizing them based on the magnitude of the need, frequency of need, and seriousness of the problem. Available resources and existing programs may also influence prioritization of needs.

Available resources such as funding allocated for programs, space allocated to house programs, program equipment needs, and personnel available to staff programs may influence which needs may be met and in what order. Also, existing programs in the community may also influence prioritization of needs related to the development of new programs.

In assessing and setting priorities, the counselor may find that some of the most pressing needs of older persons in the community are not easily resolved through community programs. For example, lack of adequate finances is a major problem for older persons, with many older persons living at or below the poverty level. However, there is little that can be done to solve this problem at a local level. Efforts may be more effectively aimed at resolving this issue through advocacy for older persons at state and national levels. At the local level, assistance with utility bills and other basic needs may help to address financial needs, but likely will not be areas where counselors invest the majority of their time and resources.

The needs assessment process usually results in the development of a report summarizing the information obtained; it concludes with recommendations based on an analysis and prioritization of needs based on this information. This report may be presented to a board, agency director, or city planning council. The information in the report should be written at a level that can be easily understood by the intended audience and that clearly demonstrates the link between existing resources, needs, and recommendations.

Program Planning

Program planning involves taking the information gained during the needs assessment process, which has resulted in a comprehensive view of the existing services available to and needs of older persons, and developing a clear picture of what needs will be met by the program to be developed. Once this has been determined, a plan of action can be developed to move service levels from where they are to where they should be. Developing clear outcome goals is critical to successful program development; program planning is based directly on achievement of desired goals. Additionally, program evaluation of the success or failure of the program will be based on the program's ability to meet the stated goals.

Program planning involves the development of an action plan and results in the development of a program or service that meets the needs the counselor has targeted. This action plan contains four components: goals and objectives, strategies for reaching these goals and objectives, a work plan to implement strategies, and a budget. As stated previously, goals allow for the development of a clear understanding of what will ultimately be accomplished by the service or program. Program objectives are different from goals in that they are short term in nature. Objectives should be specific, measurable, and contain an estimated time frame for accomplishment or review. Once objectives have been developed, they should be prioritized in terms of immediacy of unmet need, ability to organize and mobilize existing resources, and practicality of accomplishment given constraints such as staffing, politics, and availability of program housing.

Once goals and objectives have been developed, the counselor must develop strategies that will define how these goals and objectives are to be met. The first step in the development of strategies is to brainstorm possible ways in which to meet goals and objectives. Brainstorming involves writing down a list of strategies that might be used to meet the stated goals and objectives; it may include input from directors, council members, community members, and so on.

Once all possible strategies have been developed, they are then prioritized according to which strategy, or combination of strategies, best meets the stated program objectives. It is also important to evaluate the proposed strategy, or combination of strategies, in view of available resources and finances. Often the best or most ideal solutions and programs are more costly; many times, less than ideal solutions and programs must be used due to lack of available finances and resources. Therefore, it is critical that accurate information related to needed costs and resources for each strategy be obtained and included in the selection of appropriate strategies.

As discussed in the previous example, it is important to consider existing services versus establishment of a new program during the prioritization process of needs assessment. It is also an important consideration during the planning stage. That is, strategies may be aimed at revising existing programs to meet a need or solve an identified problem, or they may be aimed at developing a new program to fill unmet needs. In either case, it is important for counselors to be prepared to identify potential funding sources.

Development of funding sources may include grant writing at the local, state, and national levels. It may also include requesting funds from private agencies, such as the United Way, Salvation Army, and so on. Other sources of funding may involve cost sharing funded by local government or other community funding. Private donations from local citizens, community fundraising activities, and donations from companies in the community may also be sources of funding for developing new programs or expanding existing programs.

The development of a work plan may begin once a strategy or combination of strategies has been agreed on. The work plan specifically delineates what will be done, by whom, when, where, and how. Each stage of the work plan also includes a time frame for accomplishment of each task. The work plan will serve as a guide for program implementation and evaluation. Additionally, development of a specific work plan will facilitate the formulation of a proposed budget.

The proposed budget should reflect, as accurately as possible, costs associated with starting the program and those associated with maintaining the program once it has been established. Both parts of the budget are critical to program success. That is, if there is only enough money to start the program and run it for 1 year, what will happen at the end of that year? Given that startup costs may exceed the first year's annual operating costs, it is not an effective use of resources to establish a program that can only be expected to run for 1 year. It is important to establish both startup and maintenance costs and to develop strategies for continued funding support. This may involve a long-range plan for the program to become self-supporting eventually, until which time costs are shared with other funding sources.

Program Implementation

Program implementation involves actually putting the work plan into action and, ultimately, in the provision of services to clients. During this phase, staff are hired, facilities are secured, and equipment and supplies are obtained. Additionally, operating policies and procedures for the program are established. Other activities that may be included in this stage are the establishment of an advisory board, relationship and links with other community organizations, and program publicity. The importance of an effective publicity campaign should be stressed because even the best program in town will do no good if no one knows about it. Flyers, public service announcements, speeches given to local community groups, open houses, and participation in community health fairs are examples of avenues for publicity.

The establishment of an advisory board is especially important for service programs. Consumers as well as providers of services in the community should be included on the board. The advisory board can help with all aspects of the program, including development, publicity, recruitment, and evaluation.

Program Evaluation

Adequate program evaluation is often the missing component in program development. Once the program has been established and has begun service provision, program evaluation is often forgotten or done in a cursory manner, only to fulfill the requirements of an advisory board or funding agency. When done effectively, program evaluation allows program directors to assess the impact of the services provided on client need. This assessment allows program directors to make changes in the services provided to meet client needs more effectively. In a sense then, the entire process of program development is cyclical. Following program evaluation, needs that are not being met are assessed (needs assessment), program changes are planned to address those areas (program planning), changes are implemented (program implementation), and the entire program, including changes, are reevaluated (program evaluation).

The actual program evaluation begins at the same time the program begins, with the establishment of baseline data against which to evaluate the success of future service delivery efforts. Data are collected on a continuing basis regarding number of clients served, demographics of client population, cost of services, and so forth. In addition, client satisfaction with services may be assessed on an ongoing basis. The work plan should specify at which point program data are to be collected and an evaluation completed.

At this point, all of the data that have been collected regarding program performance are reviewed. Additionally, some organizations may seek input from clients and employees regarding service provision and satisfaction with services. This may be done through surveys, focus groups, or personal interviews. All of the input regarding program delivery and performance are then considered and evaluated in terms of the degree to which program goals and objectives have been met. Program changes, deletions, or additions may be made based on this evaluation.

As mentioned earlier, final reports of program evaluations may be required by funding agencies or advisory boards. A summary of the data gathered regarding program service delivery and outcomes of service delivery should be included, as well as a restatement of program goals and objectives. It is essential that the overall focus of the report include the relationship between service delivery and program goals and objectives and suggested program changes in order to meet the program's overall goals and objectives. It is important to note that program goals and objectives also may need to be reviewed at this point. Changes may need to be made based on current information that was unavailable at the program's inception.

Summary

Gerontological counselors must be knowledgeable and skilled in the area of program development if they are to adequately assess and meet the needs of older persons in their community. More specifically, gerontological counselors must be able to use their specialized knowledge of older people in conjunction with the processes of needs assessment, program planning, program implementation, and program evaluation to develop programs and services targeted toward the unmet needs of older persons. Program development skills may be required of gerontological counselors in settings as diverse as private practice, director of an Area Agency on Aging, or program coordinator of or consultant to a local nursing home.

Case Studies

Following are two case studies that will allow the reader to apply the knowledge and skills learned in this chapter related to development and evaluation of programs for older adults. Read each case study and think about how you would help the client. Then read the comments for further insights into the role of the gerontological counselor in each situation.

Case One

You are a gerontological counselor who has recently moved to a new community. You wish to begin a private practice that exclusively serves the needs of older persons and their families. You have had extensive experience working with older persons and their families as a counselor at a community mental health center. What are some important considerations in assessing whether your private practice is needed and will be successful?

Comments on Case One

You need to undertake an extensive needs assessment of the community. You may wish to consult the local chamber of commerce and local telephone directory to review all of the mental health services currently available to older persons in the community. In addition, you may wish to contact and meet with local service providers to older persons, such as program directors, agency counselors, and so on, to gain insight into current services provided and areas of need. You may also wish to talk with counselors already working in private practice in the community to assess the number of counselors working with older persons and to assess the community's openness to counseling in general. Professional networking with counselors, physicians, nurses, social workers, case workers, and other service providers may be beneficial in establishing potential referral sources and/or potential sources for collaboration. After assessing all available resources, you may decide that, rather than opening an individual private practice exclusively focusing on the needs of older persons and their families, you would be more effective by joining an established group of private practitioners and focusing on the needs of older persons and their families.

Case Two

You are a program coordinator at a local Alzheimer's Association chapter. You have recently been asked to write a grant to obtain federal money for a respite program. What steps should you take to obtain the necessary information to write the grant?

Comments on Case Two

As part of a needs assessment, you may want to send a survey to participants or persons on your mailing list to document the need for respite services. Additionally, you may organize focus groups of caregivers, older persons, and service providers in the community to discuss the need for respite services, and to document existing community need for such services. Information regarding the lack of currently existing programs that provide respite services is also important to establishing need for the program.

In addition, it is important to thoroughly research existing respite programs in other communities. This might be done through a literature search. It might also include correspondence with other programs providing respite programs to ascertain the successes of such programs and program structure. Barriers to implementation of such programs and program expenses should be researched as well.

Once appropriate needs assessment has been conducted and a need established, program planning and suggestions for implementation can be developed. This includes answers to questions such as: Who will provide the service? Will the program need additional paid staff or volunteers? What are the insurance costs for such a program? Where is the best place to house such a program? Is in-home respite better than a group day care format? What are the benefits of such a program?

Seeking a funding source may include consideration of local, state, and national private and public sources. You may contact the U.S. Administration on Aging or your state office on aging, the National Institute of Mental Health, your state program office for mental health, and national and state foundations that fund research and service programs for older persons. Your local public or university library can assist you in locating appropriate funding sources.

Discussion Questions

1. Briefly discuss the importance of program development for gerontological counselors.
2. What are some important sources and methods for obtaining information related to needs assessment?
3. What are the necessary components of effective program development?
4. In what settings and roles might gerontological counselors be required to demonstrate program development skills? How does the training of professional gerontological counselors contribute to successful program development in these settings?

Supplemental Reading List

Adelman, R. (1988). A well elderly program: An intergenerational model in medical evaluation. *The Gerontologist, 28*(3), 409–413.

Agresti, A. A. (1992). Counselor training and ethical issues with older clients. Special section: Training in gerontological counseling. *Counselor Education and Supervision, 32*(1), 43–50.

Allers, C.T. (1990). AIDS and the older adult. *Gerontologist, 30*(3), 405–407.

Anastas, J. W., Gibeau, J. L., & Larson, P. L. (1990). Working families and eldercare: A national perspective in an aging America. *Social Work, 35*(5), 405–411.

Aranda, M.P. (1990). Culture-friendly services for Latino elders. *Generations, 14*(1), 55–57.

Atchley, R. C. (1992). What do social theories of aging offer counselors? *Counseling Psychologist, 20*(2), 336–340.

Babins, L.H., Dillion, J.P., & Merovitz, S. (1988). The effects of validation therapy on disoriented elderly. *Activities, Adaptation, and Aging, 12*(1–2), 73–86.

Barclay, T.A., & McDougall, M. (1990). Older worker programs. *Generations, 14*(1), 53–54.

Barstow, C. (1986). Tending body and spirit: Counseling with elders. *Hakomi-Forum, 4*, 42–51.

Bornstein, J.M. (1986). Retraining the older worker: Michigan's experience with senior employment services. *Journal of Career Development, 13*(2), 14–22

Bowman, G. (1992). Using therapeutic metaphor in adjustment counseling. *Journal of Visual Impairment and Blindness, 86*(10), 440–442.

Bratter, B., & Freeman, E. (1990). The maturing of peer counseling. *Generations, 14*(1), 49–52.

Brown, L. (1989). Is there sexual freedom for our aging population in long term care institutions? *Journal of Gerontological Social Work, 13*(3–4), 75–93.

Burgener, S., & Logan, G. (1989). Sexuality concerns of the post-stroke patient. *Rehabilitation Nursing, 14*(4), 178–181.

Burlew, L.D., Jones, J., & Emerson, P. (1991). Exercise and the elderly: A group counseling approach. *Journal for Specialists in Group Work, 16*(3), 152–158.

Burlingame, V.S. (1988). Counseling an older person. *Social Casework, 69*(9), 588–592.

Burr, E.W. (1986). What next after fifty? *Journal of Career Development, 13*(2), 23–29.

Butler, R. (1984). Senile dementia: Reversible and irreversible. *Counseling Psychologist, 12*(2), 75–79.

Cahill, M., & Salamone, P. (1987). Career counseling for work life extension: Integrating the older worker in the labor force. *Career Development Quarterly, 35*(3), 188–196.

Capuzzi, D. (1990). Recent trends in group work with the elderly. *Generations, 14*(1), 43–48.

Capuzzi, D., & Friel, S.E. (1990). Current trends in sexuality and aging: An update for counselors. *Journal of Mental Health Counseling, 12*(2), 342–353.

Capuzzi, D., & Gossman, L. (1982). Sexuality and the elderly: A group counseling model. *Journal for Specialists in Group Work, 7*(4), 251–259.

Catania, J. A. (1989). Issues in AIDS primary prevention for late-middle-aged and elderly Americans. *Generations, 13*(4), 50–54.

Cavallero, M.L., & Ramsey, M. (1988). Ethical issues in gerocounseling. *Counseling and Values, 32*(3), 221–227.

Cavallero, M. (1991). Curriculum guidelines and strategies on counseling older women. *Educational Gerontology, 17*(2), 157–166.

Centers for Disease Control. (1988). *Behavioral risk factor surveillance.* Atlanta, GA: Author.

Charlton, R. (1992). Palliative care in non-cancer patients and the neglected caregiver. *Journal of Clinical Epidemiology, 45*(12), 1447–1449.

Cohen, P. M. (1983). A group approach for working with families of the elderly. *Gerontologist, 23*(3), 248–250.

Combs, D.W., Miller, H.L., Alarcon, R., Herlihy, C., Lee, J.M., & Morrison, D.P. (1992). Presuicide attempt communications between parasuicides and consulted caregivers. *Suicide and Life Threatening Behavior, 22(3),* 289–302.

Corey, K.M., & Cryns, A.G. (1991). Group work as interventive modality with older depressed clients. *Journal of Gerontological Social Work, 16(1–2),* 137–157.

Covey, S. (1989). *The seven characteristics of highly effective people.* New York: Simon & Schuster.

Crane, F.W., & Kramer, B.J. (1987). Perceptions of losses in the later years. *Counseling and Values, 31(2),* 185–189.

Crenshaw, T.L. (1986). Dyspareunia due to senile vaginitis and vaginal atrophy. *Medical Aspects of Human Sexuality, 20(9),* 22–28.

Crose, R. (1990). Reviewing the past in the here and now: Using Gestalt therapy techniques with life review. *Journal of Mental Health Counseling, 12(3),* 279–287.

Crose, R. (1991). What's special about counselling older women? *Canadian Journal of Counselling, 25(4),* 617–623.

Crose, R. (1992). Gerontology is only aging, it's not dead yet! *Counseling Psychologist, 20(2),* 330–335.

Cross, R., & Drake, L.K. (1993). Older women's sexuality. *Clinical Gerontologist, 12(4),* 51–56.

Cubillos, H.L., Prieto, M.M., & Paz, J.J. (1988). Hispanic elderly and long term care: The community's response. *Pride Institute Journal of Long Term Home Health Care, 7(4),* 14–21.

D'Eramo-Melkus, G. A., Wylie-Rosett, J., & Hagan, J. A. (1992). Metabolic impact of education in NIDDM. *Diabetes Care, 15(7),* 864–869.

Decker, T. W., Cline-Elsen, J., & Gallagher, M. (1992). Relaxation therapy as an adjunct in radiation oncology. *Journal of Clinical Psychology, 48(3),* 388–393.

deMello, A. (1981). *The song of the bird.* New York: Image Books.

deMello, A. (1988). *Taking flight: A book of story meditations.* New York: Doubleday.

Denollet, J. (1993). Emotional distress and fatigue in coronary heart disease: The Global Mood Scale (GMS). *Psychological Medicine, 23(1),* 111–121.

Dickel, C. T. (1990, March). *Preserving elder autonomy: Moral and ethical considerations.* Paper presented at the annual convention of the American Association for Counseling and Development, Cincinnati, OH.

Dowd, T. (Ed.). (1984). *Leisure counseling: Concepts and applications.* Springfield, IL: C.C. Thomas.

Eisenberg, D.M., & Carilio, T.E. (1990). Friends of the family: Counseling elders at family service agencies. *Generations, 14*(1), 25–26.

Ekland, S. J., Siffin, C. F., & Stafford, P. B. (1990). Alzheimer's Awareness Days: A community education model. *Gerontology and Geriatrics Education, 10*(3), 1–10.

Eng, E. (1993). The Save our Sisters Project. A social network strategy for reaching rural black women. *Cancer, 72*(Suppl. 3), 1071–1077.

Erlanger, M.A. (1990). Using the genogram with the older client. *Journal of Mental Health Counseling, 12*(3), 321–331.

Florsheim, M. J., & Herr, J. J. (1990). Family counseling with elders: A useful and positive starting point. *Generations, 14*(1), 40–42.

Frankl, V.E. (1961). *Man's search for meaning.* New York: Pocket Books.

Fry, P. S. (1992). Major social theories of aging and their implications for counseling concepts and practice: A critical review. *Counseling Psychologist, 20*(2), 246–329.

Gafner, G. (1989). Marital therapy with an old-old couple. *Clinical Gerontologist, 8*(4), 51–53.

Garratt, J. P. (1992). Depression in the elderly. *Physician Assistant, 16*(3), 101–104, 110, 112.

Genevay, D. (1990). The aging-family consultation: A "summit conference" model of brief therapy. *Generations, 14*(1), 58–60.

Gibran, K. (1923). *The prophet.* New York: Knopf.

Gonzalez, S., Steinglass, P., & Reiss, D. (1989). Putting the illness in its place: Discussion groups for families with chronic medical illnesses. *Family Process, 28*(1), 63–87.

Gotterer, S.M. (1989). Storytelling: A valuable supplement to poetry writing with the elderly. *Arts in Psychotherapy, 16*(2), 127–131.

Grady, S. (1990). Senior centers: An environment for counseling. *Generations, 14*(1), 15–18.

Green, C.P. (1991). Clinical considerations: Midlife daughters and their aging parents. *Journal of Gerontological Nursing, 17*(11), 6–12.

Hanson, R.O., Briggs, S.R., & Rule, B.L. (1990). Old age and unemployment: Predictors of perceived control, depression, and loneliness. *Journal of Applied Gerontology, 9*(2), 230–240.

Hargrave, T.D., & Anderson, W. (1990). Helping older people finish well: A contextual family therapy approach. *Family Therapy, 17*(1), 9–19.

Hedenstrom, J., & Ostwald, S.K. (1988). Adult day care programs: Maintaining a therapeutic triad. *Home Health Care Services Quarterly, 9*(1), 85–102.

Hereford, R.W. (1989). The market for community services for older persons. *Pride Institute Journal of Long Term Home Health Care, 8*(1), 44–51.

Hernan, J. A. (1984). Exploding aging myths through retirement counseling. *Journal of Gerontological Nursing, 10*(4), 31–33.

Hinkle, S. (1990). An overview of dementia in older persons: Identification, diagnosis, assessment, and treatment. *Journal of Mental Health Counseling, 12*(3), 368–383.

Hinkle, S.J. (1991). Support group counseling for caregivers of Alzheimer's disease patients. *Journal for Specialists in Group Work, 16*(3), 185–190.

Hollis, J. (1988). Standards for practicum and internship. In J.C. Boylan, P.B. Malley, & J. Scott (Eds.), *Practicum and internship: Textbook for counseling and psychotherapy* (pp. 6–8). Muncie, IN: Accelerated Development.

Hopper, S. V. (1993). The influence of ethnicity on the health of older women. *Clinical Geriatric Medicine, 9*(1), 231–259.

James, S. (1994). Expectations versus reality: Assisting the older job seeker in a changing job market. *Career Planning and Adult Development Journal, 10*(4), 15–17.

Jamuna, D. (1985). Self-concept among middle-aged and older women. *Journal of the Indian Academy of Applied Psychology, 11*(2), 16–18.

Janocko, K.M., & Lee, S.S. (1988). Ethical implications of deinstitutionalization and moves of the institutionalized elderly. *Professional Psychology Research and Practice, 19*(5), 522–526.

Johnson, R.P., & Stripling, R.O. (1984). Bridging the gap between counselor educators and the administrators of programs for the elderly. *Counselor Education and Supervision, 23*(4), 276–289.

Johnson, S. (1984). *The precious present.* New York: Doubleday.

Johnson, W.Y., & Wilborn, B. (1991). Group counseling as an intervention in anger expression and depression in older adults. *Journal for Specialists in Group Work, 16*(3), 133–142.

Kalymun, M. (1990). Toward a definition of assisted living. *Journal of Housing for the Elderly, 7*(1), 97–132.

Kampfe, C. (1990). *Dignity versus dehumanization in long term care settings for older persons.* Greensboro, NC: ERIC/CASS.

Kampfe, C. (1994). Vocational rehabilitation and the older population. *The Southwest Journal on Aging, 9,* 65–69.

Kampfe, C. (in press). *Empowerment in residential rehabilitation. Handbook on counseling adolescents, adults, and older persons.* Alexandria, VA: Association for Counselor Education and Supervision.

Kane, R., & Kane, R. (1983). *Assessing the elderly: A practical guide to measurement.* Lexington, MA: Lexington Books.

Kellett, J.M. (1991). Sexuality of the elderly. *Sexual and Marital Therapy, 6(2),* 147–155.

Kent, K.L. (1990). Elders and community mental health centers. *Generations, 14(1),* 19–21.

Kieffer, J.B. (1986). Kicking the premature retirement habit. *Journal of Career Development, 13(2),* 39–51.

Kirwin, P. M., & Kaye, L.W. (1991). Service consumption patterns over time among adult day care program participants. *Home Health Care Services Quarterly, 12(4),* 45–58.

Koenig, H.G. (1986). Shepherds centers: Helping elderly help themselves. *Journal of the American Geriatrics Society, 34(1),* 73.

LaBarge, E., Rosenman, L.S., Leavitt, K., & Cristiani, T. (1988). Counseling clients with mild senile dementia of the Alzheimer's type: A pilot study. *Journal of Neurologic Rehabilitation, 2(4),* 167–173.

Lipsman, R., Fader, D., & Harmon, J.S. (1992). Developing home-based mental health services for Maine's older adults. *Pride Institute Journal of Long Term Home Health Care, 11(1),* 29–38.

Lloyd, G. A. (1989). AIDS & Elders: Advocacy, activism, & coalitions. *Generations, 13(4),* 32–35.

Lurie, A., & Rich, J.C. (1984). The medical center's impact in the network to sustain the aged in the community. *Journal of Gerontological Social Work, 7(3),* 65–73.

Lustbader, W. (1990). Mental health services in a community health center. *Generations, 14(1),* 22–23.

McCarthy, B., Kuipers, L., Hurry, J., & Harper, R. (1989). Counseling the relatives of the long-term mentally ill: A low cost supportive model. *British Journal of Psychiatry, 154,* 775–782.

McCloskey, L.J. (1990). The silent heart sings. *Generations, 14(1),* 63–65.

McCoy, H.V., Kipp, C.W., & Ahern, M. (1992). Reducing older patients' reliance on the emergency department. *Social Work in Health Care, 17(1),* 23–37.

McIntosh, J. (1988–1989). Official U.S. elderly suicide data bases: Levels, availability, omissions. *Omega Journal of Death and Dying, 19*(4), 337–350.

Morgan, L.A. (1986). The financial experience of widowed women: Evidence from the LRHS. *Gerontologist, 26*(6), 663–668.

Morse, R.L. (1989). Roles of the psychotherapist in family financial counseling: A systems approach to prolongation of independence. *Journal of Psychotherapy and the Family, 5*(1–2), 133–147.

Mulligan, T., & Palguta, R.F. (1991). Sexual interest, activity, and satisfaction among male nursing home residents. *Archives of Sexual Behavior, 20*(2), 199–204.

Myers, J.E. (1988). The mid/late life generation gap. Adult children and aging parents. *Journal of Counseling and Development, 66*(7), 331–335.

Myers, J. E. (1990a). Aging: An overview for mental health counselors. *Journal of Mental Health Counseling, 12*(3), 245–259.

Myers, J.E. (1990b). *Empowerment for later life*. Greensboro, NC: ERIC/CASS.

Myers, J.E., & Blake, R. (1984). Employment of gerontological counseling graduates: A follow-up study. *Personnel and Guidance Journal, 62*, 333–335.

Myers, J.E., Loesch, L.C., & Sweeney, T.J. (1991). Trends in preparation of gerontological counselors. *Counselor Education and Supervision, 30*(3), 194–204.

Myers, J.E., Poidevant, J.P., & Dean, L. (1991). Groups for older persons and their caregivers: A review of the literature. *Journal for Specialists in Group Work, 16*(3), 197–205.

Myers, J.E., & Salmon, H. (1984). Counseling programs for older persons: Status, shortcomings, and potentialities. *Counseling Psychologist, 12*(2), 39–53.

Myers, J.E., Witmer, J.M., & Sweeney, T.J. (1993). Spirituality: The core of wellness. *Wellness Connections, 4*(2), 1, 6–8.

Neihardt, J.G. (1979). *Black Elk speaks*. Lincoln, NE: University of Nebraska Press.

Nelson, R.C. (1989). Choice awareness: A group experience in a residential setting. *Journal for Specialists in Group Work, 14*(3), 158–169.

Olson, S.K., & Robbins, S.B. (1986). Guidelines for the development and evaluation of career services for the older adult. *Journal of Career Development, 13*(2), 63–73.

Osgood, N., & McIntosh, J. (1986). *Suicide and the elderly*. New York: Greenwood.

Paulus, T. (1972). *Hope for the flowers*. New York: Paulus.

Payne, S. (1989). Anxiety and depression in women with advanced cancer: Implications for counselling. *Counselling Psychology Quarterly, 2*(3), 337–344.

Peck, M.S. (1978). *The road less traveled*. New York: Touchstone.

Penn, N.E., Levy, V.L., & Penn, B.P. (1986). Professional services preferred by urban elderly Black women. *American Journal of Social Psychiatry, 6*(2), 129–130.

Penning, M., & Wasyliw, D. (1992). Homebound learning opportunities: Reaching out to older shut-ins and their caregivers. *Gerontologist, 32*(5), 704–707.

Piktialis, D.S. (1990). Employers and elder care: A model corporate program. *Pride Institute Journal of Long Term Home Health Care, 9*(1), 26–31.

Ponzo, Z. (1981). Counseling the elderly: A lifetime process. *Counseling and Values, 26*(1), 68–80.

Powell, J. (1976). *Fully human, fully alive*. Allen, TX: Tabor.

Powers, J. S. (1989). Helping family and patients decide between home care and nursing home care. *Southern Medical Journal, 82*(6), 723–726.

Qualls, S.H. (1992). Social gerontology theory is not enough: Strategies and resources for counselors. *The Counseling Psychologist, 20*(2), 341–345.

Reever, K.E., & Thomas, E. (1985). Training facilitators of self-help groups for caregivers to elders. *Generations, 10*(1), 50–52.

Ribeiro, V. (1989). The forgotten generation: Elderly women and loneliness. *Recent Advances in Nursing, 25*, 20–40.

Riensche, L.L., & Lang, K. (1992). Treatment of swallowing disorders through a multidisciplinary team approach. *Educational Gerontology, 18*(3), 277–284.

Riverin-Simard, D. (1990). Adult vocational trajectory. *Career Development Quarterly, 39*(2), 129–142.

Russell, N. K., & Roter, D. L. (1993). Health promotion counseling of chronic-disease patients during primary care visits. *American Journal of Public Health, 83*(7), 979–982.

Scharlach, A.E. (1989). Social group work with the elderly: A role theory perspective. *Social Work With Groups, 12*(3), 33–46.

Scharlach, A.E., Mor-Barak, M., Katz, A., Birba, L., Garcia, G., & Sokolov, J. (1992). Generation: A corporate sponsored retiree health program. *Gerontologist, 32*(2), 265–269.

Schwiebert, V.E., & Myers, J.E. (1995). *Counseling older persons: An annotated bibliography.* New York: Greenwood.

Shamoian, C.A., & Thurston, F.D. (1986). Marital discord and divorce among the elderly. *Medical Aspects of Human Sexuality, 20*(8), 25–34.

Sherman, E. (1987). Reminiscence groups for community elderly. *Gerontologist, 27*(5), 569–572.

Smedly, G. (1991). Addressing sexuality in the elderly. *Rehabilitation Nursing, 16*(1), 9–11.

Sommerstein, J.C. (1986). Assessing the older worker: The career counselor's dilemma. *Journal of Career Development, 13*(2), 52–56.

Sommerstein, J.C. (1994). Career development and the mature worker [Special issue]. *Career Planning and Adult Development Journal, 10*(2).

Szwabo, P., & Thale, T. T. (1983, November). *Expressive group psychotherapy with the older adult.* Paper presented at the annual scientific meeting of the Gerontological Society, San Francisco, CA.

Thomas, M.C., & Martin, V. (1992). Training counselors to facilitate the transitions of aging through group work. *Counselor Education and Supervision, 32*(1), 51–60.

Tincher, B. J. (1992). Retirement: Perspectives and theory. *Physical and Occupational Therapy in Geriatrics, 11*(1), 55–62.

Tomine, S. (1986). Private practice in gerontological counseling. *Journal of Counseling and Development, 64*(6), 406–409.

Toseland, R.M., Rossiter, C.M., & Labrecque, M.S. (1989). The effectiveness of three group intervention strategies to support family caregivers. *American Journal of Orthopsychiatry, 59*(3), 420–429.

Toseland, R.W., & Smith, G.C. (1990). Effectiveness of individual counseling by professional and peer helpers for family caregivers of the elderly. *Psychology and Aging, 5*(2), 256–263.

U.S. Department of Health and Human Services, Public Health Service. (1991). *Healthy people 2000: National health promotion and disease prevention objectives.* Washington, DC: U.S. Government Printing Office.

Van Auken, E. (1991). Crisis intervention: Elders awaiting placement in an acute care facility. *Journal of Gerontological Nursing, 17*(11), 30–33.

Waltman, R. (1992). When a spouse dies. *Nursing, 22*(7), 48–51.

Waters, E., & Goodman, J. (1991). *Empowerment of older adults*. St. Louis: C.V. Mosby.

Waters, E.B. (1984). Building on what you know: Techniques for individual and group counseling with older people. *Counseling Psychologist, 12*(2), 63–74.

Webster, J.D., & Young, R.A. (1988). Process variables of the life review: Counseling implications. *International Journal of Aging and Human Development, 26*(4), 315–323.

Weisman, C.B., & Schwartz, P. (1989). Worker expectations in group work with the frail elderly: Modifying the models for a better fit. *Social Work With Groups, 12*(3), 47–55.

Whanger, A.D., & Myers, A.C. (1984). *Mental health assessment and therapeutic intervention with older adults*. Rockville, MD: Aspen Systems.

White, D., & Ingersoll, D.B. (1989). Life review groups: Helping the member with an unhappy life. *Clinical Gerontologist, 8*(4), 47–50.

Wickwire, P.N. (1994). Assessment of mature workers in career counseling. *Career Planning and Adult Development Journal, 10*(2), 25–34.

Wilbur, K., & Zarit, S. (1987). Practicum training in gerontological counseling. *Educational Gerontology, 13*(1), 15–32.

Williams, W.C., & Lair, G.S. (1988). Geroconsultation: A proposed decision-making model. *Journal of Counseling and Development, 67*(3), 198–201.

Woodruff, J.C., Donnan, H., & Halpin, G. (1988). Changing elderly persons' attitudes toward mental health professionals. *Gerontologist, 28*(6), 800–802.

Wright, B., Thyer, B.A., & DiNitto, D. (1985). Health and social welfare needs of the elderly: A preliminary study. *Journal of Sociology and Social Welfare, 12*(2), 431–439.

Youssef, F. A. (1990). The impact of group reminiscence counseling on a depressed elderly population. *Nurse Practitioner: American Journal of Primary Health Care, 15*(4), 32–38.

Zisook, S., Shuchter, S., Sledge, P., & Mulvihill, M. (1993). Aging and bereavement. *Journal of Geriatric Psychiatry and Neurology, 6*(3), 137–143.

Index

abuse, elder, 53–54, 170–71, 201, 202
Activity Theory, 33
Adams, D., 106
Adopt-a-Grandparent program, 197
adult day care services, 157
Adult Development, Aging, and
  Counseling Interest Network, 67
African American elders, 46, 47,
  148–49
Age Discrimination in Employment
  Act, 25, 90–91
aging
  ageism, 19–21
  gender and, 36–38
  national aging projects, 4–7
  normal vs. pathological, 36
  physical and mental health and,
    34–36
  theories of, 33–34
  See also research and aging; social
    and cultural foundations of
    aging
aging network, 36
  case studies, 158–59
  continuum of care, 156–58
  formal, 154–56
  informal, 153–54
alcohol misuse and abuse, 54
Alzheimer, Alois, 146
Alzheimer's disease, 108–9, 144,
  146–47, 150, 189, 192–93
American Association of Retired
  Persons (AARP), 91, 156, 169
American Counseling Association
  (ACA), 1, 118, 156

advocacy efforts, 15
  Committee on Adult Development
    and Aging, 3
  ethical standards, 117, 191, 196, 197
  national aging projects, 4–7
American Personnel Guidance
  Association (APGA). *See*
  American Counseling
  Association (ACA)
appraisal of older persons, 99–100
  assessing depression, 106–7
  assessing life satisfaction, 105–6
  case studies, 108–10
  clinical assessment, 104–5
  ethical issues in testing, 107
  interpreting test results, 103–4
  purposes of assessment, 100–101
  reliability and validity issues, 102–3
  test construction and use, 101–2
  types of tests, 103
Ardell, D. B., 125
Area Agencies on Aging (AAAs),
  155, 197
Association for Adult Development
  and Aging (AADA), 7, 8, 63, 67,
  119
Association for Counselor Education
  and Supervision, 67
Association for Gerontology in Higher
  Education (AGHE), 15, 118
autonomy, 195

Beck Depression Inventory (BDI),
  107